THE
Crisis
OF THE
End Time

Luellyn Barrett

April, 1992

THE
Crisis
OF THE
End Time

**Keeping Your Relationship With Jesus
in Earth's Darkest Hour**

Marvin Moore

Pacific Press Publishing Association
Boise, Idaho
Oshawa, Ontario, Canada

Unless otherwise indicated, Scripture references in this book are from the New International Version.

The author assumes full responsibility for the accuracy of all facts and quotations cited in this book.

Edited by B. Russell Holt
Designed by Tim Larson
Cover by Tom Ives © The Stock Market
Typeset in 10/12 Century Schoolbook

Library of Congress Cataloging-in-Publication Data
Moore, Marvin, 1937-
    The crisis of the end time: keeping your relationship with Jesus in earth's darkest hour / Marvin Moore.
        p.   cm.
    ISBN 0-8163-1085-8
    1. Second advent. 2. White, Ellen Gould Harmon, 1827-
1915—Prophecies. 3. Christian life—Seventh-day Adventist authors. 4. Seventh-day Adventists—doctrines. I. Title.
BT886.M64   1992
236'.9—dc20   91-40487
                                                          CIP

92 93 94 95 96 • 5 4 3 2 1

Dedication

To Lois
Loving Wife
Faithful Friend

Table of Contents

Introduction

For some time I have conducted Sabbath seminars on the end time in churches throughout North America. Typically, I speak on Sabbath morning and conduct two seminars on Sabbath afternoon. Among other things, I explain how to be ready to live without a Mediator after the close of probation, and I discuss the judgments of God that are soon to come on the earth—both topics that you will read a great deal about in this book. (Don't worry! I think I can promise that you will feel better about these things, not worse, when you have finished.)

I have a strong conviction that the final events of world history are upon us and that most Adventists have no idea what is about to happen. That's why I dedicate my time to travel wherever I am invited to speak; and that's why I have devoted the major part of a year to writing this book. *I want our people to know.*

I urge you to read this book prayerfully. Suggest to your pastor that he conduct a series of prayer meeting talks based on this book. Get a small group together in your home to discuss these issues.

Four people in particular deserve thanks for their help in the production of this book. The first is my wife Lois, who spent many hours as a "computer widow" while I wrote. She also spends many weekends alone when I travel to churches and camp meetings to speak about the end time. However, we both believe the signs of the times tell us the end is near, and we are committed to doing whatever is necessary to help God's people understand that.

I would also like to thank three other people who contributed significantly to the production of this book. Comments by Dr. Robert Olson, former secretary of the Ellen G. White Estate, were particularly valuable. He is an expert on Ellen White's teachings about last-day events, and his criticism of the manuscript, as well as his editing skills, have made this book not only much more accurate but also much more readable.

Dr. George Knight, professor of church history at the Seventh-day Adventist Theological Seminary in Berrien Springs, Michigan, is a close friend, both personally and professionally. He made the reading of my manuscript a top priority, and his helpful suggestions have also significantly improved what you will read on the pages that follow.

For several years Elder Russell Holt has been a friend and colleague at Pacific Press, and with this book he has become my editor as well. His skillful touch has also made this book easier for you to read.

I pray that the time you spend with this book will help you find a place in God's kingdom. I am looking forward to meeting you there. I don't think I'll be waiting very long!

Marvin Moore
Caldwell, Idaho
January 1, 1992

CHAPTER

1

Why Talk About the End Time?

The last half of 1989 seemed to wake up Seventh-day Adventists. Over and over, as I spoke with church members in various parts of the United States and other areas of the world, I heard them say, "The dramatic events in Eastern Europe are prophetic." Time and again I read in Adventist magazines that Eastern Europe's total break from the Communist orbit in less than a year fulfilled Ellen White's prediction that "the final movements will be rapid ones" (*Testimonies*, vol. 9, p. 11).

Hard on the heels of those developments came Iraq's invasion of Kuwait, Desert Storm, and George Bush's talk about a "new world order." Again, startled Seventh-day Adventists sat up and said to themselves, "Something's going on here. The time of the end is upon us!"

The dust had scarcely settled on Desert Storm when the Soviet Union erupted again. Hard-line Communists attempted a coup, and the Russian people exploded. They took their political future into their own hands, and, as it appears at this writing, set their nation on a permanent course to democracy.

Such rapidly multiplying signs of the end threaten to put Adventists and other Christians into sensory overload! Who knows what will happen next? By the time you read these words, the events I just mentioned may have been superseded by other developments far more dramatic and far more prophetic.

In light of this growing sense of the approaching end of the world, it seems appropriate to examine again what Scripture and

Ellen White tell us the end time will be like, and to ask ourselves, Are the final events really upon us? As the future unfolds, this understanding of last-day events can help us relate to them with maturity rather than fanaticism.

Webster defines a *primer* as "a textbook giving the first principles of any subject" (*Webster's New World Dictionary*, third college edition). If I were to give one reason above all others why I wrote this book, it would be to provide Adventists in the last decade of the twentieth century with a primer on eschatology—a textbook giving the first principles of end-time events as Adventists have historically understood them.

Something a friend told me recently impressed on my mind the need for this review of our teachings about the end time. In the course of our conversation, I mentioned the latter rain, and she asked me what that meant. I explained to her briefly about the outpouring of the Holy Spirit in the last days.

"I remember talking about that in academy Bible class," she replied, "but that's been a long time ago. I don't always remember what those things mean."

I believe many Adventists, like my friend, are not familiar with the understanding of end-time events as it was taught by our pioneers, especially Ellen White. Perhaps a majority in our church today have not had the advantage of attending an Adventist academy or college, either because as Adventist young people they attended public schools or because they joined the church as adults. Their exposure to the Adventist understanding of end-time events has been limited to Sabbath School, the pastor's sermon, and an occasional magazine article. And, as my friend confessed, many Adventists who studied these things years ago in academy or college have forgotten what they mean.

I want this book to help fill that gap in our understanding.

What about Ellen White?

Adventist eschatology has been profoundly influenced by Ellen White. Here probably more than in any other area of study, we turn to her writings in combination with Scripture when we want an authoritative opinion from the Lord. I believe this is perfectly appropriate. God gave us a prophet at this time to help us prepare for the final days of earth's history. It should come as no surprise, then, to find that prophet expanding greatly our understanding of what is to happen just before Jesus comes and how to prepare ourselves and others to meet the crisis.

I recognize that in the past some of us exaggerated Ellen White's infallibility and attempted to give her an authority over our understanding of Scripture that she herself did not claim. For example, the church's leadership during the late 1880s tried repeatedly to get her to take a position on the identity of the law in Galatians, but she refused. She told the brethren to ask the Bible that question.

I believe we should do the same with prophecy. We must search Daniel, Revelation, the Old Testament prophets, and the prophetic views of the apostle Paul for ourselves, and not let Ellen White be our primary interpreter of these books. However, we need a balance. Some Adventists today almost seem embarrassed and apologetic about Ellen White. That, too, is unfortunate. I agree that we should use the Bible and the Bible only when we are writing and speaking to those who are not Adventists. However, Ellen White received specific instruction about end-time events, and if she was God's messenger to the remnant, then we who are the remnant ought to take her seriously.

I believe it is perfectly valid to interpret current events in light of what Ellen White foretold. If God really did tell her what the world will be like at the end of time, then we ought to be able to see trends in current events that are a fulfillment of what she wrote. So please do not be troubled when I quote a great deal from Ellen White. One important reason I am writing this book is to help Adventists understand what she said about the end time. My purpose is to organize her thoughts about the future together with Scripture to make them more easily understood.

In some cases Ellen White unfolded in great detail ideas that Scripture only suggests. That bothers some people, because they think she is adding to the Bible. They don't want to believe anything she said unless it can be found stated just as clearly in the Bible. I disagree with such restrictions on Ellen White. Why would God have bothered to give us another prophet if all she ever did was to repeat what Scripture says? New light has to be truly new light, and not simply a repeat of the old light.

Unfortunately, some Adventists have fallen into the trap of interpreting prophecy by the headlines in the newspaper. Adventists aren't the only ones who do that. In fact, we probably do it less than dispensationalist evangelical Protestants of other faiths who tend to interpret every event in the Middle East as a sign that the Russians are about to descend on Israel or that the temple is about to be rebuilt in Jerusalem. Some dispensationalists got so excited over the war in Iraq and Kuwait that they almost lost their ability to reason sensibly. I'm glad Adventists didn't do that.

Yet we scarcely fare better when it comes to future events that are meaningful to us. Let the slightest hint of a Sunday law show up in the news, and out come the charts of last-day events. All of a sudden some of us have it figured out down to the year when the latter rain will be poured out and probation will close.

Events or trends?

I believe we should be very cautious about interpreting any one event as *the* fulfillment of a particular Bible prophecy. Trends are much more valid than single events as indicators of the fulfillment of Bible prophecy. For example, when Mussolini returned the Vatican to Rome in 1929, many Adventists said, "The deadly wound is healed." No it wasn't. That was only one small piece very early in a long process that is still going on. Ronald Reagan's appointment of an ambassador to the Vatican in 1984 was not the healing of the deadly wound either, nor was Gorbachev's reconciliation with Rome in 1989. But, taken together, these events form a trend that is leading toward the healing of the deadly wound. And that, in my opinion, *is* a valid way to interpret prophecy, whether from the Bible or Ellen White.

Viewed in this way, I believe it is possible even to see the world's conflict with Iraq in 1991 as a fulfillment of Bible prophecy. With all due respect to the dispensationalists, that war is not mentioned in Daniel or Revelation or the major and minor prophets of the Old Testament. But the context of the war and the alignment of nations that arose out of it are significant as trends that appear to be fulfilling Bible prophecy. I will have more to say about that later in this book.

While I believe we need to be careful *how* we interpret, I believe that we *must* interpret. Interpretation of Ellen White's views on last-day events is even more important today because we live between 70 and 140 years from the time she wrote. I think most Adventist scholars would agree that she wrote of earth's final events in the context of her own time. Now we must understand her predictions in the light of what is happening in our day, which is significantly different from hers in a variety of ways, not the least of which is the much greater speed with which history is unfolding today.

You will find that I have done considerable interpretation in this book—considerable application to our own time of what Scripture and Ellen White say about the end time. I do not claim that my conclusions are 100 percent accurate. However, I believe we have a responsibility to try to understand our own times in light of Bible prophecy. This book is my effort to fulfill that responsibility. I present my views both to encourage God's people to prepare for the end time and also with the hope that where my interpretations are unwarranted, others will provide the needed correction. I hope you will not hesitate to do that. For my part, I promise not to argue.

Chronological charts

A word about charts. Because of the misuse some Adventists have made of them, I am a bit reluctant to create charts. I am particularly opposed to charts that try to fit every last detail into one single flow of events. I find Ellen White quite consistent in her view of the broad sweep of end-time events but often rather hazy about the details. I don't think, for example, that it's possible to nail down exactly when the shaking, the latter rain, and the loud cry will begin or end in relation to a supposed first, second, or third national Sunday law.

However, there is a certain chronological order to Ellen White's view of the end time, and in some cases diagramming this broad outline on a chart can aid understanding. For that reason, where it seems that a chart or diagram would help the reader to understand a point, I have provided one.

You will find, however, that I have not combined the information from the individual charts scattered throughout the book into a single "master chart" at the end. Such a chart would no doubt satisfy some people's curiosity, but I don't think it would make the points I stress in the various chapters any easier to understand. If you would like to have such a chart, I encourage you to create your own. The review of the evidence and the effort to put everything together will fix the chronology of the end time in your mind much better than had I done it for you.

Spiritual issues of the end time

"But our salvation doesn't depend on understanding every jot and tittle of end-time events," you say. "Why not focus on the love of God and developing a relationship with Jesus?"

That very question brings into focus the dual purpose of this book: prophetic events *and* the spiritual message that arises out of them. Unfortunately, in their fascination with the "what" and the "when" of last-day events, Adventists have too often ignored the spiritual issues involved. Understanding the order of events is important. It's just not *most* important. Most important is developing a relationship with Jesus that will see us through those times. In the context of spiritual relationships, understanding the order of last-day events can be very helpful. In the following statement Ellen White stressed this combination of prophetic events and their spiritual implication:

The student . . . should understand the nature of the two principles that are contending for supremacy, and should learn to trace their working through the records of history and prophecy, to the great consummation. He should see how this controversy enters into every phase of human experience; how in every act of life he himself reveals the one or the other of the two antagonistic motives; and how, whether he will or not, he is even now deciding upon which side of the controversy he will be found (*Education*, p. 190).

Notice the two points Ellen White emphasized: Tracing the great controversy through history and prophecy, and recognizing its influence in one's own life. Prophetic events and spiritual life are the theme of this book. And nothing is more important than the last sentence of Ellen White's paragraph: "Whether he will or not, *he [the student] is even now deciding upon which side of the great controversy he will be found.*" The choices you and I are making today, this very moment, will become the determining factors in the ultimate choices we make when the end time is upon us.

I hope you find this book interesting and informative, but most of all, I hope you find it spiritually uplifting. My greatest hope is that it will help many of God's people to keep their relationship with Jesus who otherwise might fall by the way in earth's darkest hour.

CHAPTER

2

Will We Keep Our Faith?

Several years ago my wife Lois and I decided that it might be wise for us to sell our house in Boise, Idaho, and move to Caldwell. Lois taught nursing at a junior college just across the state line in Ontario, Oregon, which meant driving an hour to work each day and an hour back. Moving to Caldwell would cut her driving time almost in half. Since we weren't sure a move would be best, we prayed about it. We told the Lord how much we felt our house was worth and asked Him to send us a buyer willing to pay that price if it would be in our best interest to move.

Within two months of the time we listed our house, we were signing the papers to sell. Then we started looking for a house in Caldwell, and within one week we found exactly what we wanted. It had an assumable loan at 8 percent interest that cost us only $45 in closing costs. Unbelievable!

Lois and I were sure the Lord was leading.

And then the strangest thing happened. Less than a year after we moved to Caldwell, Lois terminated her employment at the college in Ontario—before she had another job to take its place! Because of the circumstances, we both felt she should quit her job, but now we were scratching our heads, wondering whether the Lord had really led us to move to Caldwell.

Lois began looking for work, and within a week she found an opening at the department of public health in Caldwell—a five-minute drive from our home—for which she was perfectly qualified. The director hired her on the spot.

17

Needless to say, Lois and I have no doubt that God led us to sell our house in Boise and gave us the house in Caldwell. We will always remember those events as proof positive that God was leading in our lives.

Let me ask you, though, were the events themselves proof of God's leading? Lots of people buy and sell houses each day with no thought whatsoever about God. A secular-minded person looking at our situation would call it good luck. How could we prove otherwise? It takes faith to see God's involvement in the events of our lives. To those who have faith, certain events take on a whole new meaning.

What is true of our personal lives is also true of history. We look back on certain events in history, and we say, "God intervened there, and there, and there."

The Exodus was one of those times in human history when we believe God intervened in the lives of His people in a most dramatic way. Moses said, "The Lord took you and brought you out of the iron-smelting furnace, out of Egypt, to be the people of his inheritance." "Because he loved your forefathers and chose their descendants after them, he brought you out of Egypt by his Presence and his great strength" (Deuteronomy 4:20, 37).

Forever after that, certain events were burned into the minds of the Israelites as evidence of God's leading—the ten plagues in Egypt, the crossing of the Red Sea, God's appearance in thunder and lightning on Mount Sinai, water from the rock in the wilderness, the manna that fell every day for forty years, and the fall of Jericho, to name a few. Pharaoh looked at the plagues and denied that God was at work, but the Israelites had no doubt.

Yet they did doubt. When the wilderness got hot enough and dry enough, they complained to Moses that *he*, not God, had brought them out there to die. Never mind the dramatic events— ten plagues, the Red Sea, and Sinai. *When the Israelites' faith grew weak, the events took on a different meaning.*

A series of events occurred 2,000 years ago that Christians and Jews interpret in opposite ways. Christians believe that Jesus Christ was born of a virgin, that during His ministry He performed miraculous signs, and that He died on the cross to save us from our sins. We believe that the greatest event in all history occurred three days later, when He rose from the dead.

Jews today admit that Jesus died on a cross, but they deny that God had anything to do with it. Christians, on the other hand, believe that through the Crucifixion, God put an indelible mark on human history. But that's faith, not proof.

From the Bible we understand that the high points in salvation history have always been marked by dramatic events that tell us God has intervened in human affairs. We have every reason to believe, then, that the next great step in the plan of salvation, the second coming of Christ and the weeks and months leading up to it, will also be marked by dramatic events.

Think about it: plagues, earthquakes, hailstones, and a great battle. Those are events yet to happen. Adventists have never believed that the Bible described the future in symbols only. We have always recognized the Lisbon earthquake and the falling of the stars as literal events that fulfilled predictions made by John in Revelation 6:12, 13, and we have also believed that the seven last plagues will be fulfilled quite literally. Though we recognize certain symbols in the Bible's description of the Battle of Armageddon, we generally agree that the battle itself will in some way be a literal event. And the great earthquake at Christ's second coming, as described in Revelation 16:18, will be a literal catastrophe that shatters the earth's crust and destroys the things human beings have made. How much more powerful can an event be than that?

Just as God's people in the past have commemorated His great acts in salvation history with songs of praise, so we, when we get to heaven, will praise Him for His great acts in connection with the end of the world and the second coming of Christ. Notice this song from Revelation 15:3, 4, sung by "those who had been victorious over the beast and his image and over the number of his name":

> Great and marvelous are your deeds,
>   Lord God Almighty.
> Just and true are your ways,
>   King of the ages.
> Who will not fear you, O Lord,
>   and bring glory to your name?
> For you alone are holy.

All nations will come
  and worship before you,
  for your righteous acts have been revealed (emphasis
  supplied).

We sometimes think back to the events surrounding the Exodus or the life of Christ and wonder what it would have been like to witness them. Moses said, "The Red Sea split in half," and we say, "Wow! I'd like to have seen that happen!" It seems real to us because someone who saw it wrote it down and we can read about it.

Can you imagine what the events in the near future will be like? God's deliverance of the Israelites involved only one nation at a time in history when human technology was primitive by our standards. When God delivers us in the near future, on the other hand, it will be from a worldwide enemy that has the most sophisticated equipment ever available for communication and persecution, when Satan will direct the battle in person. The most awesome events will take place in connection with our deliverance, and we will see and hear and feel them. I get excited just thinking about it!

Let me warn you, though, not to get too excited too soon.

The events will be the most dramatic in human history. They will be evidence on the grandest scale that God is at work. And they will be truly exciting to live through—if you and I are spiritually right with God. But if we are not, we had better watch out, for two reasons.

First, the final events of earth's history won't come with a tag on them that says, "Final events." Scientists will be able to give a perfectly reasonable explanation of every one, I'm sure. By themselves, the events will not be evidence that God is at work. In fact, I'd like to suggest to you that it will be easier to disbelieve at that time than to believe!

Second, it won't be enough to *know* about the final events of earth's history or even to *believe* they are coming. Unless we have developed a personal faith relationship with Jesus *before* these events occur, we will be overcome even while we recognize what's happening around us.

Does that sound strange? Think about the experience of the children of Israel for a moment. God delivered them from Egypt with ten terrible plagues. He brought them through the Red Sea and appeared to them in thunder and lightning on Sinai. He brought them bread from heaven and water from a rock. Yet when the going got tough, the people said, "Moses, why did *you* bring us out here to die in the wilderness? We wish we were back in Egypt!" (see Numbers 11:5, 18; Acts 7:39). They forgot all about God's part in their escape from Egypt. Instead, they reinterpreted those awesome events to match their disbelief.

Or think about the Jews at Christ's time. They knew the prophecies of His coming perfectly well. When He came they saw the same miracles that everyone else saw, but only the disciples recognized the Messiah in those events. *The events were not enough to convince people who refused to believe in the first place.* Jesus said, "They will not be convinced even if someone rises from the dead" (Luke 16:31). To prove the point, He raised a man from the dead, yet less than a week later the Jews were saying, "Come down from the cross and we'll believe you" (see Matthew 27:42). But they wouldn't have.

Our hearts beat a little faster when we see indications that the last days are upon us. Let me tell you, one of these days your heart will race. The events in the near future won't be a glorified Disneyland. They will be the most terrible experience you and I or anyone else has ever been through, and unless our faith is strong *before* they begin, when those events come, we, like the Israelites, will blame God instead of thanking Him. Like the Jews, we will curse Him instead of praising Him.

That's why the parable of the ten virgins is so important. It tells us we must be ready before the bridegroom arrives. Once He arrives, it's too late, no matter how eagerly we have anticipated His arrival. Prophetic events that we had formerly believed would be from God we will reinterpret to match the disbelief we've actually had all along. In other words, final events of this earth's history will determine those who have true faith and those who do not; they will separate the genuine from the false. Unless we have a strongly developed faith before the final events happen, we will be sorted into the group of disbelievers because we *will* be disbelievers, in spite of our prior claim to believe.

God told the Israelites that He brought them out of Egypt with "miraculous signs and wonders, by war, by a mighty hand

and an outstretched arm," "by great and awesome deeds" (see Deuteronomy 4:34). One of these days He will deliver His people from earth's final war with similar spectacular events. But don't count on events alone to persuade you to do anything but curse God—even if you know about them ahead of time!

If you get nothing else out of this book, I hope you learn that *now is the time to get ready for the future*, because when the future comes, it will be too late to prepare.

CHAPTER

3

The Final Crisis

When the door closed on Noah's ark, the probation of those who stood on the outside closed along with it. They had squandered their last opportunity to enter the ark and be saved. Yet for another seven days, they danced and played around the ark, while nature continued as it had from the beginning. Nothing in the world around them so much as hinted that doomsday was just around the corner. Not until the lightning began to flash, the thunder began to roll, and the rain began to fall, did they realize anything was wrong.

That will not be the case the next time God destroys the world. Christ's coming will not interrupt a world that is partying. It will interrupt a world in severe trauma. Prior to the second coming of Christ, the entire planet will be engulfed in disaster more severe than anything the world has ever known. Scripture calls it "a time of trouble, such as never was since there was a nation" (Daniel 12:1, KJV). Ellen White often spoke of it as "the crisis ahead," "the final crisis," and "the final conflict."

The purpose of this chapter is to introduce you to the concept of a final crisis, and the purpose of this book is to describe that crisis in detail. An introduction doesn't have to be long, and this chapter isn't long. But don't let its shortness fool you. It summarizes one of the major themes of this book—the theme stated in the title itself: *The Crisis of the End Time*.

Though they don't all call it that, the following cryptic statements from Scripture and Ellen White predict a final crisis:

- He was given power to give breath to the image of the first beast so that it could speak and cause all who refused to worship the image to be killed (Revelation 13:15).

- If anyone worships the beast and his image and receives his mark on the forehead or on the hand, he, too, will drink of the wine of God's fury, which has been poured full strength into the cup of his wrath (Revelation 14:9, 10).

- The coming of the lawless one will be in accordance with the work of Satan displayed in every sort of evil that deceives those who are perishing (2 Thessalonians 2:9, 10).

- We are standing on the threshold of the crisis of the ages (*Prophets and Kings*, p. 278).

- A storm is gathering, ready to burst upon the earth; and when God shall bid His angels loose the winds, there will be such a scene of strife as no pen can picture (*Education*, p. 180).

- The crisis is fast approaching. The rapidly swelling figures show that the time for God's visitation has about come. Although loath to punish, nevertheless He will punish, and that speedily (*Testimonies*, vol. 5, p. 209).

Of course, the question uppermost in every Adventist mind, including yours and mine, is, How much longer do we have? When will the final crisis begin? I cannot give you a date because God has not given anyone the date. However, the signs I point out in the next chapter suggest to me that we have very little time left before the final crisis bursts upon the world.

There is one way, however, in which I want to answer quite specifically the question of when the final crisis will begin. While I cannot point to a date, I can tell you when the final crisis will begin in relation to other major end-time events.

Most Adventists probably don't have any trouble with the idea that the final crisis will precede the second coming of Christ, but many of us, if asked, would probably say that it will commence with the close of probation and the seven last plagues. Scripture and Ellen White both state quite clearly, however, that the final crisis will commence some time *before* the close of probation. Ellen White adds to our understanding of the final crisis by informing us that it will include a series of devastating natural disasters. The purpose of these disasters will be to warn the world, and especially the wicked, of the close of probation and Christ's return. Here is a simple diagram of the final crisis:

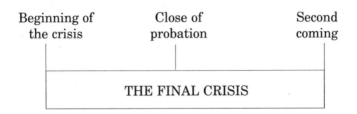

Beginning of the crisis	Close of probation	Second coming
	THE FINAL CRISIS	

The most important point to understand about the final crisis is the reason why it will happen: It will be the conclusion of the great controversy between Christ and Satan.[1] Satan thought he had conquered the world when he tempted Adam and Eve to sin, but he quickly discovered that God had a plan for saving those who place their trust in Him. For 6,000 years now, Satan has been trying to defeat that plan. The final crisis will be a short period, just before Christ returns, when Christ and Satan will make an all-out, final effort to win as many adherents as possible, each to his own side.

The reason we don't read about a similar crisis just before the Flood is that Satan's kingdom was not in jeopardy at that time. He knew there would still be many years after the Flood for him to seduce the human race. He could afford to let a few of God's people get past the Flood. He'd catch them later. In fact, the Flood made his task easier. After the Flood he had only eight righteous people to seduce!

But today Satan is battling for his very life. He is fighting to preserve his kingdom. He knows that his time is short, and Scripture says that the shorter his time gets, the more angry he

---

1. The conclusion of the great controversy won't come until the end of the millennium, of course, but its last phase in earth's history as we know it will be the final crisis that this book is about.

becomes (see Revelation 12:12). During the final crisis Satan will do everything in his power to wipe God's people off the face of the earth so that he can rule supreme. This will be war—literally, as you will see in the chapter on the Battle of Armageddon. God will protect His people, of course, and He will also punish Satan and his followers for their apostasy and their persecution of His followers.

The rest of this book describes this final crisis—the crisis of the end time—in detail. It is a fascinating study, and a sobering one, as we realize the seriousness of the times we face. The final crisis will test our faith more severely than Christians have ever been tested in the history of Christianity. That is why the question above all questions that we will address in this book is how to keep our relationship with Jesus in earth's darkest hour.

4

Signs That Jesus Is Coming Soon

My mother tells me that when she was a little girl she said something to her mother one day about "when I get married." Her mother said, "Oh, honey, you'll never get married. Jesus will come before then."

That was 1915. Today my mother has grandchildren and may have great grandchildren someday.

The apostles believed Jesus was coming in their day. Paul told his readers, "The time is short," and Jesus told John, "I am coming soon" (1 Corinthians 7:29; Revelation 22:20).

Our pioneers who went through the 1844 Disappointment preached the soon coming of Jesus with deep conviction. For nearly 150 years this church has preached the soon coming of Jesus all over the world. From about a dozen people in 1845, our movement has grown to more than six million in the early 1990s.

Yet Jesus still has not come!

By the time you read this, I will probably have preached fifty sermons all across North America in less than two years, telling Seventh-day Adventists everywhere that "Jesus is coming very soon." Yet I would be less than honest if I did not admit to you that I sometimes ask myself, "Am I building up my listeners for another letdown? If John, Paul, our pioneers, and my grandmother all thought Jesus was coming in their day and we're still waiting, who am I to pound the pulpit and tell Seventh-day Adventists that 'Jesus really is coming soon'?"

I cannot prove that Jesus is coming soon. I believe it. That's faith. However, my faith is not blind. It is informed by at least three contemporary signs of the end. I'm not thinking about the Lisbon earthquake, the Dark Day, or the falling of the stars. Those events happened between 150 and 250 years ago. They were important signs that the time of the end had begun, but we now realize that the time of the end is a fairly long period— nearly 200 years now since it began in 1798. The three signs I will share with you in this chapter lead me to the conviction that the time of the end has just about reached its conclusion, and that Jesus is about to come.

1844

Church-state separation under attack

For 150 years Seventh-day Adventists have predicted that church-state separation would come to an end in America, to a great extent through the insistence of conservative Protestants. This idea didn't make sense in the late 1800s. For example, Rev. Theodore Nelson, writing in the introduction to Dudley Canright's *Seventh-day Adventism Renounced*, said:

> Nothing can be more absurd than their [the Adventists'] interpretation of current events, and, especially, their belief that our general and state governments are about to be converted into engines of religious persecution and despotism. . . .
> Such a change would be a great[er] miracle than for God to grow a giant oak in an instant (pp. 20, 23).

As recently as 1960, American Protestants forced John F. Kennedy to support separation of church and state as a condition of winning their votes. But please notice the status of church-state separation in America today:

> Contrary to contemporary belief, the "separation of church and state," as defined by recent United States Supreme Court decisions, is not in keeping with the beliefs and desires of the framers and ratifiers of the Constitution and the First Amendment. . . .
> Not only is the word *separation* absent from it [the first amendment], there is no reference or allusion to it. Their amendment did not mandate separation in 1787; it does not

authorize it now (*Fundamentalist Journal*, July-August 1984, pp. 28, 30).

Did you notice where that statement appeared? Not in a Catholic book or magazine article. It appeared in the *Fundamentalist Journal*, published by none other than Jerry Falwell, one of the most prominent leaders in right-wing American Protestantism today. The new Religious Right, which is spearheaded by conservative American Protestants with strong Catholic support, has declared open war on America's foundational principle of separation of church and state.

Baptist support for church-state separation has a long and honorable history. Baptists originated in England in the 1600s, when as a persecuted minority they took a firm stand on church-state separation. Roger Williams, one of the first Baptists to arrive in America, championed church-state separation in this land, and Baptists have continued their strong support of that principle almost to the present time.

Unfortunately, Southern Baptist support for church-state separation has eroded seriously in the last few years.

W. A. Criswell was for many years the pastor of the First Baptist Church of Dallas, Texas—the largest church in the Southern Baptist Convention. Southern Baptists are also the largest conservative Protestant denomination in the world. On one occasion, when he was asked by a reporter what he thought about church-state separation, Criswell shot back the reply, "I believe this notion of the separation of church and state was the figment of some infidel's imagination" (*Church and State*, October 1984, p. 23).

A number of years ago the various Baptist groups in the United States pooled their resources to form the Baptist Joint Committee on Public Affairs—the Baptist Joint Committee for short. The purpose of this joint committee was to represent all Baptist denominations in matters pertaining to religious liberty. Because they were the largest group represented, Southern Baptists naturally contributed the largest amount.

For years and years, the Baptist Joint Committee has stood shoulder-to-shoulder with Seventh-day Adventists in support of church-state separation. Often, we would defend church-state separation together in the courts of law. The Baptist Joint Committee still defends church-state separation as strongly as we do.

However, the Southern Baptist Church recently did a complete about-face. For years, Southern Baptists contributed $400,000 a year to the Baptist Joint Committee. But at their annual session in New Orleans in 1990, Southern Baptists cut their support to the Baptist Joint Committee from $400,000 to just $50,000 a year, and in 1991 they eliminated the $50,000. The reason? "The BJC, a pro-separationist agency, was too liberal and out of touch with the reigning ideology among Southern Baptists" (*Church and State*, July-August, 1990, p. 15).

Unfortunately, conservative Protestants are not the only force trying to break down church-state separation in America today. All three branches of the American government have gotten into the act. President Bush has jumped onto the "parochiaid"[1] bandwagon. Lamar Alexander, the U.S. Secretary of Education under George Bush, said, "Choice plans that would funnel tax aid to parochial and other private schools are 'absolutely fundamental' to [the president's] education legislation" (*Church and State*, July-August 1991, p. 3). In addition, both President Reagan and President Bush have gone on record supporting prayer in the public schools and condemning abortion. Both of these are high on today's conservative Protestant agenda, and both are a major threat to church-state separation.

Congress has also gotten into the anti-separation act:

> Support for church-state separation has reached disappointingly low levels in the Congress. . . . In its rush to enact some type of federal day care subsidy, Congress has caved in to pressure from religious lobbies and "all but abandoned strict separation. . . . America [has], for the first time in your lifetime, . . . moved in the Congress of the United States to pay churches to provide education to America's young citizens. My own view is that the wall of separation is seriously jeopardized" (U.S. Rep. Pat Williams [D, Mont.], quoted in *Church and State*, November 1990, pp. 4, 5).

---

1. A term coined by Americans United for Separation of Church and State that means state financial aid for parochial schools.

Most ominous of all, however, is the situation in the United States Supreme Court. Ronald Reagan appointed three justices to the Supreme Court, and, so far, George Bush has appointed two. All five of these justices are known for their conservative views. Reagan also elevated William Rehnquist, a conservative who was on the court when Reagan took office, to the position of chief justice. These recent appointees will be transforming this country's understanding of religious liberty for years to come.

According to *U.S. News & World Report*, the new Supreme Court "is blasting fissures in the church-state barrier and rewriting longstanding rules on religion's role in public life" (18 June 1990, p. 22). *U.S. News* calls Reagan appointee Anthony Kennedy "a persistent advocate of weakening the separation between church and state," and quotes Kennedy as saying that " 'substantial revision' of church-state law may be in order" (ibid.)

The following statement by Chief Justice William Rehnquist would have been utterly unacceptable to America's Protestant community thirty years ago. Today, a significant number of Protestants are cheering the chief justice on:

> The "wall of separation between church and state" is a metaphor based on bad history, a metaphor which "has proved useless as a guide to judging. It should be frankly and explicitly abandoned (*Church and State*, July-August 1985, p. 14).

Following Clarence Thomas's confirmation as a Supreme Court justice, Gary Ross, an Adventist expert on government affairs, commented that "it would take a miracle to reverse" the court's present drift away from church-state separation (Gary M. Ross, "Stark New Realities," *Adventist Review,* 14 November 1991, p. 15).

A number of years ago I was pastor of the Adventist church in Waco, Texas. Waco is the home of Baylor University, the largest Southern Baptist university in the world—and the only university in the United States where students can earn a degree in church-state studies. On one occasion I had the opportunity of visiting with Dr. John Wood, chairman of the department of church-state studies at Baylor. In the course of our conversation, Dr. Wood said to me, "Mr. Moore, it's not a question of *whether* church-state separation will end in this country, but only *when*."

Ten years later we are seeing a dramatic fulfillment of Dr. Wood's prediction.

And now I want you to notice something that I believe is extremely significant. As recently as 1960, American Protestants firmly supported church-state separation, and the United States Supreme Court was utterly committed to that principle. *Only since about 1975 have conservative American Protestants begun demanding an end to church-state separation*, and the trend in the Supreme Court is even more recent than that.

Spiritualism

For nearly 150 years Seventh-day Adventists have predicted that at the very end of time, just before the second coming of Christ, spiritualism would be one of the most dominant religious forces in the world, including the United States. This seemed preposterous when we first began predicting it. American Protestants of the 1850s "had an aversion to this spectral cult comparable to the horror of [their] Puritan forebear[s] of the 1690's over witchcraft" (Arthur W. Spalding, *Origin and History of Seventh-day Adventists*, vol. 1, p. 133).

As recently as the late 1950s, when I was a senior theology student at Union College in Lincoln, Nebraska, I remember scratching my head as I read Ellen White's statements in *The Great Controversy* about the dominant role of spiritualism in the world at the end of time. How, I wondered, could rationally minded Westerners—scientists, bankers, lawyers, and business executives—ever fall for such foolishness as crystal balls and séances in dark back rooms? Our culture is based on science, and science demands objective proof—evidence that can be seen and measured and tested by many scientists. It isn't interested in magic and the occult. As recently as the late 1950s Ellen White's prediction about the dominant role of spiritualism at the end of time just didn't make sense.

But the last quarter of the twentieth century has brought a dramatic fulfillment to Ellen White's words. Today the New Age, the modern name for spiritualism, is the fastest-growing religious movement in the world. New Age terms such as *channeling* and *astral projection* have become household words. Back in the late 1950s, I thought bankers, lawyers, and business executives would never fall for such nonsense as crystal balls and séances in dark back rooms. But according to a leading proponent of today's New Age movement, it's happening:

[Actress Shirley MacLaine] believes not only in reincarnation, but is convinced of the reality of "spiritual guides" who speak to humans through psychics.

[She] believes the world is on the brink of a spiritual rebirth. . . . [And] although many people are hesitant to admit publicly that they believe in this rebirth, Shirley knows they are there. "I have seen leading bankers and doctors and executives visiting psychics for advice. I sit in on these channeling sessions where they ask the soul entities about economics, the stock market, projections for world depression and OPEC" (*Ladies' Home Journal*, June 1983, pp. 26, 33).

And for those who are persuaded only by what science itself tells them, Satan has yet another deception: extraterrestrials.

What have extraterrestrials to do with science? you ask. Please read on:

Scientists are making major strides in answering the tantalizing question of whether humans are the only intelligent beings in the universe.

The Harvard Project, sponsored by the Planetary Society, a private group interested in space exploration, is only one of several intense new searches for extraterrestrial intelligence . . . started around the world in recent months.

"If anyone is trying to get in touch with us, we're ready to listen," says Paul Horowitz, the Harvard University physicist in charge of the Project.

Last year [1982], the scientific community, including 68 renowned scientists in a letter to *Science* magazine, urged an international effort to listen for other civilizations in the universe (*U.S. News & World Report*, 2 May 1983, p. 36).

Well, that was 1983, you say. Yes. Back then scientists were urging "an international effort to listen for other civilizations in the universe." Today they're doing it.

Right now, two radio telescopes are operating in the United States—one at Ohio State University and the other at Harvard's Oak Ridge Observatory in Massachusetts—and NASA is building a third that is projected to begin operating in 1992. In 1990 Harvard also began operating a radio telescope in Argentina to cover the Southern skies. And all of these radio telescopes are dedicated to just one purpose—the search for extraterrestrial intelligence.

The Skeptical Inquirer, a quarterly journal that is endorsed by the American Humanist Association, is dedicated to debunking claims of the supernatural. Normally, *SI* is very skeptical of reports about UFOs, communication with spirits, and Ouija boards. But it is utterly committed to the search for extraterrestrial intelligence. In a recent article, Thomas R. McDonough, director of the Planetary Society's search for extraterrestrial intelligence, confessed in the pages of *The Skeptical Inquirer* that he will be "very depressed" if no signals are picked up from intelligent beings in outer space within ten years—by the year 2001 (*The Skeptical Inquirer*, Spring 1991, p. 261).

The overwhelming mass of "star wars" science fiction that is flooding the entertainment market today adds to this picture. Science and contemporary science fiction meet at one point: Both are intensely interested in intelligent beings beyond our own planet and solar system. Fiction writers dream about them. Today's scientists are searching for them.

And whether it's genuine science or fiction science, I am fully persuaded that Satan is using these means to "soften up" the world for his masterpiece of deception. When Satan appears as Christ, I fully expect that he will introduce himself as ET. If not, he's going to have to ignore all the genuine scientific search for extraterrestrials and all the science fiction, all the star wars movies and videos and books and magazine articles that have flooded the entertainment market during the last several decades. *But Satan isn't going to ignore all of that.* He's the one behind it all, and I'm convinced it's part of his strategy to prepare the world for his masterpiece of deception.

Almost 150 years ago Seventh-day Adventists began to predict that at the very end of time, just before Jesus returns, spiritualism would be a dominant religious force in the world. This prediction made absolutely no sense back then, but please notice that *it has begun to be fulfilled since about 1975.*

Roman Catholic political power

On January 1, 1076, Henry IV, emperor of the Holy Roman Empire, attempted to depose Pope Gregory VII. Then he called a meeting of twenty-six bishops and persuaded them to refuse obedience to the pope.

That was the wrong thing to do!

The pope promptly excommunicated Henry and absolved his subjects of their oath of allegiance. Henry had only two choices: bow to the pope or lose his throne.

He bowed.

In the winter of 1077 he traveled to Canossa in northern Italy and stood outside barefoot in the snow while the pope enjoyed the warmth of his castle. After three days the pope finally granted Henry an audience, heard his confession, and reinstated him into the church. Whereupon Henry returned to his throne in Germany.

For several hundred years a struggle had been going on in Europe over who had the greater authority, the king or the pope. This event settled that question:

> By doing penance Henry had admitted the legality of the Pope's measures and had given up the king's traditional position of authority equal or even superior to that of the church. The relations between church and state were changed forever (*Encyclopædia Britannica*, 15th ed., s.v. "Henry IV").

It is common knowledge that the Roman Catholic Church held political control over Europe during most of the first half of the second millennium. However, by the year 1500, the church's control over Europe had slipped to the point that when a German monk and professor at the University of Wittenberg nailed ninety-five theses to the church door in 1517, the church could not force the emperor or the German princes to hand him over for trial in Rome.

The church's political power in Europe continued to slip, until in 1798 the French general Berthier, under orders from Napoleon, entered Rome and took the pope prisoner. Yet Rome's political power had still not come to a complete end. The church continued to control large tracts of land in central Italy, which she governed until 1870, when the modern nation of Italy was established.

What's the point of all this?

The point is that in the early 1850s, Seventh-day Adventists began predicting that at the very end of time, just before the second coming of Christ, the political power of the Roman Catholic Church would be restored. Please notice that when we began making this prediction, the deadly wound was still hemorrhaging!

It didn't make sense, back then, to say that the Roman Catholic Church would regain its political power in the world. People thought Adventists were crazy. As recently as 1951 it didn't make sense. In that year, President Harry Truman appointed an ambassador to the Vatican, and American Protestants rose up in arms. Truman quickly withdrew his appointment. In America, at least, the Roman Catholic Church did not have political power.

Were Seventh-day Adventists mere dreamers to predict the restoration of Rome's political power in the world at the very end of time, just before Jesus comes?

Please read on.

By 1980 more than 100 countries around the world had recognized the Vatican as a legitimate political state, but the world's two superpowers still had not.

Then, in 1983—you probably remember it well—President Ronald Reagan secretly and swiftly pushed a bill through the U.S. Senate establishing diplomatic relations with the Vatican. *And America's Protestants scarcely whimpered.*

Still, the world's other superpower held out—until late 1989. Early in December of that year President George Bush and Soviet Premier Mikhail Gorbachev met on a ship near the island of Malta, off the coast of Italy. On the way to attend that meeting, Mr. Gorbachev stopped by for a visit with Pope John Paul II in Rome. And when the pope and the Soviet premier emerged from that meeting, they announced that the Vatican and the Kremlin would establish diplomatic relations.

The other giant had capitulated! Commenting on that event *Time* magazine said:

When the Holy Roman Emperor Henry IV decided to seek the pardon of Pope Gregory VII in 1077, he stood barefoot for three days in the snow outside the papal quarters in Canossa, Italy. Gorbachev's concordat with the church was no less significant in its way (*Time*, 11 December 1989, p. 36).

And that's not all. The whole world watched in awe as Eastern Europe crumbled during the last half of 1989. Yet most of the world probably was not aware of the crucial role the Roman Catholic Church, and particularly Pope John Paul II, played in those events. But the world's politicians knew, and *Time* magazine knew:

John Paul helped inflame the fervor for freedom in his Polish homeland that has swept like brush fire across Eastern Europe. . . . While Gorbachev's hands-off policy was the immediate cause of the chain reaction of liberation that has swept through Eastern Europe in the past few months, *John Paul deserves much of the longer-range credit* (*Time*, 4 December 1989, p. 74, emphasis supplied).

One of the most fascinating books I've read in recent months was written by a former Jesuit priest named Malachi Martin. The title of the book, *The Keys of This Blood*, seems innocent enough—till you read the subtitle: *The Struggle for World Dominion Between Pope John Paul II, Mikhail Gorbachev and the Capitalist West.* Now do you understand why that book has become one of the most widely read books in the Adventist Church since its publication in September 1990?

Please read the following paragraphs from the first two pages of Martin's book:

Willing or not, ready or not, we are all involved in an all-out, no-holds-barred, three-way global competition. Most of us are not competitors, however. We are the stakes. For the competition is about who will establish the first one-world system of government that has ever existed in the society of nations. It is about who will hold and wield the dual power of authority and control over each of us as individuals and over all of us together as a community; over the entire six billion people expected by demographers to inhabit the earth by early in the third millennium.

The competition is all-out because, now that it has started, there is no way it can be reversed or called off. . . .

It is not too much to say, in fact, that the chosen purpose of John Paul's pontificate—the engine that drives his papal grand policy and that determines his day-to-day, year-by-year strategies—is to be the victor in that competition, now well under way (*The Keys of This Blood*, pp. 17, 18, emphasis supplied).

The rest of Mr. Martin's book—all 700 pages of it—backs up these introductory paragraphs. It is fascinating reading.

My point is this. Nearly 150 years ago, Seventh-day Adventists began to predict that the political power of the Roman Catholic Church would be restored in the last remnant of time, just before the second coming of Jesus. That prediction made absolutely no sense back then. And please notice that *it has begun to make sense only since 1975*.

You probably have noticed by now that all three of the contemporary signs of Christ's soon coming that I mentioned have begun to develop since 1975. Prior to that they did not make much sense. Please keep 1975 firmly fixed in your mind because we're going to talk about it in the next chapter.

CHAPTER

5

So Where Are We Now?

Imagine that you are hiking across the western part of the United States. Anyone familiar with that part of the world knows it is a combination of mountains and deserts. Suppose that you are walking across a hot, dry desert, longing for the cool mountain breezes. At the beginning of your journey is a sign that says, "Antelope Mountains—100 miles."

Just thinking about a hike like that is enough to make me tired, but you are determined to make the trip, so you start across the desert. Several times a day you come to landmarks that you can locate on your map, and each time you check to see how much progress you've made. At the end of each day you wonder, "Will I see the Antelope Mountains tomorrow?" But you can believe that the mountains are up ahead only because the map says so. You haven't actually seen them yet.

And then one day it happens. Toward the end of the day, you think you can make out the shape of the mountains in the distance. The next morning you get up early, anxious to make as much progress as possible, and sure enough, by the middle of the day it's obvious that the mountains really are up ahead. Now you don't have to believe they're there because the map says so. You know they're there because you can see them. By the end of the day, you can even begin to make out different colors and shades. Mostly the mountains are dark

39

blue, but there is a streak of white here and a splotch of pink there. Maybe the white is shale, you say to yourself. Maybe the pink is sandstone. And as you get closer, you think perhaps there is snow on the peaks.

By the middle of the next day it's very evident that the higher elevations of the mountains are covered with trees, so what looked like snow must have been clouds. By the end of the day you're climbing the foothills, and you can tell that at least one of those white streaks is a huge granite cliff.

Our journey to the second coming

Your imaginary journey to the Antelope Mountains is a parable of the journey of God's people toward the second coming of Jesus. Our pioneers who came out of the Great Disappointment believed the second coming of Jesus was very near because the stars had fallen less than fifteen years before; the sun had turned dark and the moon had turned to blood scarcely more than fifty years before; and it was less than one hundred years since the Lisbon earthquake. Our pioneers didn't realize that these events were a signpost at the very beginning of their journey that said, "Second coming of Jesus—100 miles." They didn't know that there was still a lot of hiking to do before they could see the mountains.

I am convinced, however, that today we can see the outline of the mountains up ahead. I base that conclusion on the evidence I discussed in the last chapter. For nearly 150 years, Seventh-day Adventists have predicted that at the very end of time, just before the second coming of Jesus, three important trends would develop in the world:

- The Protestant disavowal of church-state separation in America.
- The rise of spiritualism as a world religion.
- The restoration of the political power of the papacy.

And, as I pointed out in the previous chapter, each of these signs began to manifest itself openly to the world about 1975—just as the final quarter of the twentieth century was getting underway.

In my story about your hike, I had you saying to yourself one day, "That looks like the Antelope Mountains up ahead!" After another half day's walk it became evident that the mountains really were up ahead.

I can still remember, about 1975, noticing each of these trends in the world and saying to myself, "That looks like what we've said all along would happen just before Jesus comes!" Now, several years later, it is very evident that if present trends continue, earth's final events really are up ahead.

For most of our history we've had to believe these things would happen. Now they are happening! Now we can see the end approaching.

That's where we are today.

Is it appropriate for Seventh-day Adventists to interpret trends in the world, and particularly trends in the United States, in this way? I believe it's our responsibility to do so. We have the road map. Let's use it! God wants us to know where we are in the stream of time. That's why He gave us the map.

And now I'd like you to think about this whole question from another perspective.

The delay

In His sermon about His second coming, Jesus told a story about ten girls. Five were wise, He said, and five were foolish. You know the story well enough; I hardly need to repeat it here. The point of the story was that the five wise girls carried extra oil to replenish their lamps when they began to go out, but the five foolish girls did not. As a result, the five foolish girls missed out on the wedding banquet.

Let's assume it was about six o'clock in the evening when these girls arrived at the place where they were to await the bridegroom. They confidently expected that he would be there by seven. However, seven o'clock came and went, then eight, then nine—and still no bridegroom. One by one the girls dozed off, and soon all ten of them were fast asleep.

Please notice that *there was a delay in the arrival of the bride-groom.*

Ellen White said that this story illustrates "the experience of the church that shall live just before His [Christ's] second coming" (*Christ's Object Lessons*, p. 406).

Imagine yourself boarding a time machine and going back to

the 1844 Disappointment and the years immediately following. You meet James White, and you say, "James, is Jesus coming soon?"

"Oh, absolutely!"

"How soon?"

"Oh, no more than a few years now."

"Well, say, by 1860?"

"Oh, much sooner than that!"

Yet you know as well as I do that our church didn't even organize until 1863.

So you attend the 1863 General Conference session where we organized, and you approach John Byington, the first General Conference president. "Elder Byington, when do you think Jesus will come?"

"Oh, any time now."

"How soon is that?"

"Just a few years at the most."

"Maybe by the year 1900?"

"Oh, long before that!"

Yet you and I are pushing the year 2000, and Jesus still has not come!

At the very least we have to say that there has been a delay. This seems to perplex some Adventists. But why should it? Jesus said a delay would happen. In Jesus' parable, the delay of the bridegroom was a type, a prophecy, if you please, of the experience of the church in our day. Instead of being discouraged that there has been a delay, we should rejoice that prophecy has been fulfilled!

In the Bible, oil represents the Holy Spirit. The lesson of the parable is that the delay is not simply procrastination or indifference on God's part. The delay has a distinct purpose: To give His people time to obtain the Holy Spirit. Perhaps as late as eleven forty-five the foolish girls could have slipped away, bought their oil, and returned in time to attend the banquet.

The question "So where are we now?" is crucial to those who live during the delay, and the closer we come to the second coming of Christ, the more compelling that question becomes. By eleven forty-five the clock is screaming at us, "Wake up! Wake up! Time is almost gone!"

I cannot guarantee that Jesus is coming soon. However, I can tell you that some of the most specific signs of the end, which Adventists have preached for 150 years, have all but exploded in our faces since about 1975. Those trends are an undeniable fact, and there is every reason to believe that they will continue to develop in the same direction they have been going.

Because of these trends, it is my personal conviction that the end is very near. I wouldn't be writing this book if I didn't hold that belief with full confidence.

Keeping your relationship with Jesus

I would like to close this chapter by raising the most important question this book addresses: How can you and I keep our relationship with Jesus in earth's darkest hour? And here's my answer: You and I must have a relationship with Jesus *before* we enter earth's darkest hour if we expect to have it *in* earth's darkest hour.

Please get used to reading that, because I'll be saying over and over again that those who don't know Jesus before the end time will never know Him at all. That's the message of the parable of the ten virgins. Ellen White does not mention this parable in the quotation below, but the lesson is the same:

> Many have in a great measure failed to receive the former rain [the Holy Spirit]. They have not obtained all the benefits that God has thus provided for them. They expect that the lack will be supplied by the latter rain. When the richest abundance of grace shall be bestowed, they intend to open their hearts to receive it. They are making a terrible mistake (*Testimonies to Ministers*, p. 507).

Adventists have an intense fascination with the signs of Christ's soon coming. We want the assurance that it's just around the corner. I'm glad of that. It means we haven't forgotten. I believe the closer we get to the end, the more God wants us to know where we live in the stream of time. All those time charts we've prepared over the years are good.

But God is not interested in merely satisfying our curiosity about the order of end-time events. If that's all we get out of the charts, then they do more harm than good. Unless those charts cause us to open our Bibles and fall on our knees, unless they lead us to develop a close relationship with Jesus, we would be better off without them.

Now that you and I understand where we live in the stream of time, I urge you to join me in using the few remaining days and months of the delay for the purpose God gave it—to bring the Holy Spirit into our hearts, to develop a closer relationship with Jesus than we've ever had before.

CHAPTER

6

The Close of Probation

When I was a freshman in college, I had a Bible teacher named Morris Lewis—"the Elder" we called him—who was a favorite with all the students. I took a class in Daniel and Revelation from "the Elder" that year, and one of our assignments was to prepare a chart of last-day events based on both the Bible and the writings of Ellen White. That class has influenced my understanding of earth's final events from that time to the present. In this book I am sharing with you some of the things I learned back then, together with what I've learned from my study since.

The close of probation is one of the most unique features of the Adventist view of the end time. Probation is a period of time granted to sinful human beings in which they can choose to accept God or Satan. The simplest way to define the close of probation is to say that it is the time when Jesus ceases His mediatorial ministry in the heavenly sanctuary and human beings no longer have an opportunity to change their decision for or against God.

Probation will close before Christ returns

Adventists believe that probation will close a short time before Christ returns, just before the seven last plagues begin to fall:

The probation of those who choose to live a life of sin, and

45

neglect the great salvation offered, closes when Christ's ministration ceases just previous to His appearing in the clouds of heaven (*Testimonies*, vol. 2, p. 691).

Probation is ended a short time before the appearing of the Lord in the clouds of heaven (*The Great Controversy*, p. 490).

Many of our beliefs about the end time are similar to those of other Christians, but as far as I know, Adventists are the only ones who talk about a preadvent close of probation. Yet if we are right, the world faces one of the most awesome events in all of history—Christ's cessation of ministry in the heavenly sanctuary just before the time of trouble—and most people don't even know about it.

That's sobering to think about.

Here's a simple chart of last-day events as taught by Adventists. Please fix it firmly in your memory, because even though it's simple, it is basic to nearly everything else you will read in this book.

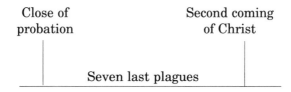

	Close of probation		Second coming of Christ
		Seven last plagues	

The close of probation is a great prophetic landmark that divides human history into two parts. No point in the Adventist view of last-day events is more important than the close of probation. We mark off prophetic events according to whether they come before the close of probation or after. We do not do that with the second coming of Christ so much, because the second coming ends history on this earth as we know it. But a short period of history is still left after the close of probation during which there will be no opportunity for unrepentant sinners to accept Christ and be saved. That's what makes the close of probation such a momentous landmark, such a pivotal point in history and prophetic interpretation.

The biblical evidence

For years I thought that the only evidence Seventh-day Adventists had for probation's closing a short time before Christ's second coming came from Ellen White. Fortunately, more recently I have discovered ample evidence for this concept in Scripture.

I would like to divide our discussion of the biblical evidence for a preadvent close of probation into several parts. First we will examine the evidence from Christ's parables. Then we will look at types of the close of probation in both the Old and New testaments. And, finally, we will examine the evidence in the book of Revelation for a preadvent close of probation.

Christ's parables. There are three classes of people in the world today: those who have accepted Christ, those who have rejected Him, and those who have not made a decision one way or the other. However, Adventists teach that when probation closes, there will be just two classes: the righteous and the wicked.

This concept of only two groups at the end of time—righteous and wicked—is one of the most consistent teachings of Christ's parables, particularly the following:

- The wheat and the weeds (Matthew 13:24-30, 36-43).
- The fish in the net (Matthew 13:47-50).
- The ten virgins (Matthew 25:1-13).
- The men with talents (Matthew 25:14-30).
- The sheep and the goats (Matthew 25:31-46).

The significance of these parables is that even church people will be divided into two classes. It's not enough to have accepted Jesus Christ, to have been baptized and joined the church. Many lifelong Christians will say to Jesus in that day, "Lord, Lord, did we not prophesy in your name, and in your name drive out demons and perform many miracles?" And Jesus will unfortunately have to say to them, "I never knew you. Away from me, you evildoers!" (Matthew 7:22, 23).

Old Testament types of the close of probation. Several stories and one prophecy in the Old Testament are types of the close of probation at the end of the world:

- *The story of Noah.* The whole world was divided into two classes—those who served God and those who did not. The ark created a physical barrier between them.
- *The destruction of Sodom and Gomorrah.* Before the city was divided into two classes, Abraham interceded for the people (see Genesis 18:22-33). This was a type of Christ's intercessory ministry in heaven. Abraham's intercession ceased one afternoon, and the cities were not destroyed until the next morning. This is a type of intercessory ministry ceasing a short time before the final reward is given.
- *The Jewish people.* God gave the Jews 490 years of probationary time (see Daniel 9:24). An important lesson here is that the probation of the Jewish nation ended in A.D. 34 at the conclusion of the seventy weeks, but not the probation of individual Jews. This point will be significant later in this book.

The close of probation in Revelation

Adventists have always understood Revelation 22:11 to be a reference to the close of probation:

> He that is unjust, let him be unjust still: and he which is filthy, let him be filthy still: and he that is righteous, let him be righteous still: and he that is holy, let him be holy still (KJV).

This verse comes at the very end of Revelation, in a collection of verses that form what we might call "concluding remarks." Because it speaks of a final division of the entire human race into two classes, it is a definite reference to the close of probation. However, its location among Revelation's "concluding remarks" provides us with no help whatsoever in determining when that division will occur in relation to other end-time events. To find out, we must examine other evidence in Revelation.

Two classes of people. I pointed out earlier that Christ's parables show a division of the world into two classes, the righteous and the wicked, at the end of time. Revelation teaches the same lesson; here the two classes of people receive either the seal of God (see Revelation 7:1-4; 14:1-5) or the mark of the beast (see chapter 13:16, 17; 14:9, 10).

I think most Christians, including Seventh-day Adventists, understand that the seven last plagues immediately precede the second coming of Christ, and Revelation clearly teaches that the wicked will receive the mark of the beast before the seven last plagues begin to fall (see Revelation 14:9, 10; 15:1; 16:2).

If there will be only two classes of people at the end of time, and if the plagues fall on only one class, then logic forces us to the conclusion that both classes must be defined before the plagues fall. Thus the close of probation—the division of the righteous and the wicked into two classes—must occur before the seven last plagues begin to fall, which is a short time before the second coming of Christ. Let's put that on a diagram:

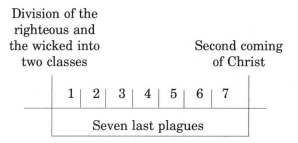

Division of the
righteous and
the wicked into
two classes

Second coming
of Christ

| 1 | 2 | 3 | 4 | 5 | 6 | 7 |

Seven last plagues

The cessation of Christ's mediatorial ministry. There is also evidence in Revelation 15 that Christ's mediatorial ministry will end before the seven last plagues begin to fall. I will mention two points. The first is in verse 5: "After this I looked and in heaven the temple, that is, the tabernacle of Testimony, was opened." A similar text in Revelation 11:19 says, "Then God's temple in heaven was opened, and within his temple was seen the ark of his covenant." Clearly, we are looking into the Most Holy Place of the heavenly sanctuary.

In the earthly sanctuary, when was the Most Holy Place opened to view? At the death of Christ, when the temple veil was torn in two by an unseen hand (see Matthew 27:50, 51). At that moment the services in the earthly sanctuary came to their end.

I believe that the exposure of the Most Holy Place of the heavenly sanctuary just before the seven last plagues are poured out indicates that Christ's mediatorial ministry there has ceased.

The second point in Revelation 15 that suggests that Christ's ministry in the heavenly sanctuary ceases before the plagues fall is the statement in verse 8:

> The temple was filled with smoke from the glory of God and from his power, and no one could enter the temple until the seven plagues of the seven angels were completed.

This statement has a parallel in the Old Testament story of the dedication of Solomon's temple:

> When Solomon finished praying, fire came down from heaven and consumed the burnt offering and the sacrifices, and the glory of the Lord filled the temple. The priests could not enter the temple of the Lord because the glory of the Lord filled it (2 Chronicles 7:1, 2).

Notice that in both Revelation and 2 Chronicles, the priests could not enter the temple because of the glory of God. Two other Old Testament passages about the dedication of Solomon's temple say the same thing and more:

> Then the temple of the Lord was filled with a cloud, and *the priests could not perform their service* because of the cloud, for the glory of the Lord filled the temple (2 Chronicles 5:13, 14, emphasis supplied).

> When the priests withdrew from the Holy Place, the cloud filled the temple of the Lord. And *the priests could not perform their service* because of the cloud, for the glory of the Lord filled his temple (1 Kings 8:10, 11, emphasis supplied).

In both of these texts, the priests could not carry on their mediatorial ministry as long as the cloud and the glory of God filled the temple. This biblical parallel to Revelation 15:8 provides the strongest possible evidence that Christ's mediatorial ministry will cease just before the seven last plagues are poured out.

The close of probation as a process

Most Adventists have always thought of the close of probation as an event that will occur at a particular point in time. However, careful study has led me to the conclusion that the close of probation will be both a point in time and a process. Let me explain in some detail what I mean.

Adventists have always had two thoughts in mind when they speak of the close of probation:

1. The close of probation will be the time when people all over the world make their final decisions about the truth, thereby sealing their eternal destiny.
2. The close of probation will be the time when Jesus ceases His mediatorial ministry in the heavenly sanctuary.

I would like to suggest that *the time when each of these events will happen is different*. Jesus will cease His mediatorial ministry at the point we have traditionally called "the close of probation," but the probation of individual human beings all over the world will already have closed when Jesus ceases His ministry in the heavenly sanctuary.

Let me explain. We know that the seal of God and the mark of the beast will be the close of probation for the righteous and the wicked respectively. Every human being will receive one or the other of these marks, depending on his or her final decision about the truth. Obviously, in order for the righteous to receive the seal of God and be saved, Jesus must still be ministering in the heavenly sanctuary at the time they make their decision to remain loyal to Him. Thus the close of probation as a person's final choice for or against the truth will precede the conclusion of Christ's ministry. The following statement by Ellen White supports this thought:

> Reference to our published works will show our belief that the living righteous will receive the seal of God prior to the close of probation (*Selected Messages*, book 1, p. 66).

But, you say, I thought it was at the point that He closes His ministry that Jesus will pronounce the fateful words, "He that is unjust, let him be unjust still: . . . and he that is righteous, let him be righteous still" (Revelation 22:11, KJV).

That is correct. But notice that according to Jesus' own words, the wicked will already be unjust and the righteous will already be righteous at the time He makes that pronouncement. His words will not close anyone's probation. Every human being will already have closed his or her own probation by the choice made regarding the truth. Jesus' words will simply be a formal declaration that the choices made are now eternal; there will never again be an opportunity to change sides.

The close of probation *as a point in time* will occur when Jesus ceases His mediatorial ministry. However, individual probations will be closing throughout the final crisis, before Jesus ceases His mediatorial ministry.

Thus the close of probation is a process as well as a definite point in time. If what I have said is true, then some people will make their final choice earlier than others, and Jesus will not cease His ministry until every choice has been made. Thus, the close of probation as the time when both the righteous and the wicked are making final decisions will occur over a period of time, not all at once. *In this sense, the close of probation will be a process.*

Ellen White clearly supported the idea that some people will make their final choice before others:

> The time of God's destructive judgments is the time of mercy for those who have [had] no opportunity to learn what is truth. Tenderly will the Lord look upon them. His heart of mercy is touched; His hand is still stretched out to save, while the door is closed to those who would not enter (*SDA Bible Commentary,* vol. 7, p. 979).

The point of this whole discussion has been that the close of probation will be both a point in time and a process. The following chart illustrates what I mean:

	Close of probation as a point in time
Close of probation as a process	
People everywhere are making final decisions	
	Jesus ceases His mediatorial ministry

As a point in time, the close of probation will occur when Jesus ceases His ministry in the heavenly sanctuary. As a process, it will occur during the weeks and months that people are receiving the mark of the beast and the seal of God.

God's decision or ours?

The Adventist teaching that probation will close a short time before Christ's second coming has created a lot of needless anxiety in many minds. We fear that we might not be quite good enough when God closes probation, or that probation might close and *then* we will discover some sin that we were not aware of.

I am convinced that these fears are groundless, particularly in light of the idea that the close of probation will be a process. The basic issue is this: Will the close of probation be God's decision or ours? And the answer is, It will be ours. The actual close of probation—the time when Jesus ceases His ministry in the heavenly sanctuary—will simply be God's recognition that all final choices have been made and no one is left to decide for Jesus; no one is left to be converted. If one person remains who is still not quite ready, probation will remain open. There can be no such thing as even one soul who wants to be ready not being ready for the close of probation.

That's fantastic news for Adventists who've always been frightened to death they might not be "good enough" for the close of probation!

I like to think of the close of probation as Jesus turning to God and saying, "Father, everyone who is going to accept Me has done so, and all the rest have rejected Me. There's no one left to be saved, no one left to benefit from My intercession. Since there's nothing more to do, I guess I'll have to stop my mediatorial ministry."

Surely those will be among the most painful words Jesus ever utters—similar to the time when He wept and said, "O Jerusalem, Jerusalem, . . . how often I have longed to gather your children together, as a hen gathers her chicks under her wings, but you were not willing. Look, your house is left to you desolate" (Matthew 23:37, 38).

The close of probation will not be God's decision at all. It will be God's recognition of our decision—the collective decision of the entire human race. Christ's ministry will stay open till the last person has made his or her final choice and closed his or her own probation. *Jesus will not cease His ministry as long as one soul is left to decide.*

If you and I want nothing more than to spend eternity in heaven with Jesus, and if we are keeping our relationship with Him and doing our best to serve Him, then He is not going to close probation until we are ready.

The judgment of the living

One of the distinctive Seventh-day Adventist teachings is that God's final judgment began in heaven in 1844 and will continue to the close of probation. Ellen White had an interesting variation on this theme which she referred to as "the judgment of the dead" and "the judgment of the living." Though she said very little about this during her seventy-year career, she said enough that we can conclude she was not just making a passing comment. Following are two of her statements:

> The cases of the righteous dead have been passing in review before God. When that work shall be completed, judgment is to be pronounced upon the living (*Selected Messages*, book 1, p. 125).

> The judgment has been over forty years in progress on the cases of the dead, and we know not how soon it will pass to the cases of the living (*Testimonies*, vol. 5, p. 692).

The first statement suggests that the judgment of the living will be God's verdict, which He will give at a certain moment in the future. However, in the second statement Ellen White suggests that the judgment of the living will be a process, which, like the judgment of the dead, will take place over a period of time. It is this latter idea that I want to pursue here.

Ellen White never explained the difference between the judgment of the dead and the judgment of the living. However, I would like to suggest that the judgment of the living has to do with the close of probation as a process. Since 1844 God, Christ, and the watching universe have been passing final judgment on people after they die. But when the judgment of the living begins, that final judgment will be pronounced upon people while they are still alive. It will happen as people close their own probations by the choices they make.

My conclusion is that the judgment of the living and the close of probation as a process are essentially the same thing. You may disagree; I don't mind that. Ellen White did not tell us what she meant by "the judgment of the living." The explanation above is my present understanding. I will mention it from time to time and put it on time charts during the remainder of this book.

Let's put on a chart the various ideas about the close of probation that we've discussed in this chapter:

Judgment of the living begins	Close of probation as a point in time	Second coming
Close of probation as a process	Time of trouble	
People making final decisions Judgment of the living	Seven last plagues	

Jesus ceases
His ministry

The Adventist mission

Mission statements are very common these days. Even secular industries are creating these short declarations—usually no more than a paragraph—that summarize an organization's reason for existing as the members themselves understand it.

Since you are reading this book, you are probably a member of the Seventh-day Adventist Church, which means you have every reason to be a part of this church's process of formulating a mission statement. So let me ask, Can you state the Adventist Church's mission to the world in one sentence? I'll share mine with you shortly, but before you read mine, take a minute to think about your understanding of the Adventist Church's reason for being here. See if you can formulate your mission statement in one sentence, and then compare it with mine.

I can give you my Adventist mission statement in just nine words: To prepare the world for the close of probation.

Perhaps you've always thought our mission was to prepare the world for the second coming of Christ, and that is correct. But think of this: Anyone who is ready for the close of probation will be ready for the second coming of Jesus, and anyone who is not ready for the close of probation won't be ready for the second coming of Jesus. Therefore, our real goal is not so much to prepare people for the second coming of Jesus as it is to prepare them for the close of probation.

Adventists know that the final crisis is coming. We know a time is ahead when every human being will be forced to make certain choices, and that those choices will be eternal. We also know that Satan will present the most subtle lies in order to deceive people into making the wrong choices. And we know that the truths contained in our message, especially the Sabbath and the state of the dead, will protect people from accepting Satan's deceptions and making the wrong choices.

Our mission is to warn the world of the coming crisis and to share with them the truths that will enable them to make the right choices during that crisis, so they can be ready for the close of probation.

That's why our teachings about the final crisis and the close of probation are so important.

CHAPTER

7

Preparing for the Close of Probation

In her book *The Great Controversy*, Ellen White gave an important reason why Jesus did not return on October 22, 1844: "The people were not yet ready to meet their Lord. There was still a work of preparation to be accomplished for them" (pp. 424, 425). That's strange, considering the fact that these people had just come out of one of the most spiritually invigorating experiences in Christian history. What kind of preparation did God's people still lack? Here is how she explained it:

Those who are living upon the earth when the intercession of Christ shall cease in the sanctuary above are to stand in the sight of a holy God without a mediator. Their robes must be spotless, their characters must be purified from sin by the blood of sprinkling. Through the grace of God and their own diligent effort they must be conquerors in the battle with evil. While the investigative judgment is going forward in heaven, while the sins of penitent believers are being removed from the sanctuary, there is to be a special work of purification, of putting away of sin, among God's people upon earth (*The Great Controversy*, p. 425).

Ellen White then said, "When this work shall have been accomplished, the followers of Christ will be ready for His appearing" (ibid.). Later in the same book, she made a similar statement:

Now, while our great High Priest is making the atonement for us, we should seek to become perfect in Christ. Not even by a thought could our Saviour be brought to yield to the power of temptation. Satan finds in human hearts some point where he can get a foothold; some sinful desire is cherished, by means of which his temptations assert their power. But Christ declared of Himself: "The prince of this world cometh, and hath nothing in Me." John 14:30. Satan could find nothing in the Son of God that would enable him to gain the victory. He had kept His Father's commandments, and there was no sin in Him that Satan could use to his advantage. *This is the condition in which those must be found who shall stand in the time of trouble* (ibid., p. 623, emphasis supplied).

Nothing is more clear from a study of Ellen White's teaching about end-time events than her conviction that God's people must put forth deliberate effort to obtain perfection of character in order to be prepared for earth's final conflict.

Unfortunately, many Adventists, misunderstanding what she said, and fearful that they might not be "good enough," have become obsessively perfectionistic. In this chapter I want to present perfection in such a way that it maintains the same high standard that Ellen White envisioned, while removing the fear so many of us have held that preparation for the end time is an impossible dream.

What is perfection?

The first thing we need to discuss is the nature of perfection. If we are ever to achieve it, we must have a correct idea of what it is.

I have found three analogies to be very helpful in understanding character perfection. These analogies have taught me that character perfection is nothing to be afraid of.

The rainbow analogy. Have you ever tried chasing a rainbow? Let's say you're standing on top of a hill, and you can see a rainbow that ends "right at that tree in the valley." So you run down to the tree, but when you get there, where is the rainbow? It's at the top of the next hill. So you run to the top of that hill, but now the rainbow is in the next valley! You could chase the end of the rainbow over hills and valleys till sundown and never find it, because it always moves ahead of you. That's the reason for the proverbial saying about the pot of gold at the end of the rainbow. There is no such thing.

Perfection is like that. Just when you think you've gotten there, it moves ahead of you. You can chase it until the Lord comes, and you'll never find it. I don't mean that it's impossible to be perfect. I mean that you and I will never know when we have reached perfection. That's what 1 John 1:8 means: "If we claim to be without sin, we deceive ourselves and the truth is not in us."

The Columbus analogy. When he left Spain with three little ships, Columbus did not set out to find America. He went in search of a shorter route to India. When he finally landed, he thought he had found India. He even called the native people of that place "Indians." Only after several years did Columbus realize that he had not found India at all. India was still halfway around the world from the land he had found.

Perfection is like that. Even if you think you've achieved it, you will discover sooner or later that you really haven't. It's still "halfway around the world."

The Abraham analogy. My favorite analogy of perfection is Abraham's trip to Canaan. When God first came to Abraham in Ur of the Chaldees, He told him to go to a country that He would show him (see Genesis 12:1). The author of Hebrews tells us that when Abraham left Ur, he did not know where he was going (see Hebrews 11:8).

Let's imagine Abraham's reaction when God said, "I want you to go to a country that I will show you."

Abraham probably said, "Sure, God. Where is it?"

And God told him something very strange. He said, "I'm not going to tell you where it is."

Now let me ask you, Did Abraham reach the promised land?

Of course. But how did he get there if God didn't tell him where it was? First Abraham had to start walking. When he did that, God guided his steps.

Now please notice this principle, because it's crucial to everything else I'll say in this chapter:

**Abraham walked
God guided him**

Character perfection is like that. We don't know where it is or what it is, and God hasn't told us, but that doesn't mean that getting there is impossible. Like Abraham, we have to start walking. We have to put one foot ahead of the other. When we do that, God makes Himself responsible for getting us to perfection.

Some people would like us to believe that our trip to perfection is like God's spreading a magic carpet on the floor in Abraham's home in Ur and saying, "You and your family lie down on this carpet tonight, and when you wake up in the morning you'll be there." In other words, our journey to heaven is all God's responsibility.

Others think our journey to perfection is like God's handing Abraham a map and saying, "Here's the road to take. I'll be waiting for you when you get there." In other words, getting there is all our responsibility.

The truth is that Abraham's trip to Canaan was neither fully his responsibility nor fully God's. Abraham had to put one foot ahead of the other and walk. That was his part. God's part was to guide Abraham's steps. Once Abraham did his part, God guaranteed to do His part, and Abraham's arrival in Canaan was assured.

It's the same with our trip to perfection. It's neither God's exclusive responsibility nor ours. Rather, it's a cooperative venture between us and God. Like Abraham, we don't know where we're going. We will never know when we are perfect. But when we do our part—when we "put one foot ahead of the other" the way Abraham did—God makes Himself responsible for getting us to perfection. This point is an extremely important principle:

We don't know what perfection is or how to get there, but when we do our part, God is responsible for getting us there.

What is our part in this matter of reaching character perfection? I will mention three things, and we will spend the rest of this chapter discussing them. They are conviction, conversion, and resistance. God has a part in each of these, and so do we, like this:

	God's part	Our part	Change
Conviction			
Conversion			
Resistance			

What about the column on the far right? Each step you and I take, which God guides, will bring about a certain change in us. This will be especially important to understand when we come to the last two steps.

I need to explain one other thing before we get started. What I say in the rest of this chapter has to do entirely with sanctification. I know exactly what justification is and how important it is to salvation. In a later chapter I'll discuss it in detail. If this were a book about the doctrine of salvation I would discuss justification first, since it not only precedes sanctification in Christian experience, but is also a requirement for sanctification. However, the focus of this book is eschatology—the doctrine of last things—and I trust you will allow me to present justification and sanctification in the way that fits best with my main point.

Conviction

Conviction means to have a strong feeling or impression about something. A conviction is a strongly held belief. Christians use the word *conviction* to express the idea of God trying to get them to do or believe a particular thing. Jesus said, "When he [the Holy Spirit] comes, he will *convict* the world of guilt in regard to sin and righteousness and judgment" (John 16:8, emphasis supplied).

If conviction were just a matter of imparting information, God could easily help us. However, more often than not, we humans think we are quite all right and God is all wrong. For example, when I really get angry at someone, there's no question in my mind that I'm absolutely right, my antagonist is absolutely wrong, and I am perfectly justified to punch him in the nose! However, a day or two can make a great deal of difference in how I feel toward that person. Calm reflection after I've cooled down often helps me to understand that my anger really was quite uncalled for. But nobody could have persuaded me that I was wrong at the moment I was flushed with anger.

God's problem is how to persuade us stubborn humans that we are wrong when we are so sure that we're right. The fact that God manages to do it as often as He does proves that conviction—one of the things He does in our character development—is very powerful.

God's part in conviction is to show us our sins. So what's our part? The best Bible passage I've found on that is Psalm 139:23, 24:

> Search me, O God, and know my heart;
>   test me and know my anxious thoughts.
> See if there is any offensive way in me,
>   and lead me in the way everlasting.

Notice that David *asked* God to convict him. He said, in effect, "Please search my mind, test my thoughts, and if You find anything wrong in my life, tell me what it is."

Our part in obtaining conviction is to ask for it. We can ask God to show us whatever we need to know in order to be perfect, and He will do it. That's what Paul told the Philippian believers:

> One thing I do: Forgetting what is behind and straining toward what is ahead, I press on toward the goal to win the prize for which God has called me heavenward in Christ Jesus.
>
> All of us who are mature should take such a view of things. *And if on some point you think differently, that too God will make clear to you* (Philippians 3:15, 16, emphasis supplied).

Some people worry that they might not think of all the sins they need to confess and overcome before the close of probation. They're afraid that probation might close and *then* they'll think of an unconfessed or unconquered sin in their life. That's a useless fear. In the text above Paul assures us that if you and I need to know about it, God will reveal it to us. Anything God doesn't bring to our minds we don't need to know.

I'm going to repeat that last statement because it's so important:

Some people worry that they might not think of all the sins they need to confess and overcome before the close of probation. That's a useless fear. If you and I need to know about it, God will reveal it to us. Anything God doesn't bring to our minds we don't need to know.

Here's another extremely important thought that Adventists need to understand as they anticipate the close of probation and living without a Mediator:

Jesus will bring to your mind any sin that you need to know about, and He will do it in time for you to deal with it before probation closes.

Remember that the close of probation is a process as well as a point in time. During the final crisis, when the close of probation as a process is taking place, God will bring to your mind everything—yes, everything—you need to know in order to be ready to live without a Mediator. There will be no such thing as discovering, after the close of probation, a secret sin that should have been dealt with before the close of probation.

Now let's fill in the first part of our diagram—God's part and our part in conviction:

	God's part	**Our part**	**Change**
Conviction	Show us our sins	Ask for it	Insight
Conversion			
Resistance			

Conversion

The next step we take with God is conversion. When God made Adam and Eve, they were perfect. The Bible says, "God saw all that he had made, and it was very good" (Genesis 1:31). Ellen White says:

> Man was originally endowed with noble powers and a well-balanced mind. He was perfect in his being, and in harmony with God. His thoughts were pure, his aims holy (*Steps to Christ*, p. 17).

Adam and Eve were perfect on the inside. From the deepest part of their being, they loved God and wanted to obey Him. God's way of life was built into their desires. Unfortunately, when they sinned, a change came:

> Through disobedience, his powers were perverted, and selfishness took the place of love. His nature became so weakened through transgression that *it was impossible for him, in his own strength, to resist the power of evil* (ibid., emphasis supplied).

Now, from the deepest part of their being, Adam and Eve were selfish. Sin was built into their desires. And the trouble was, they were trapped. They had gotten themselves into a situation from which they could not get out on their own. You and I can jump into a well all by ourselves, but we can't get out without help. Adam and Eve jumped into sin on their own, but they had to have help to get out, and so must you and I. I find the following statement by Ellen White to be particularly helpful in understanding this problem:

> It is impossible for us, of ourselves, to escape from the pit of sin in which we are sunken. Our hearts are evil, and we cannot change them. . . . Education, culture, the exercise of the will, human effort, all have their proper sphere, but here they are powerless. They may produce an outward correctness of behavior, but they cannot change the heart; they cannot purify the springs of life (ibid., p. 18).

Notice that last sentence: "They cannot purify the springs of life." What are the "springs" of life? A spring in real life is a place where water bubbles to the surface from deep down in the earth.

An impure spring is either bitter or poisonous—perhaps both. One of the tourist attractions in Yellowstone National Park is a bitter spring. I tasted the water once, and it was awful! Presumably, deep down in the earth, the water passes through a stratum of sulfur, making it bitter before it reaches the surface. Can you imagine the president of the United States ordering the Army Corps of Engineers to dig under Yellowstone Park, remove the sulfur, and purify that spring? That would be ridiculous, wouldn't it?

That's how impossible it is for you and me to purify the springs of our lives.

Obviously, it's crucial that we understand what are the springs of our lives. I believe they are the deepest motives of our hearts, our strongest desires, our most basic priorities. And only God can change those desires. That's His part. Jesus called this change the "new birth." Please read how Ellen White explained it:

> The Saviour said, "Except a man be born from above," unless he shall receive a new heart, *new desires, purposes, and motives,* leading to a new life, "he cannot see the kingdom of God" (*Steps to Christ*, p. 18, emphasis supplied).

God has to change for us that which we can't change for ourselves—our desires, purposes, and motives. We can't create these new desires, purposes, and motives in ourselves. We receive them from God.

Let's pause and change directions just slightly. I need to introduce you to another piece of this puzzle, and then we'll come back to this matter of God's changing our desires.

There are two things in our lives that need changing. One is our desires and the other is our behavior. Unfortunately, in trying to overcome sin, most Christians get these two mixed up. They ask God to help them change their sinful *behavior* when they need to ask Him to change their sinful *desire*. I don't mean that Christians shouldn't ask God for help with behavior change—I'll talk about that in a moment. My point is that we shouldn't begin by asking for help with our behavior. Our first prayer should be for God to change our desires.

I heard a story once that illustrates the futility of trying to overcome sin on the behavioral level only. There was a woman who prayed, "Lord, please remove the cobwebs from my life." Day after day she said that prayer till finally her exasperated husband said, "Lord, please kill the spider."

As long as we fight sin at the behavioral level only, sooner or later we are almost certain to fail, because we're only sweeping out the cobwebs. We haven't killed the spider. Killing the spider means changing the source of sin, the desire for sin, deep down in our hearts. But we can no more do that than the U.S. Army Corps of Engineers could remove the sulfur that makes the spring in Yellowstone Park bitter. *Only God can change the evil desires in our hearts.* We will begin to gain true victories over sin when we begin asking Him to change our wrong motives and desires.

The next time Satan comes to you with your most difficult temptation, instead of saying, "Lord, help me to stop doing such and such," say, "Lord, please take away my *desire* for such and such." I find that when I pray that prayer, I gain the victory, and when I don't, I don't.

I must warn you, though, that this can be an extremely difficult prayer to say. The problem is illustrated by an experience I had with a church member I'll call Gary. Gary said to me one day, "Pastor, I have a problem. I like coffee. I have to have a cup of coffee every morning before I go to work. I love that early morning cup of coffee. I've tried to quit, but I can't. Can you help me?"

Analyze with me what Gary said. He told me that he had a strong desire for coffee—he loved it. And then he said, "I've asked God to help me stop drinking it." Gary was asking God for help to change his behavior—"help me to stop *drinking* coffee"— when he needed to ask God to change his desire—"help me not to *want* coffee."

I explained this to Gary, and then I said, "Tomorrow, instead of asking God to help you not to drink coffee, try saying, 'Please help me not to want coffee right now.' "

Gary thought a moment, and then he said, "But if I did that, I might not get my cup of coffee!"

That's your problem and mine. We enjoy our sins, and we don't want God taking away that pleasure.

A cherished sin is one we're willing to ask God to help us with when we're in church. It's one we're willing to pray about during our morning and evening devotions. But we are not willing to pray about it at the moment of temptation. We like it too much. If God took away the desire for it, we wouldn't get to enjoy it.

The key to overcoming these sins is to make a conscious choice at the moment the temptation is strongest. That choice is to say a very specific prayer: "God, please help me not to want this sin. Take away the desire right now."

For myself, I do not know of any spiritual battle that is more difficult than asking God to change my desire for a particular sin when I want nothing more right then than to do it. However, I have found that when I say that prayer at my moment of strongest temptation, I gain the victory. I've also found that if I keep asking Him to change my desire each time that temptation presents itself to me, eventually I come to the place that I no longer want that sin.

Now let's put God's part and our part in this matter of conversion on our chart:

	God's part	Our part	Change
Conviction	Show us our sins	Ask for it	Insight
Conversion	Change our desires	Ask for it	Desire
Resistance			

Please notice that conversion changes desire. It does not change behavior. We come to that next.

Resistance

In one sense it is incorrect to call this section "resistance," because one of the most powerful ways you and I resist is when, at the moment of temptation, we ask God to remove our desire for that sin. However, the prayer for a change in the desire for sin is not quite the same as the prayer for help not to do it, and at the moment of strongest temptation, we need help with both. We need God to remove the desire, and we need His help so we won't do the wrong behavior. However, we need the desire removed first, or else we'll be left struggling not to do something we very much want to do. So the prayer for a change in our desire has to come first. But as soon as we've said that prayer, we immediately need to deal with the deed itself—the wrong behavior.

"Well," you say, "if the desire is gone, the behavior change will be automatic."

Often that will be true. I believe that a lot of sin is indeed conquered simply by the change in our desire for it. However, I've found that when I'm struggling with a deeply ingrained sin, I often need God's help with the behavior too, even after I've asked Him to change my desire. The reduced or transformed desire makes behavior change possible. It does not necessarily make it inevitable.

Furthermore, the change in our behavior comes about through an entirely different process than the change in our desire. God has to change our desire. We cannot do that. But God will not change our behavior. This principle is important:

Only God can change our desire.
Only we can change our behavior.

In the rest of this section of the chapter, I want to give you some practical ideas on how to resist so that your behavior really does change.

Some people would like God to change both their desires and their behavior. However, God cannot change our behavior without violating our free will. In fact, I can prove to you that God won't change your behavior. Did you ever see God reach down from heaven and take the cigarette out of a smoker's mouth? Did you ever hear of His pulling a couple apart who were engaged in a lustful relationship? Did you ever see Him clap His hand over the mouth of a person about to take His name in vain? Of course not. God will take away the desire, but *we* must change the behavior.

Fortunately, God doesn't say to us, "I gave you a new set of desires. Now you change the behavior." He helps us with that too. God's help in our behavior change is summarized in a very short Bible verse:

I can do all things through Christ which strengtheneth me (Philippians 4:13, KJV).

Notice that Paul is talking about behavior here. He says, "I can *do* all things"—and not just a few things, but *all* things. That means you can overcome any sin, regardless of how impossible it may seem.

And whom does Paul say "does" it? "*I* can do all things through him who gives me strength." Paul says that he changes his own behavior—with Christ's strength. So God's part in behavior change is to give us the power.

And what do you think your part and mine is? I'm sure by now you've guessed it: *Ask for it.*

Let's add that to our chart:

	God's part	**Our part**	**Change**
Conviction	Show us our sins	Ask for it	Insight
Conversion	Change our desires	Ask for it	Desire
Resistance	Give us the power	Ask for it	Behavior

There's one more part to this matter of resistance for behavior change that we need to discuss. I'm sharing it with you because I've found that it works beautifully. The best way to explain it is to give you an illustration.

Have you ever seen a child nag his parents for something?

"Dad, may I go to the swimming hole at the river this afternoon?"

"No, not today."

"But, Dad, all the other guys will be there."

"Well, yes, Son, but Mother and I can't go with you today, and we don't think you should be there alone."

"But, Dad, all the other guys go alone. Their parents don't have to stay with them."

"Well, yes, but Mother and I think, uh, maybe you shouldn't do that any more."

"But I'll be really careful."

"Well, yes, but, well, Mother and I would rather . . ."

"Please, Dad?"

"Well, uh . . ."

"Just this once, Dad? I'll promise never to ask you again."

Do you get the point? Junior will keep pestering his father as long as he thinks there's the slightest chance he might get his way. But notice this scenario, which works beautifully for every parent who's ever tried it:

"Dad, can I go to the swimming hole this afternoon?"

"No, not today."

"But, Dad, all the other guys will be there."

"I understand, Son, but Mother and I can't go with you today, and we don't want you there alone."

"But, Dad, all the other guys go alone. Their parents don't have to stay with them."

"Did you hear me, Son?"

"But, Dad . . ."

"I said No, and I mean it. Now go outside and play in the yard. You can invite Billy over if you like."

"But . . ."

"I said No. I'm not discussing it any further. Go outside."

So Junior marches outside, muttering under his breath about how unfair parents are, but five minutes later, when Dad looks out the window, he sees Junior and Billy playing happily together, as though neither of them had ever thought about the swimming hole.

The psychology behind these two scenarios is utterly simple, and it works just as well with adults as it does with children: As long as your mind thinks there's the slightest chance it might get the sin it wants, your desire for it will remain white hot. But once your mind accepts the fact that it really is not going to get what it wants, your desire will disappear very rapidly.

I conducted a Five-Day Plan to Stop Smoking once, and Joan attended faithfully. On the first night she shared with the group how she had quit several times in the past, but had always gone back. However, on the last night she said, "This time I've quit for good."

I said, "Joan, you told us on the first night that you had quit several times before and always went back. What makes you so sure you won't go back to smoking this time?"

I'll never forget her answer. Joan said, "Always in the past I knew there would be another cigarette in my life—maybe a month later, maybe a year later. And there always was. But this time I know there will never be another cigarette in my life."

That's the principle: *When your mind really accepts the fact that you're not going to get what you want, your desire fades very rapidly.* When you learn to tell yourself No! the way you'd say No to a kid who was pestering you for something you didn't want him to have, you will discover that victory comes much more easily. This is an important key to changing your behavior.

The following statement by Ellen White summarizes this principle beautifully:

> It is an important law of the mind—one which should not be overlooked—that when a desired object is so firmly denied as to remove all hope, the mind will soon cease to long for it and will be occupied in other pursuits. But as long as there is any hope of gaining the desired object, an effort will be made to obtain it (*Mind, Character, and Personality*, vol. 2, p. 419).

Say No! to temptation, and the desire for it will go away much more rapidly. I've already filled in the "resistance" part of our chart, but let's add this last bit of strategy to it:

	God's part	**Our part**	**Change**
Conviction	Show us our sins	Ask for it	Insight
Conversion	Change our desires	Ask for it	Desire
Resistance	Give us the power	Ask for it Say No!	Behavior

You may wonder how you can tell the difference between the desire going away because God changed your heart and the desire going away because you told yourself No!

You can't.

At the pool of Bethesda Jesus healed a paralytic, and the man put forth the effort to walk (see John 5:1-9). The paralytic probably could not tell, within himself, the difference between God's healing and his own effort to walk, but with the two combined, he walked.

That's how it is with victory at the moment of temptation. You won't be able to tell which of these ways is working, because they both are. Trying to figure out which is which is like trying to figure out which eye you're looking out of. What you see comes through both eyes, and you can't tell the difference between the sight from one and the sight from the other.

Use this formula the next time a temptation comes on strong. Begin by saying, "Lord, change my heart so I don't want this sin any longer," and immediately follow that prayer with another one: "Lord, give me the power not to do it." Then tell yourself No! very firmly, the way you would say No to a child who was nagging you. This may be the toughest choice you ever made, but it will work. I know. It has worked for me many times.

important

Abraham got to the promised land by putting one foot ahead of the other. When Abraham did his part, God did His. You put one foot ahead of the other by asking God to convict you and convert you. You put one foot ahead of the other by asking God for strength to change your behavior and telling yourself No! That's your part. Once you do your part, then getting you to that great unknown called perfection is God's responsibility. You don't have to worry about whether you're good enough. He'll take care of that.

By asking for the Holy Spirit in the ways we have talked about in this chapter, you will discover significant, and often rapid, character development in your life. Begin taking those steps. I guarantee you, God won't close probation until you're ready.

CHAPTER

8

The Season of Calamity

The headline caught my attention: "A World of Hurts Stretches Relief Groups and Givers to Their Limits."

The article stated that an unusually large number of natural disasters occurred in the spring of 1991—earthquakes in Costa Rica, Soviet Georgia, and Peru; a deadly cholera epidemic in South America in the wake of the Peruvian quake; a cyclone in Bangladesh that left more than 150,000 people dead; and, though not the result of a natural disaster, the plight of the Kurdish refugees following Operation Desert Storm. The author of the article said that "relief veterans agree the past three months have been unprecedented in the number and severity of disasters coming so close together" (*Christianity Today*, 24 June 1991, p. 48).

Adventists have always considered natural disasters to be a sign of the end, especially earthquakes, famines, and pestilences (epidemics), since these are mentioned in the Bible (see Luke 21:11). However, I would like to suggest that the end-time natural disasters God is about to bring on the world will make today's worst disasters seem like a stubbed toe.

I will begin by sharing with you my most basic conclusions about these calamities, and then I will give you the evidence to substantiate them. My conclusions are as follows:

1. A period of terrible natural disasters is coming upon the world.

2. This period of disaster will coincide with the final crisis.
3. It will begin before the close of probation.
4. These disasters will come very suddenly.
5. They will be a major cause of the final crisis for God's people.
6. At a certain time God will change His relationship to the world very suddenly, and that is the time when these disasters will fall.

Let's examine these conclusions point by point. I will discuss the first two together.

A period of disaster and the final crisis

The following statement makes it very clear that the time of the final crisis will also be a time of terrible natural disasters:

> The time is nearing when the great crisis in the history of the world will have come, when every movement in the government of God will be watched with intense interest and inexpressible apprehension. In quick succession the judgments of God will follow one another—fire and flood and earthquake, with war and bloodshed (*Testimonies*, vol. 9, p. 97).

Ellen White's expression "the great crisis in the history of the world" can refer to nothing other than the final crisis we are discussing in this book. And notice that during this time, terrible natural disasters will be coming upon the world, including fire, flood, and earthquake. She also mentions "war and bloodshed," but in this chapter I am primarily concerned about the judgments of God in the form of natural disasters.

Here is another statement in which Ellen White predicted judgments from God in the form of natural disasters during the final crisis:

> There are many souls to come out of the ranks of the world, out of the churches—even the Catholic Church—whose zeal will far exceed that of those who have stood in rank and file to proclaim the truth heretofore. . . . When the crisis is upon us, when the *season of calamity* shall come,

they [the souls from other churches] will come to the front, gird themselves with the whole armor of God, and exalt His law (*Selected Messages*, book 3, pp. 386, 387, emphasis supplied).

In this statement Ellen White again combined the final crisis with terrible natural disasters. Her words "the crisis" are almost certainly a shortened version of her more common "the final crisis," and her expression "season of calamity" undoubtedly refers to natural disasters. A season is a three-month period we call winter, spring, summer, or fall. However, it can also mean any short period of time, and that seems to be Ellen White's meaning in her expression "season of calamity." The point is, there will be a short period in the future when calamities will be coming on the world one after the other, and this will coincide with the final crisis.

Disasters before the close of probation

Because the seven last plagues will be such terrible natural disasters, some Adventists, in reading these statements, have concluded that Ellen White was describing the calamities we know will come after the close of probation, during the time of the plagues. There can be no doubt, of course, that the plagues will be terrible natural disasters. However, notice carefully exactly what Ellen White said in that last statement:

When the crisis is upon us, when the season of calamity shall come, they [the souls from other churches] will come to the front, gird themselves with the whole armor of God, and exalt His law.

Ellen White clearly had in mind calamities before the close of probation, because she said they will occur during the time when people are coming out of other churches to join with God's people in exalting His law. Thus, the "season of calamity" she spoke of will begin before the close of probation.

From now on in this book I will use the expression "season of calamity" in a rather technical sense to refer to the judgments of God in the form of natural disasters during both the little time of trouble before the close of probation and the great time of trouble after the close of probation.

I could share with you a number of statements in which Ellen White makes it clear that the season of calamity will begin before the close of probation. However, one more will suffice. Though it is rather lengthy, I suggest you read it in its entirety:

> I am bidden to declare the message that cities full of transgression, and sinful in the extreme, will be destroyed by earthquakes, by fire, by flood. All the world will be warned that there is a God who will display His authority as God. His unseen agencies will cause destruction, devastation, and death. All the accumulated riches will be as nothingness. . . .
>
> Calamities will come—calamities most awful, most unexpected; and these destructions will follow one after another. . . .
>
> Strictly will the cities of the nations be dealt with, and yet they will not be visited in the extreme of God's indignation, because some souls will yet break away from the delusions of the enemy, and will repent and be converted, while the mass will be treasuring up wrath against the day of wrath (*Evangelism*, p. 27).

Ellen White does not use the expression "final crisis" or "last great crisis" in this statement, but there can be no doubt that is the time she had in mind. Her statement essentially substantiates the points we've already noted: (1) terrible natural disasters are coming; (2) they will follow one after another—that is, over a period of time; and (3) they will occur before the close of probation, because "some souls will yet break away from the delusions of the enemy, and will repent and be converted."

From these statements we can conclude that before the close of probation, the world will enter into a period of terrible natural disasters, and this season of calamity will coincide with the final crisis.

Disasters will be sudden

Paul warned the Thessalonian Christians that "when they shall say, Peace and safety; then sudden destruction cometh upon them" (1 Thessalonians 5:3, KJV). I have already quoted one statement by Ellen White in which she said that the disasters during the season of calamity will be "most awful, most unexpected." Here are three other short statements that suggest the same thing:

I knew that time was short, and that the scenes which are soon to crowd upon us would at the last come very suddenly and swiftly (*Selected Messages*, book 3, p. 413).

We who know the truth should be preparing for what is soon to break upon the world as an overwhelming surprise (*Testimonies*, vol. 8, p. 28).

The work of the people of God is to prepare for the events of the future, which will soon come upon them with blinding force (*Selected Messages*, book 2, p. 142).

Ellen White spoke of these events coming upon *God's people*. This does not mean the wicked won't experience them. Her point is that God's people should be preparing for them, and especially for the test of faith these disasters will create.

The crisis for God's people

The season of calamity will create a terrible crisis for God's people. This is particularly evident in the following statement:

It is in a crisis that character is revealed. When the earnest voice proclaimed at midnight, "Behold the bridegroom cometh; go ye out to meet him," and the sleeping virgins were roused from their slumbers, it was seen who had made preparation for the event. Both parties were taken unawares; but one was prepared for the emergency, and the other was found without preparation. So now, a sudden and unlooked-for calamity, something that brings the soul face to face with death, will show whether there is any real faith in the promises of God. It will show whether the soul is sustained by grace. The great final test comes at the close of human probation, when it will be too late for the soul's need to be supplied (*Christ's Object Lessons*, p. 412).

The crisis for God's people that will test their faith, and following which their probation will close, must obviously come before the close of probation, not after. That is why I believe the statements I quoted earlier, referring to a crisis that will come upon God's people "suddenly and swiftly" as an "overwhelming surprise," and "with blinding force," speak of events that will occur before the close of probation.

However, I don't believe these natural disasters will take us by surprise quite the way they will the world. Commenting on his statement about "sudden destruction," Paul said, "But you, brothers, are not in darkness so that this day should surprise you like a thief" (1 Thessalonians 5:4). I believe the crisis for us will not be the sudden destruction, which we know is coming, but the aftermath of that destruction. Ellen White makes it very clear that the world will blame God's people for these disasters:

> Those who honor the law of God have been accused of bringing judgments upon the world, and they will be regarded as the cause of the fearful convulsions of nature and the strife and bloodshed among men that are filling the earth with woe. The power attending the last warning has enraged the wicked; their anger is kindled against all who have received the message, and Satan will excite to still greater intensity the spirit of hatred and persecution (*The Great Controversy*, pp. 614, 615).

This statement appears in the chapter in *The Great Controversy* on the time of trouble, which is after the close of probation. However, a careful examination reveals that it primarily refers to judgments before the close of probation—those who honor God "have *been* accused of bringing judgments upon the world"—and God's people will be blamed for those judgments and persecuted because of them. This will be the great crisis for God's people, and not the judgments themselves.

God will change His relationship to the world

Ellen White makes several statements which suggest that a decision by God to remove His protection from the world—a change in His relationship to the world—will initiate the season of calamity. Here is one of them:

Do you believe that the Lord is coming, and that the last great crisis is about to break upon the world? There will soon come *a sudden change in God's dealings.* The world in its perversity is being visited by casualties—by floods, storms, fires, earthquakes, famines, wars, and bloodshed. The Lord is slow to anger, and great in power. . . . But His forbearance will not always continue. Who is prepared for *the sudden change that will take place in God's dealing* with sinful men? (*Fundamentals of Christian Education*, pp. 356, 357, emphasis supplied).

Ellen White began this statement with a reference to Christ's second coming and "the last great crisis" that is "about to break upon the world." We have already seen that the final crisis will begin some time before the close of probation. In this statement Ellen White again suggests that judgments from God in the form of natural disasters will initiate the final crisis. And notice that twice she said a "sudden change" in God's dealings with sinful men will bring about those disasters.

In the following statement she says essentially the same thing using different words:

It is God that shields His creatures and hedges them in from the power of the destroyer. But the Christian world have shown contempt for the law of Jehovah, and the Lord will do just what He has declared that He would—He will withdraw His blessings from the earth and remove His protecting care from those who are rebelling against His law and teaching and forcing others to do the same (*Counsels on Health*, p. 460).

Ellen White began this statement by calling attention to God's protection that shields the world from judgments. But a time is coming when God will "remove His protecting care," and then the terrible calamities we've been talking about will begin—although she does not refer to those calamities in this statement.

Here is another statement that says a time is coming when God will remove His protection from the world, following which terrible calamities will occur:

When God's restraining hand is removed, then the destroyer begins his work. Then in our cities the greatest calamities will come (*Manuscript Releases*, vol. 3, p. 314).

Nature of God's judgments

What will these calamities consist of? What kinds of terrible natural disasters can we expect to occur?

My first response to that question is, Probably the same disasters we are acquainted with now, only much more frequent and far more devastating: earthquakes, volcanoes, hurricanes and tornadoes, tidal waves and floods that will claim lives by the millions rather than by the thousands as they now do. Ellen White gives us some idea of the nature of these disasters.

Tidal waves. In two places Ellen White suggested that great tidal waves will sweep over the coastal lands of the earth:

In the last scenes of this earth's history, war will rage. There will be pestilence, plague, and famine. The waters of the deep will overflow their boundaries. Property and life will be destroyed by fire and flood (*Review and Herald*, 19 October 1897).

Ellen White begins the following statement by quoting Luke 21:25, in which Jesus says that the signs in the sun, moon, and stars will cause the sea and the waves to roar and toss. Then she says:

Yes, they [the sea and the waves] shall pass their borders, and destruction will be in their track. They will engulf the ships that sail upon their broad waters, and with the burden of their living freight, they will be hurried into eternity, without time to repent (*Selected Messages*, book 3, p. 417).

Earthquakes. In the following statement Ellen White suggests that earthquakes during the final crisis will be far more severe than those we are familiar with today:

Earthquakes in various places have been felt, but these disturbances have been very limited. . . . Terrible shocks will come upon the earth, and the lordly palaces erected at great expense will certainly become heaps of ruins.

The earth's crust will be rent by the outbursts of the elements concealed in the bowels of the earth (ibid., p. 391).

A ball of fire. Ellen White made at least three statements about end-time judgments that have puzzled Adventists for the better part of 100 years. Following is one of them:

Last night a scene was presented before me. I may never feel free to reveal all of it, but I will reveal a little.

It seemed that an immense ball of fire came down upon the world, and crushed large houses. From place to place rose the cry, "The Lord has come! The Lord has come!" Many were unprepared to meet Him, but a few were saying, "Praise the Lord!"

"Why are you praising the Lord?" inquired those upon whom was coming sudden destruction.

"Because we now see what we have been looking for."

"If you believed that these things were coming, why did you not tell us?" was the terrible response. "We did not know about these things. Why did you leave us in ignorance? Again and again you have seen us; why did you not become acquainted with us, and tell us of the judgment to come, and that we must serve God, lest we perish? Now we are lost!" (Ms. 102, 1904, quoted in *Reflecting Christ*, p. 243; see also *Testimonies*, vol. 9, p. 28, and *Evangelism*, p. 29).

It is very clear from the reaction of the people that this ball of fire[1] is a part of God's judgments on the world. Personally, I believe it will happen during the season of calamity that we've been talking about.

When the atomic bomb first became known to the world in 1945, Seventh-day Adventists speculated that perhaps that's what Ellen White saw in her "ball of fire" vision. More recently, scientists have begun studying the effects of the impact of asteroids and giant meteorites on the earth, and some Adventists have speculated that that's what Ellen White saw. I can assure you that her description does *not* fit what is known about the

---

1. In *Evangelism*, p. 29, Ellen White spoke of "balls" of fire—plural.

effect of an asteroid impact. An asteroid a mile in diameter would devastate an entire continent, and an asteroid four to six miles across would very likely wipe the human race and most other living things off the face of the earth.[2] Ellen White's "ball of fire" statements describe the destruction of a few buildings—something that might be expected from the impact of a large meteorite.

However, I do believe we ought to take recent scientific conclusions about asteroids and meteorites seriously. My personal conclusion is that the following prediction by Jesus, as quoted by Luke, should cause us to consider the possibility of major devastation on the earth from meteorites and possibly asteroids:

> There will be signs in the sun, moon and stars. On the earth, nations will be in anguish and perplexity at the roaring and tossing of the sea. Men will faint from terror, apprehensive of what is coming on the world, for the heavenly bodies will be shaken (Luke 21:25, 26).

A major asteroid impact would cause terrible ecological devastation, especially in the atmosphere. Dust from the impact and smoke from forest fires would partially block the sun's rays for months, affecting weather patterns all over the world. A global cooling, together with reduced sunshine, would prevent crops from ripening for harvest, thus drastically reducing the world's food supply.

An asteroid impact would indeed leave the nations "in anguish and perplexity," and the human race would indeed faint from terror at such a "shaking" of the heavenly bodies. We know, of course, that the star shower of November 13, 1833, did not create that kind of international distress.

Although I can't speak with certainty, Luke's words cause me

---

2. Scientists now believe that a comet or an asteroid five to six miles in diameter impacted the earth sixty-five million years ago, causing the death of the earth's entire dinosaur population (I am not suggesting that the earth is sixty-five million years old). If this asteroid struck the ocean, huge tidal waves would have devastated the coastlands in that part of the world. If it impacted on the earth, it would have blasted 100 trillion tons of dust into the sky, and 90 percent or more of the earth's forests would have been destroyed by a global firestorm. The entire globe would have been covered with darkness for several months. It is now estimated that there is a slight chance of an asteroid the size of a supertanker impacting our earth within the lifetime of young people living today. Such an impact would largely wipe out a city the size of Manhattan (Clark R. Chapman and David Morrison, *Cosmic Catastrophes* [New York: Plenum Press, 1989], pp. 82-93, 77).

to believe that large meteorites and possibly asteroids may well be among the judgments God allows to come on the world during the season of calamity.

The description of future destruction in the following statement is particularly interesting even though it does not mention the cause of the destruction:

> The time is right upon us when there will be sorrow in the world that no human balm can heal. The flattering monuments of men's greatness will be crumbled in the dust, even before the last great destruction comes upon the world (*Selected Messages*, book 3, pp. 418, 419).

What are the "flattering monuments of men's greatness" that "will be crumbled in the dust"? I would suggest such things as the American and Russian space industries, our freeway system in the United States, and the world's international air transport system, to name a few. These "will be crumbled in the dust, even before the last great destruction comes upon the world"—the last great destruction being, of course, the second coming of Christ.

Will God warn His people ahead of time?

Ellen White warned that God's most severe judgments will fall on the cities in our world, especially those that have given themselves up to the greatest wickedness:

> The time is near when the large cities will be visited by the judgments of God. In a little while these cities will be terribly shaken (*Testimonies*, vol. 7, p. 83).

> I am bidden to declare the message that cities full of transgression, and sinful in the extreme, will be destroyed by earthquakes, by fire, by flood (*Evangelism*, p. 27).

> O that God's people had a sense of the impending destruction of thousands of cities, now almost given to idolatry (ibid., p. 29).

> The time is near when large cities will be swept away, and all should be warned of these coming judgments. But

who is giving to the accomplishment of this work the whole-hearted service that God requires? (ibid.).

At the present time many of God's people live in these cities. How will they fare when these judgments begin to fall? One of the principles of God's dealing with His people is that He always sends them warnings of coming judgments so they can escape. Ellen White said:

> God has always given men warning of coming judgments. Those who had faith in His message for their time, and who acted out their faith in obedience to His commandments, escaped the judgments that fell upon the disobedient and unbelieving. The word came to Noah, "Come thou and all thy house into the ark; for thee have I seen righteous before Me." Noah obeyed and was saved. The message came to Lot, "Up, get you out of this place; for the Lord will destroy this city." Gen. 7:1; 19:14. Lot placed himself under the guardianship of the heavenly messengers, and was saved. So Christ's disciples were given warning of the destruction of Jerusalem. Those who watched for the sign of the coming ruin, and fled from the city, escaped destruction. *So now we are given warning of Christ's second coming and of the destruction to fall upon the world.* Those who heed the warning will be saved (*The Desire of Ages*, p. 634, emphasis supplied).

Please notice two things in particular about this statement. First, Ellen White called attention to the fact that Christ gave a sign of the approaching destruction of Jerusalem, and she said that "those who watched for the sign . . . and fled from the city, escaped destruction." Second, she applied this principle to our own time. She said we have been warned of both Christ's second coming and "the destruction to fall upon the world." I believe this latter phrase refers to the judgments of God we have been discussing in this chapter, which will come on the cities prior to the second coming and prior to the close of probation.

I believe this because in two other places she said the very same thing—God gave the disciples a sign of the impending destruction of Jerusalem, and He has given us a sign of God's coming judgments. Furthermore, she told us exactly what the disciples' sign was and what ours will be. Their sign was the approach of the Roman armies toward Jerusalem. Ours will be the first national Sunday law in the United States.

Here is the first of her two statements:

> By the decree enforcing the institution of the papacy in violation of the law of God, our nation will disconnect herself fully from righteousness. When Protestantism shall stretch her hand across the gulf to grasp the hand of the Roman power, when she shall reach over the abyss to clasp hands with spiritualism, when, under the influence of this threefold union, our country shall repudiate every principle of its Constitution as a Protestant and republican government, . . . then we may know that the time has come for the marvelous working of Satan and that the end is near.
>
> As the approach of the Roman armies was a sign to the disciples of the impending destruction of Jerusalem, so may this apostasy be a sign to us that the limit of God's forbearance is reached, that the measure of our nation's iniquity is full, and that the angel of mercy is about to take her flight, never to return. The people of God will then be plunged into those scenes of affliction and distress which prophets have described as the time of Jacob's trouble (*Testimonies*, vol. 5, p. 451).

My personal conclusion, from this statement and other evidence presented in this book, is that when the United States government enacts its first national Sunday law, regardless of how mild it may be, God's people must take that as a warning that the final crisis and the season of calamity associated with it are near.

So how should we heed the warning? What should we do when the first national Sunday law is enacted? In her second statement Ellen White's counsel was very specific on this very point:

> As the siege of Jerusalem by the Roman armies was the signal for flight to the Judean Christians, so the assumption of power on the part of our nation in the decree enforcing the papal sabbath will be a warning to us. It will then

be time to leave the large cities, preparatory to leaving the smaller ones for retired homes in secluded places among the mountains (ibid., pp. 464, 465). *Very important*

God's judgments before the close of probation will be especially directed toward the most wicked cities in the world, but Ellen White said that before that time comes, a Sunday law in the United States—probably at that point a very mild Sunday law—will warn God's people to get out of the cities. *important*

Of course, before leaving the cities we should have a plan for housing and employment in the place where we intend to go. In view of the nearness of the final crisis, it seems to me that those of us now living in the cities should begin thinking and praying about where we might go and what we might do when we get there. If a wise move opens up, we should take the opportunity and move. Those for whom no move is apparent at the moment should pray earnestly that God will show them when to sell their property and when and where to move. God will answer those prayers in time for us to get out.

Please keep in mind the last sentence in the quote from *The Desire of Ages*: "Those who heed the warning will be saved." She does not mean "saved" from sin. She means "saved" from God's terrible judgments that are coming on the cities, which I spoke about earlier in this chapter.

Perhaps you can more easily put together in your mind all that we've discussed in this chapter if it's on a time chart where you can visualize it:

Sunday law in the U.S.	God changes His relationship to the world	Close of probation	Second coming
		Seven last plagues Great time of trouble	
	Little time of trouble		
Warning: Get out of the cities	Season of calamity Final crisis		

Warning others

You will recall that in the "ball of fire" statement I quoted earlier, the friends of God's people exclaimed, "We did not know about these things. Why did you leave us in ignorance? Again and again you have seen us; why did you not become acquainted with us, and tell us of the judgment to come, and that we must serve God, lest we perish? Now we are lost!"

I have pondered that statement many times in recent months. I think about my neighbors and ask myself, Will they confront me like that someday? What is my obligation to them and to the people in the city where I live, in the state where I live? For that matter, What is my responsibility to my nation and the world?

Ellen White stated emphatically that God holds us responsible for warning the world of coming judgments. I do not want to take a lot of time in this chapter on this point, but please consider the following statement, and ask yourself, "Is God speaking to me? Is He asking me to do something?"

> In quick succession the judgments of God will follow one another—fire and flood and earthquake, with war and bloodshed.
>
> Oh, that the people might know the time of their visitation! There are many who have not yet heard the testing truth for this time. There are many with whom the Spirit of God is striving. . . .
>
> The need of earnest laborers among the multitudes of the cities has been kept before me for more than twenty years. Who are carrying a burden for the large cities? (*Testimonies*, vol. 9, p. 97).

If these judgments from God upon the entire world are as near as they seem to be, Seventh-day Adventists ought to be the most active people in the world, warning of the destruction that is about to come. Yet most of us seem paralyzed by the fear that our prediction of coming calamities might not come to pass and we would be considered extremists. We fear that we might appear to be foolish—again. Is God going to have to dump all of us in the sea and cause all of us to be swallowed by a big fish before we will respond to His call to warn Nineveh?

I began this chapter by referring to the increasing pace of

natural disasters in our world right now. However, I want to emphasize again that none of the disasters you and I are familiar with today come anywhere near fulfilling Ellen White's terrible predictions of coming destruction. The final crisis is still ahead of us. And we can thank God for that, because Ellen White clearly suggests that when the crisis does come, many of God's people will be unprepared. The nature of these future disasters may be interesting to speculate about, but the real lesson for us is that we must prepare ourselves spiritually before these judgments happen, while there is still time.

I frankly fear that we don't have a lot of time left.

CHAPTER

9

The United States of America

Iraq invaded Kuwait on August 2, 1990. A few days later an enraged Egyptian military officer protested to an American: "You are the only superpower left in the world. We see it. The Europeans see it. The Soviets see it. Why don't you?" (*U.S. News & World Report*, 11 March 1991, p. 50).

A recent *Washington Post* article called George Bush "the world's only boss," and in an interview with a reporter, Yasir Arafat, chairman of the Palestinian Liberation Organization, called Washington "the new Rome."

To Adventists, these words have prophetic significance. We believe that America has a unique role to fill as a leader in the final events of earth's history. We have based that view on the prophecies of Revelation 12 and 13 and on the predictions of Ellen White.

The United States in Revelation 12

Revelation 12 is very familiar to Adventists, but let's look at it briefly. The vision begins with a pregnant woman about to be attacked by a great red dragon, which is Satan. The dragon is particularly intent on destroying the woman's Child, which, of course, was Jesus. Fortunately, Jesus was caught up to God in heaven, where the dragon could not destroy Him.

Satan was not about to admit defeat, though. Instead, he attacked Christ's people, His church. The dragon opened his mouth and "spewed water like a river, to overtake the woman and sweep her away with the torrent" (Revelation 12:15). However, the earth "helped the woman by opening its mouth and swallowing the river that the dragon had spewed out of his mouth" (verse 16).

Adventists believe God used America to help the woman. He raised up this country to be a haven of freedom from religious persecution. We believe God influenced the writing of the American Constitution, a unique legal document in the history of nations, which guarantees freedom of religion, speech, and assembly to every human being who lives on American soil.

The United States has become the world leader in freedom and democracy. Nearly every nation on earth has been influenced by the American model. There can be no question that this nation's example has made the world a better place to live these past 200 years. After seventy years of tyranny, even the Russians recognize how right America has been.

Seventh-day Adventists believe this was all a part of God's plan. America, Ellen White wrote, has been "an asylum for the conscience-oppressed servants of God and defenders of His truth" (*Testimonies*, vol. 5, p. 714). Roger Williams's Rhode Island was a model of the civil and religious liberty that became "the cornerstone of the American Republic" (*The Great Controversy*, p. 295).

> The United States is a land that has been under the special shield of the Omnipotent One. God has done great things for this country (Ellen G. White Comments, *SDA Bible Commentary*, vol. 7, p. 975).

> Freedom of religious faith was also granted [in America], every man being permitted to worship God according to the dictates of his conscience. Republicanism and Protestantism became the fundamental principles of the nation. These principles are the secret of its power and prosperity. . . . The United States has risen to a place among the most powerful nations of the earth (*The Great Controversy*, p. 441).

One hundred years after Ellen White wrote these words, the United States not only holds a place *among* the most powerful nations on earth—she *is* the most powerful nation on earth.

The United States in Revelation 13

However, Adventists also believe Revelation predicts that the United States will repudiate its principle of religious freedom and lead the world in religious intolerance. Revelation 13:11 says, "Then I saw another beast, coming out of the earth. He had two horns like a lamb, but he spoke like a dragon." For nearly 150 years we have taught that the lamblike character of this beast represents the United States as we have always known it—a democratic, peace-loving nation; and that the dragonlike character of the beast represents what the United States will become—a persecuting power.

> The statement that the beast with two horns "causeth the earth and them which dwell therein to worship the first beast" indicates that the authority of this nation [the United States] is to be exercised in enforcing some observance which shall be an act of homage to the papacy (ibid., p. 442).

And, as every Seventh-day Adventist knows, the observance that the United States will enforce as an act of homage to the papacy is Sunday keeping—a practice that had its origin in Roman Catholic history. And in so doing, this country will exchange the principle of religious freedom on which it was founded for the Roman Catholic principle of enforced religion:

> Sunday observance owes its existence as a so-called Christian institution to "the mystery of iniquity" [the papacy]; and its enforcement will be a virtual recognition of the principles which are the very cornerstone of Romanism. When our nation shall so abjure the principles of its government as to enact a Sunday law, ... it will be nothing else than giving life to the tyranny which has long been eagerly watching its opportunity to spring again into active despotism (*Testimonies*, vol. 5, p. 712).

> Our nation, in its legislative councils, [will] enact laws to bind the consciences of men in regard to their religious privileges, enforcing Sunday observance, and bringing oppressive power to bear against those who keep the seventh-

day Sabbath (Ellen G. White Comments, *SDA Bible Commentary*, vol. 7, p. 977).

According to Ellen White, the entire world will follow America's lead in the enforcement of Sunday observance:

> Foreign nations will follow the example of the United States. Though she leads out, yet the same crisis will come upon our people in all parts of the world (*Testimonies*, vol. 6, p. 395).

> As America, the land of religious liberty, shall unite with the papacy in forcing the conscience and compelling men to honor the false sabbath, the people of every country on the globe will be led to follow her example (ibid., p. 18).

America's end-time role

These statements suggest that the United States is to be the leader among nations during the time that history's final events are taking place—the world's only superpower.

However, only in the last few years has America been in a position to assume this role. During its first 125 years, the United States was still a child among the nations of the earth. France and England were the world's leaders. America's position grew in the world as a result of the First World War, but she turned isolationist, even refusing to support President Wilson's League of Nations. Europe continued to be the political leader of the world for another twenty years.

During World War II Hitler largely destroyed Europe's political and military power, and following the war the United States emerged as the most powerful nation on earth. However, she still was not in a position to fulfill her prophetic role. Another superpower lay across the Atlantic Ocean. For forty years, from 1950 to 1990, Seventh-day Adventists scratched their heads, trying to understand how the United States could possibly lead the world in the enforcement of a Christian observance when atheistic Communism dominated a third of the globe. I still remember, back in 1959, asking one of my professors at Union College where Communism fit into Bible prophecy.

The dramatic events in Eastern Europe during the last half of

1989 and the early part of 1990 answered that question. The world's Communist giant fell, and America became the world's only superpower. Less than a year later, a crisis arose in the world that gave the United States a chance to test her new role.

Iraq invaded Kuwait.

Please reflect with me for a moment on that event and its aftermath. In less than six months, the United States government led the world to organize a military campaign against this "villain," and the villain was defeated. America set a date and said to Saddam Hussein, "Get out of Kuwait by January 15, or we will force you to get out." America emerged from Desert Storm far more powerful, far more influential in world affairs, than ever before.

The Egyptian army officer's words truly were prophetic. America is the most powerful nation on earth. Everybody knows it, and everybody accepts it.

A new world order?

You've probably heard of George Bush's comment about a "new world order." Do you know what the president means by that? In his own words:

> Out of these troubled times . . . a new world order can emerge: a new era freer from the threat of terror, stronger in the pursuit of justice, and more secure in the quest for peace; an era in which the nations of the world, East and West, North and South, can prosper and live in harmony (quoted in *Adventist Review*, 21 March 1991, p. 11).

Please understand that Sunday laws and religious persecution are the furthest things from President Bush's mind. I have no doubt whatsoever that his intentions are totally altruistic, and I believe that every Seventh-day Adventist would agree. But let's examine a bit of history, concluding with Iraq's conflict with the world.

Following World War II the United States took on the role of the world's policeman. Perhaps that was necessary in the years immediately following the war, since Europe and Japan lay in ruins. However, as these two areas regained their strength, resentment began to grow toward America's dominant position, and during the 1970s and 1980s we heard disparaging remarks about America in various parts of the world. Much of this was undoubtedly fomented by Communism. The point is that America became self-conscious of her power and began to pull back. This was particularly evident following the Vietnam fiasco.

When Saddam Hussein invaded Kuwait, President Bush and his advisors decided that he had to be turned back, and they knew that America had the military power to do it. But they also realized that a military victory would become a political defeat if the United States were to be viewed as the world's policeman turned bully. So the president and the secretary of state put forth intense efforts to bring as much of the world along with them as possible.

The strategy worked. America led the world to victory in Kuwait, and she did it through the United Nations, the only legal body that represents the whole world.

I believe beyond a shadow of a doubt that we are headed toward a one-world government in some form. Catholic author Malachi Martin said it boldly and unequivocally:

> Willing or not, ready or not, we are all involved in an all-out, no-holds-barred, three-way global competition. Most of us are not the competitors, however. We are the stakes. For the competition is about who will establish the first one-world system of government that has ever existed in the society of nations. It is about who will hold and wield the dual power of authority and control over each of us as individuals and over all of us together as a community; over the entire six billion people expected by demographers to inhabit the earth by early in the third millennium.
>
> The competition is all-out because, now that it has started, there is no way it can be reversed or called off.
>
> No holds are barred because, once the competition has been decided, the world and all that's in it . . . will have been powerfully and radically altered forever. . . .
>
> Those of us who are under seventy will see at least the basic structures of the new world government installed. Those of us under forty will surely live under its legislative, executive and judiciary authority and control (Malachi Martin, *The Keys of This Blood*, pp. 15, 16).

Surely President Bush understands this. And, as I mentioned earlier, his motives are altruistic. He wants to see the American dream extended to all the world. He wants every human being to enjoy the freedoms—political, economic, and religious—that have made America great. He also realizes that drugs, crime, terrorism, and self-serving dictators such as Saddam Hussein pose a terrible threat to that utopian vision. And he realizes that no one nation can bring these enormous forces of evil under control. It will take the society of nations working together to do that. And, as the leader of the world's only superpower, George Bush is exercising his authority positively toward achieving that goal.

But does the president's noble vision of the future mean we have nothing to fear? Does his intention to exercise the power of his office wisely and humanely for the benefit of the human race mean that surely utopia lies in the future?

Here, I believe, is where Bible prophecy and the very specific end-time views of Ellen White help Seventh-day Adventists to interpret what is happening in the world today.

When we take what Scripture and Ellen White say—and especially Ellen White, since she lived much closer to earth's final events and spoke much more specifically about them—the conclusion is inescapable that in several significant ways, these predictions are now becoming reality.

We have already noted how her predictions in three significant areas have come to pass: the restoration of Catholic political power in the world, the rise of spiritualism under the guise of the New Age, and the right-wing Protestant demand for an end to church-state separation. All these, as I pointed out in an earlier chapter, became obvious in the fifteen years between 1975 and 1990.

Then, in the year and a half between August 1989 and February 1991, the United States of America emerged as the world's only superpower. Prior to that time there were two acknowledged superpowers. Now there is only one, and, as the Egyptian army officer said, "everyone knows it."

I am very cautious about waving a newspaper report of a single event in the air and jumping up and down, proclaiming that prophecy has been fulfilled. But I feel very comfortable looking at trends in the light of prophecy. And the trends I see tell me that so far, Ellen White's scenario for the United States as a superpower during the final days of earth's history is working out very much as she said it would.

What about the future?

Which leads to the next question: What else did Ellen White foresee? What did she predict about the United States that has not yet happened?

She said plainly that religion will control the American government:

> In order for the United States to form an image of the beast, the religious power must so control the civil government that the authority of the state will also be employed by the church to accomplish her own ends (*The Great Controversy*, p. 443).

> When Protestantism shall stretch her hand across the gulf to grasp the hand of the Roman power, when she shall reach over the abyss to clasp hands with spiritualism, when, under the influence of this threefold union, our country [the United States of America] shall . . . make provision for the propagation of papal falsehoods and delusions, then we may know that the time has come for the marvelous working of Satan and that the end is near (*Testimonies*, vol. 5, p. 451).

However, one other significant development must take place before these religious groups can influence the United States government to enforce the dogmas of the papacy. The power of secular humanism over Western life must be broken. Notice that I did not say secular humanism must be destroyed. We will always have humanists around. But they cannot dominate our culture in the future the way they have during the last fifty years if the vision of Scripture and Ellen White for the future are to be fulfilled. Christianity—a coalition of Protestants and Catholics—must gain control of society and government.

Already a union of sorts exists between Protestants and Catholics on a number of points. Right-wing Protestants have joined Catholics in their determination to obtain state aid for their parochial schools, and both groups have joined efforts to rid the United States of legalized abortion. As everyone knows, prohibition of abortion is a dogma of the Roman Catholic Church.

However, reflect for a moment on the success of these endeavors. Right-wing Protestants and Catholics have experienced significant success in obtaining state financial support for their schools, and more is surely to come, but throughout all of the 1980s and the first year or so of the 1990s *their effort to abolish legalized abortion was a dismal failure.* The pro-abortion forces in this country were far more successful than the pro-life forces.

And the reason is very simple: secularism. America today is largely a secular nation. Secularism controls the nation's communications media, its public-educational system, its scientific establishment, and its government institutions. It is also the preferred lifestyle of a majority of the American people. And secularism is pro-choice all the way. Two other major areas of Western culture, Australia and Western Europe, are even more secularized than the United States.

However, prophecy says that all the world—not part of the world but *all* the world—will wonder "after the beast" (Revelation 13:3, KJV). And they will not only wonder, but they will worship. They will worship the dragon, and they will worship the beast (verse 4). Worship, of course, is the highest form of religious activity. With secularism so dominant in the West, how can the Bible say that *all* the world will worship the dragon and the beast? That's a prediction of what is yet to come. If we believe that prediction, we can say with confidence that just before the end of time secularism will lose its power. Just before the close of probation the whole world will be dominated by religion. Ellen White said that even Satan will be converted, "after the modern order of things" (*The Great Controversy*, p. 588).

As I pointed out earlier, I believe President Bush is entirely altruistic in his vision of the coming "new world order." America's present political leadership is nowhere near to passing even mild forms of distinctly religious legislation, much less giving its approval to fines and incarceration for violation of such laws. And even if the president were not altruistic, secularists, who control the U.S. government and many other aspects of American life, do not take kindly to laws that would require them to be religious.

How, then, will the change come?

A gradual union of church and state, a gradual move to Sunday legislation through the normal political processes that we see in operation today, and a gradual buildup to religious persecution by the American government could take many decades.

However, suppose that a series of natural disasters were to shatter the world's economy and destroy a significant portion of its life-support systems. Desperate circumstances would move even some atheists into a desperate search for spiritual, religious answers. Men and women everywhere would recognize that God was trying to tell them something, and political processes that normally take several decades could easily be compressed into the same number of months, perhaps even weeks.

Ellen White suggests that that is exactly what will happen. We saw in the chapter on the season of calamity that a series of natural disasters will occur, and I believe that these disasters will shock the world's secular people so profoundly, that even in America, they will support drastic political measures to deal with the emergency in ways that under more normal circumstances would be unthinkable. In a panic, Protestants, Catholics, spiritualists, and secularists—even scientists—will unite to appease an offended God. The persecution of the last days will appear to be the sensible solution to the crisis.

It is very easy to imagine a large proportion of American secularists joining with Protestants and Catholics to seek a spiritual solution to such an emergency. It is very easy to imagine the United States, altruistically again, leading the world in search of a solution to the problem. And it is very easy to imagine the world's community of nations, under the leadership of the United States, giving the supposed "cause" of the problem another deadline: Capitulate by such and such a date, or we will destroy you.

Did Ellen White ever predict that?

Iraq was a good practice session, wasn't it?

10

Sunday Laws

Samuel Mitchel of Quitman, Georgia, was the first Seventh-day Adventist in the United States to be arrested on a charge of violating a Sunday law. In 1878 he spent thirty days in the county jail, where conditions were so filthy that his health broke. A year and a half later he died.

Most states had Sunday laws at that time, but the few cases in the North and West where Adventists were brought to trial were quickly dismissed, and the California Sunday law was repealed. The South, however, was another matter. Arkansas had a Sunday law that included an exemption clause for Sabbatarians, but in 1884 the exemption clause was repealed, and about twenty Adventists were fined.

The state of Tennessee was particularly harsh on Adventists. In 1885 William Dortch, W. H. Parker, and James Stem were fined and imprisoned and spent several weeks working in a chain gang. In 1889, and again in 1890, R. M. King was arrested for plowing corn and hoeing in his potato patch on Sunday. He was convicted, and his case eventually reached the United States Supreme Court. However, Mr. King died before the case could be heard. The case died with the defendant. Three years later five Seventh-day Adventists were brought to trial for violating the Tennessee Sunday ordinance; they also spent time on a chain gang.

Several times during this period, the advocates of Sunday laws succeeded in having bills introduced into the United States

Congress. One of their chief allies was Senator H. W. Blair, who introduced a bill in 1888, the purpose of which was "To Secure to the People the Enjoyment of the First Day of the Week, Commonly Known as the Lord's Day, as a Day of Rest, and to Promote Its Observance as a Day of Religious Worship." In early 1889 Senator Blair proposed an amendment to the U.S. Constitution that would have Christianized America's public schools. Both of these bills were defeated. Blair introduced another Sunday bill in the latter part of 1889 that was also defeated. (See Arthur W. Spalding, *Origin and History of Seventh-day Adventists* [Hagerstown, Md.: Review and Herald Publishing Assn., 1962], vol. 2, pp. 253-262, and *Seventh-day Adventist Encyclopedia*, revised edition, s.v. "Sunday Laws.")

A sign of the end

If there is one event above another that Seventh-day Adventists look for as a sign that the end is near and that Jesus is about to return, that event is the enactment of Sunday laws. We believe that the mark of the beast of Revelation 13 is the observance of Sunday when it is enforced by law. Ellen White developed this theme in great detail in her book *The Great Controversy*. Because this book was first published in 1888, it would be easy to assume that her views were an extreme reaction to the persecution of Adventists over this issue about this time. However, the Adventist understanding of the mark of the beast did not originate with Ellen White, nor did it arise out of the persecution of Adventists during the late 1880s and the early 1890s.

The first Seventh-day Adventist to suggest that the mark of the beast was Sunday observance was Joseph Bates, in the second edition of his tract, *The Seventh-day Sabbath, a Perpetual Sign*, published in 1846. Ellen White was shown by the Lord that Bates's view was correct. *A Word to the Little Flock*, published in 1847, also set forth this interpretation with Ellen White's approval, since it was written jointly by Ellen and her husband and Joseph Bates. Ellen White championed this view for nearly seventy years, until her death in 1915. Thus it is obvious that the Adventist view of Sunday laws and the mark of the beast did not originate during the Sunday-law crisis of the 1880s and 1890s. Those events merely confirmed to Adventists that they had been right all along. They also raised end-time expectations in the church to a fever pitch.

The fever died down, though. Sunday laws remained on the statute books of most states in this country, but by the year 1900 persecution against Adventists for violating these laws had ceased. Since that time, many states have repealed their Sunday laws, and enforcement by most of those that have retained them is lax. There is, frankly, little activity in the United States today toward enacting, much less enforcing Sunday laws. Our society has become so secular that few people have any desire to legislate a day of worship.

Because of this strong trend away from Sunday laws during the past 100 years, some Seventh-day Adventists are beginning to wonder whether the final conflict will involve a controversy over the fourth commandment at all. They say that Ellen White described how the end time would have developed had it come in her day. A hundred years later, the issues may be significantly different, some suggest. "Could it be," questioned an Adventist scholar in a letter to me, "that history has continued beyond the Sunday issue, and that something else might show up as the final test?"

There is an element of truth to the idea that a prophecy that is predicted to be fulfilled in a particular way at one time may work out differently if it is fulfilled at a later date. However, Scripture itself, and not just Ellen White, makes it clear that the issue in the final conflict will involve the law of God:

> The dragon was enraged at the woman and went off to make war against the rest of her offspring—those who obey God's commandments and hold to the testimony of Jesus (Revelation 12:17).

> This calls for patient endurance on the part of the saints who obey God's commandments and remain faithful to Jesus (Revelation 14:12).

Revelation also informs us that the final conflict will center around true and false worship—the worship of the beast and his image on the one hand (see Revelation 13:4, 8, 15; 14:9, 10) and the worship of God on the other (see Revelation 14:6, 7). True worship is also defined in language so reminiscent of the fourth commandment that it is almost impossible not to make the connection: "Worship him who made the heavens, the earth, the sea and the springs of water" (Revelation 14:7).

Furthermore, Ellen White's views on the Sabbath/Sunday conflict at the end of time are inextricably bound up with everything else she taught about the last days. The following positive statements are representative of dozens she made during her seventy-year ministry:

The Sabbath is the great test question. It is the line of demarkation between the loyal and true and the disloyal and transgressor (*Selected Messages*, book 3, p. 423).

The Sabbath question is to be *the* issue in the great final conflict, in which all the world will act a part (Ellen G. White Comments, *SDA Bible Commentary*, vol. 7, p. 977, emphasis supplied).

A time is coming when the law of God is, in a special sense, to be made void in our land. The rulers of our nation will, by legislative enactments, enforce the Sunday law (ibid.).

This question [Sunday legislation] will soon be before us. God's Sabbath will be trampled under foot, and a false sabbath will be exalted (*Selected Messages*, book 2, p. 375).

With all this evidence, it is difficult to escape the conclusion that the Sabbath/Sunday conflict will be a major political issue during the final crisis.

Why no Sunday laws?

My personal conclusion, after examining all the evidence, is that the question is not: *Will* the final crisis focus on the fourth commandment? The real question is: *Why,* in view of Ellen White's unequivocal predictions, has the trend gone the other direction these past 100 years?

And the answer is, I believe, that Satan learned two great lessons from the Sunday-law crisis of the late 1800s. He learned first that Seventh-day Adventists take Sunday laws very seriously. We fight them. In 1892, following the arrest of five Seventh-day Adventists in Tennessee for working on Sunday, we distributed 300,000 tracts that explained our position to government officials, lawyers, and the citizens of the state. As a result, the persecution stopped. On the national level, A. T. Jones was a fearless opponent of the Sunday bills that came before the U.S. Congress during the late 1880s and early 1890s. Again, as a result, every one of these bills was defeated.

We fought Sunday laws, and we won.

I can imagine Satan retreating from the Sunday-law conflict of the late 1800s licking his wounds. I expect he said to himself, "Next time I won't give them a chance to fight!"

Satan also learned that because Sunday laws are *the* Adventist sign of the end, these laws will stir us to prepare for the second coming of Christ like nothing else could. And the last thing Satan wants is Adventists who are on fire. So he keeps Sunday laws way in the background, where we can't see them. That way we'll think we have lots of time. Instead, Satan quietly works in the background, removing the legal barrier (church-state separation) that stopped Sunday laws 100 years ago. The business of life will seem much more urgent to us, and we'll go on as usual until it's too late. Then he'll pounce on us like a cat sneaking up on a mouse. Like a chess player who fails to pay attention, we'll discover too late that we've been checkmated. One short move, and the Sunday laws we've anticipated will stare us in the face, and there won't be a thing we can do to stop them.

That, in my opinion, is why the trend has been away from Sunday legislation during the last 100 years.

The Sabbath/Sunday crisis—gradual or sudden?

Three chapters in *The Great Controversy* discuss the final conflict before the close of probation—"God's Law Immutable," "The Impending Conflict," and "The Final Warning." Reading through these chapters, one gets the distinct impression that the Sabbath/Sunday crisis in the United States will develop somewhat gradually. Each of the following statements suggests that Sunday laws will be a hot issue in American politics, and that Sunday legislation will develop over a period of time. Notice especially the italicized words:

Political corruption is destroying love of justice and regard for truth; and even in free America, *rulers and legislators*, in order to secure public favor, *will yield to the popular demand* for a law enforcing Sunday observance (*The Great Controversy*, p. 592, emphasis supplied).

As *the question of enforcing Sunday observance is widely agitated*, the event so long doubted and disbelieved *is seen to be approaching*, and the third message will produce an effect which it could not have had before (ibid., p. 606, emphasis supplied).

As *the movement for Sunday observance gains favor*, he [the papist] rejoices, feeling assured that it will eventually bring the whole Protestant world under the banner of Rome (ibid., p. 448, emphasis supplied).

As *the movement for Sunday enforcement becomes more bold and decided*, the law will be invoked against commandment keepers (ibid., p. 607, emphasis supplied).

Let's review the italicized phrases in each of these statements. Each one suggests legislation that arises out of political processes, such as campaigning and debating, rather than out of administrative fiat.

- *The first statement.* Ellen White said that "rulers and legislators . . . will yield to the popular demand." How much campaigning does it take to create a popular demand? And how much more campaigning does it take to get rulers and legislators to yield to that demand? A lot.
- *The second statement.* Ellen White said that "as the question of enforcing Sunday observance *is widely agitated* . . ." Agitation doesn't happen overnight. Even with today's instantaneous means of mass communication, changing the public's attitude to the point that national policies are reversed takes a lot of time. The abortion conflict of the 1980s and 1990s is an excellent case in point. And after all this, "the event so long doubted and disbelieved *is seen to be approaching*." It isn't here yet. It's still on the way.

3. *The third statement.* Ellen White said, "As the *movement* for Sunday observance *gains favor* . . ." Again, we are dealing with a period of time. *Webster's New World Dictionary* defines *movement* as "a tendency or trend in some particular sphere of activity" (Third College Edition). A trend, by its very definition, takes time to develop. Ellen White says this trend, this movement, "gains favor."

4. *The fourth statement.* Ellen White said that the movement for Sunday observance will become "more bold and decided." Again, the idea of protracted time is clearly suggested.

However, I believe it is entirely possible that the Sabbath/Sunday crisis will confront God's people suddenly, with little or no warning. I say this for two reasons.

First, in the late 1800s, when Ellen White wrote these words, she and Adventists in general expected the demand for Sunday legislation to be the issue that would destroy the wall between church and state in the United States. Time was needed not only to agitate Sunday laws, but to break down church-state separation with Sunday laws.

However, as I pointed out earlier, 100 years later Satan has changed his strategy. Now he is using other issues to break down the wall separating church and state—particularly the abortion conflict and the demand for government aid to parochial schools. A national Sunday law today will require much less political action for its enactment than would have been required 100 years ago, because if present trends continue, by the time agitation for Sunday laws comes on the scene, the Supreme Court will have removed church-state separation—the only legal barrier that would prevent them.

The second reason why Sunday laws may come much more quickly today is the speed with which the world moves—much faster than 100 years ago. With international direct dial, anyone who has access to money and a telephone can communicate in about one minute with just about anyone anywhere in the world who also has a telephone. People who have the money can travel to most places in the world within twenty-four hours, and even the remotest parts of the world are theoretically accessible within forty-eight hours.

As fast as the Communist countries of Eastern Europe fell in late 1989, as fast as the United States and its allies conquered Iraq in early 1991, and as fast as the Soviet Union disintegrated in late 1991, why should it take years to initiate the final crisis? The world in which we live is so vastly different from Ellen White's world, that I suspect, while she would maintain her basic view of a coming Sabbath/Sunday conflict, her understanding of how long it will take for that conflict to work itself out would be considerably different today than it was 100 years ago.

Nor is the idea of Sunday laws coming quickly to the forefront inconsistent with what she herself wrote. She spoke many times about the suddenness of God's future judgments. She spoke of "the events of the future, which will soon come upon [God's people] with blinding force" (1903), and of "what is soon to break upon the world as an overwhelming surprise" (1904).

I believe that the forces of good and evil in the world are on a collision course. Especially since the 1960s, evil has become more bold and unrestrained. Secularism dominates nearly every phase of American and Western public life, including government, science, education, the arts, and journalism. On the other hand, evangelical and fundamentalist Christians are struggling mightily to restore some semblance of Judeo-Christian values to our culture.

While some things about their approach trouble me, conservative Christians are pointing out very real sin problems in our society: pornography, homosexuality, sexual child abuse, free love, drugs, alcoholism, violent and lustful TV programs—the list goes on and on. Sooner or later, genuine religion on the one hand and the religion of secularism and the New Age on the other must confront each other in a final conflict for the control of our planet.

If this conflict is to be resolved gradually, then political reality suggests that it may require several more decades to bring on the final crisis. However, a supernatural intervention by God in the form of catastrophic, worldwide natural disasters could force the human race into a moral self-examination overnight. Disasters of the magnitude Ellen White saw coming would jolt even the most secular person into recognizing that "God is trying to tell us something."

I fear that the protracted political activity Ellen White foresaw in her Sunday-law predictions is taking place right now, but not in the context of Sunday laws. Even as you read these words, rulers and legislators are yielding to a popular demand by Protestants, exactly the way Ellen White said they would (see *The Great Controversy*, p. 592). They are not yielding to the demand for Sunday laws, but they are rapidly yielding to the demand to destroy our only protection against such laws: the separation of church and state. I believe we are seeing Ellen White's prediction fulfilled before our very eyes, and the vast majority of us don't realize it because it isn't happening the way we thought it would. That's a trick Satan used on the Jews 2,000 years ago. We shouldn't be surprised to see him try the same thing on the people of God today.

Ellen White's predictions about end-time politics in the United States foresaw a gradual process. Because that process is being fulfilled right now, apart from Sunday laws, I suspect that when they come, Sunday laws will be passed fairly quickly. We simply must not wait for agitation to develop over Sunday laws, as though that will be soon enough to get right with God. It is utterly imperative that we prepare for the final crisis as though it will come suddenly, "as an overwhelming surprise," and "with blinding force." Those who wait for the gradual development of end-time events may wait too long.

A suggested scenario

From my analysis of Ellen White's comments on Sunday laws and the coming "season of calamity," and from my knowledge of current events, I would like to suggest a scenario that seems very likely to me. Please bear in mind that this is only my personal interpretation of the evidence. Yours may be different.

During the past ten years the American government has been moving at an accelerating pace toward undoing its historic policy of keeping church and state separate. If this trend continues, as seems likely, then, in spite of the fact that there is no significant activity toward Sunday legislation on either the state or the national level at the time I am writing this book, I believe it is entirely possible that a mild form of Sunday legislation in the United States could be enacted fairly quickly in the near future. According to the prophetic guidance we have been given, such legislation, whenever it is enacted, will have a profound impact on this country's relationship with God:

When the Protestant churches shall unite with the secular power to sustain a false religion, for opposing which their ancestors endured the fiercest persecution; when the state shall use its power to enforce the decrees and sustain the institutions of the church—then will Protestant America have formed an image to the papacy, and there will be a national apostasy which will end only in national ruin (Ellen G. White Comments, *SDA Bible Commentary*, vol. 7, p. 976).

Notice that when the United States enacts even a mild form of Sunday legislation, she will radically alter her relationship with God. The inspired evidence that has been given to Seventh-day Adventists suggests that such legislation will be heaven's signal to allow disasters to fall, probably on the United States first, and then on other parts of the world.

Suppose, for instance, that a series of earthquakes were to destroy several of the major cities in the world and thousands of smaller ones. Suppose that several hundred "freak" storms were to destroy a major share of the earth's food crops the way a single storm devastated the crops in Egypt 3,500 years ago. And suppose that on top of all that a small asteroid were actually to impact in the heart of Brazil, destroying 95 percent of the Amazon jungle and seriously compromising the world's oxygen supply. Can you imagine the reaction of the world's politicians and scientists? I believe that's the kind of crisis Luke had in mind when he said that at the end of time "nations will be in anguish and perplexity" and "men will faint from terror, apprehensive of what is coming on the world" (Luke 21:25, 26).

While we can only speculate about what they will actually be, natural disasters of that magnitude *are* coming, and many of them will come suddenly and without warning. The world's statesmen will be forced to declare a state of emergency in order to provide everyone with the basic necessities of life. Ellen White's statements about coming disaster compel me to think in these stupendous terms.

People everywhere will recognize that "God is trying to tell us something." The world as a whole will seek a spiritual solution, and secular people, who heretofore have been a powerful force in support of religious freedom, will find their power gone. As a horrified reaction to catastrophic, worldwide natural disasters, the public as a whole will demand, and get, religious laws that a freedom-loving people would never before have considered possible, even in their worst nightmares. These laws will be enacted very quickly, and everyone will agree that "it had to be done." A religious "new world order" will be established that will make President Bush's political new world order seem like child's play. Fundamentalism that would have made the Ayatollah Khomeini proud will take control of government in the United States.

Does all that sound unreal to your ears? It's simply the picture I get when I take the predictions of Scripture and Ellen White interpreted in the light of current trends, and apply a little contemporary terminology. Some thinking non-Adventists, reading these current trends, are also expressing their concern. Please read the following statement by Barry Lynn, an ordained minister in the United Church of Christ and an attorney, who for several years was legislative counsel to the Washington, D.C., office of the American Civil Liberties Union:

> It's very easy for Americans to think that the problems of the Ayatollah Khomeini . . . are not problems that will ever be replicated here in the United States. They think this country somehow at some point down the road won't let things get out of hand. I think that's a very dangerous and false idea. All you need to do is to read the books and the writings of people like Randall Terry, head of Operation Rescue. He's a man who radically wants to transform America on the basis of the biblical understanding that he and many people share. He's not going to be satisfied by outlawing abortion because he will admit to an agenda that's far more far-reaching than that (*Church and State*, July-August 1991, p. 9).

I want to repeat my personal conviction that the present willingness by the American government, especially the administration, to yield to right-wing Protestant demands to dismantle church-state separation, may very well result rather quickly in a mild form of Sunday legislation in the not-too-distant future. However, I do not believe the harsh form of Sunday legislation that Ellen White predicted will happen apart from the catastrophes associated with the season of calamity.

When these catastrophes do begin to happen, they will prompt the world's religious people, especially Protestants and Catholics, to unite around a "program" to restore God to His rightful place in society. That's exactly what Ellen White predicted:

> It will be declared that men are offending God by the violation of the Sunday sabbath; that this sin has brought calamities which will not cease until Sunday observance shall be strictly enforced; and that those who present the claims of the fourth commandment, thus destroying reverence for Sunday, are troublers of the people, preventing their restoration to divine favor and temporal prosperity (*The Great Controversy*, p. 590).

> Satan puts his interpretation upon events, and . . . [the leading men] think, as he would have them [think], that the calamities which fill the land are a result of Sunday-breaking. Thinking to appease the wrath of God, these influential men make laws enforcing Sunday observance (Manuscript 85, 1899, quoted in *Maranatha*, p. 176).

That is how I believe Ellen White's prediction of sudden and unlooked-for calamities that bring God's people face to face with death will be fulfilled.

One hundred years ago, when Adventists were being persecuted in various parts of the United States for "working" on Sunday, and when a national Sunday law was being agitated in the United States Congress, second-coming fever burned hot in our brains. Today, however, with no sign of a Sunday law in the offing, the evidence of our proximity to the final crisis is much greater than it was 100 years ago. Americans back then were still strongly anti-Catholic. The papacy wasn't anywhere near reestablishing control over the world. And spiritualism was practically a non-issue. Most significantly, as I pointed out earlier in this chapter, the American people strongly supported church-state separation, which spelled the doom of any national Sunday law. The *only* evidence of the fulfillment of our unique prophetic understanding during the late 1880s and early 1890s was state Sunday laws and agitation for a national Sunday law.

Today we do not see any significant activity toward enacting a national Sunday law, but we do see the four major Adventist predictions of the end-time roaring into our lives: New-age spiritualism, a revitalized Roman Catholic Church, church-state separation under severe attack by American Protestants, and the United States as the world's only superpower.

These signs of the end are far more significant than Sunday laws, because they provide the context that make possible not only Sunday laws but the entire final crisis that Ellen White predicted.

I believe that we are on the verge of stupendous events in the world. I believe that Ellen White's prediction that "the final movements will be rapid ones" (*Testimonies*, vol. 9, p. 11) is already being fulfilled.

It's time Seventh-day Adventists woke up. It's time we began seeking the Lord for the latter rain and for the transformed hearts we will need to see us through earth's darkest hour with our relationship with Jesus intact.

I also believe it's time we started telling the world what's ahead. If we don't, God is going to raise up others who will.

CHAPTER
11
Could It Really Happen Here?

Early on Wednesday morning, December 18, 1991, I picked up the newspaper that had been delivered to my home an hour before and read the headline: "New Year Will Bring End to the Soviet Union."

I had known it was coming. We could all see it coming, following Boris Yeltsin's initiative a few days earlier to establish a commonwealth of former Soviet republics. But to read in the newspaper that seventy-four years of Communist domination had come to an end, that the Soviet Union we had all known for as long as most of us could remember had ceased to exist—that was truly awesome.

Yet think about this: A scant three years earlier, if anyone had told us that Communism in Eastern Europe and Russia would be dead by the end of 1991, we would have told them they were crazy.

Three months prior to the startling news about the demise of the Kremlin, the headline in my paper had said, "Human Rights Top Agenda in U.S.S.R." The news story went on to report that the Soviet Union was calling an international forum on human rights "to serve as a bulwark for its newfound freedoms" (*The Idaho Statesman*, 8 September 1991, p. A-1).

Three years earlier, few people in the West would have taken an announcement like that out of Moscow as anything more than a Communist propaganda ploy. Today we know it's true. Democracy and freedom are on a roll around most of the world, and it seems to be only a matter of time until even China joins in.

But reflect with me for a moment on the statement by attorney Barry Lynn that I quoted in the previous chapter. Mr. Lynn began by saying:

> It's very easy for Americans to think that the problems of the Ayatollah Khomeini . . . are not problems that will ever be replicated here in the United States. They think this country somehow at some point down the road won't let things get out of hand (*Church and State*, July-August 1991, p. 9).

That statement makes sense to me as an American living in America during the early 1990s. It does seem that the freedoms we enjoy are eternal, that our leaders are committed to them, and that by their vote Americans will always support them. With freedom and democracy increasing around the world, we wonder how the intolerance Mr. Lynn fears and that Ellen White predicts could ever break out in America. It still seems, in the words of a nineteenth-century critic of Adventism, that such a development "would be a great[er] miracle than for God to grow a giant oak in an instant." Yet Mr. Lynn said that to suppose that a Khomeini-type revolution couldn't happen in America is "a very dangerous and false idea."

We need to keep several points in mind before we brush aside Mr. Lynn's warning. First, I would like to suggest that if the forty-five-year Communist grip on Eastern Europe can be broken in six months, and if the seventy-four-year Communist grip on Russia can be broken in just two years, then couldn't the American system of government be destroyed also, and just as rapidly?

Unaccustomed as we Americans are to the Dark Ages, we tend to forget that there is tremendous political power locked up in organized religion. Given the right circumstances, that power could be unleashed very quickly. We need to ask two questions as we contemplate that possibility. First, what circumstances would be required for organized religion to dominate the American government, and second, what religious forces, if any, would be interested in doing so?

What circumstances?

Two circumstances would be required for a rapid takeover of the American political system by organized religion. The first would be the breaching of the wall that presently separates church and state in this country. And this, as I have already pointed out, is near to being accomplished by the Supreme Court as reconstituted by presidents Ronald Reagan and George Bush. Yet this, of itself, seems hardly likely to bring about the severe persecution that Adventists have predicted will occur in the United States and other parts of the world shortly before the end of time. Many other countries have some form of government cooperation with religion while still protecting the rights of minorities. The shift in church-state relations that we see coming is probably not a major threat to our freedoms if all things continue as they have in this country for the past 200 years.

If all things continue as they have.

That's a big IF.

Which brings me to the second circumstance that would be required for organized religion to take over America's political institutions: a time of dire national and international emergency. The political balance of power in any country can shift very quickly in a crisis, and if what I have said earlier in this book is true, an international crisis of unimaginable proportions lies just ahead of us. I will not trouble you with additional quotations by Ellen White regarding the judgments of God during the final crisis, but I would like to remind you of these words by Jesus:

> There will be signs in the sun, moon and stars. *On the earth, nations will be in anguish and perplexity. . . . Men will faint from terror, apprehensive of what is coming on the world* (Luke 21:25, 26, emphasis supplied).

You don't have to read between the lines of that statement to know that a terrible international crisis awaits the world shortly before the end of time. This is exactly the kind of crisis that makes massive shifts in political power possible. A religious power that was intent on gaining political control could do so in such a context. Jesus associated that crisis with signs in the sun, moon, and stars, which, as I have already pointed out, could easily be a part of the natural disasters God allows to come on the world during the final crisis. If Adventists haven't thought about that possibility, the world's scientists certainly have.

Which organized religions?

But even if such a crisis were to occur, are there religious organizations in the world prepared to step into the political power vacuum and take over? I see two religious groups that aspire to political power: Right-wing Protestantism and Roman Catholicism.

Right-wing Protestantism. It's no secret that ever since the late 1960s and the early 1970s, America's right-wing Protestants have been organizing, training, and working behind the scenes to take control of this country's governmental institutions. America's secular humanists still sniff at their fundamentalist Protestant countrymen, but if they will stop sniffing and start looking, they'll realize that, as of this writing, the fundamentalists have been influential in putting three American presidents in the White House—Carter, Reagan, and Bush—and through those presidents they have transformed the Supreme Court into their own image. Furthermore, they are gaining ground on their chief political objective of the 1980s and early 1990s—overturning *Roe v. Wade,* the Supreme Court's landmark pro-abortion decision of 1971.

Unfortunately, anti-abortionism is only the tip of the iceberg.

I remember several years ago reading in a news magazine that the power of right-wing Protestantism in this country was a fad that had run its course. America, the report claimed, was returning to its more sane roots.

As it turns out, this kind of disdain that secularists hold for right-wing Protestantism will very likely prove the undoing of secularism, and worse, the undoing of the freedoms that secularists and all the rest of us have cherished these 200 years. The guard who's in the greatest danger is the one who thinks there is no danger because he can't see any.

The Christian right correctly identifies the moral problems that plague this country, but its solution is chilling. The most extreme form of right-wing Christianity, called Christian Reconstructionism, advocates that " 'legitimate civil government is the police department within the Kingdom of God on earth,' and 'it is to impose God's vengeance upon those who abandon God's laws of justice' " (*Church and State*, October 1991, p. 4).

According to *Church and State* magazine, "The virulently political theology of Christian Reconstructionism and its variants are gradually influencing many churches, some profoundly. The goal of the Reconstructionists is to create as soon as possible a Kingdom of God on Earth operating under Old Testament law" (ibid.).

Rousas J. Rushdoony, the father of Christian Reconstructionism, claims that eighteen Old Testament sins were punishable by death, including adultery, homosexuality, and Sabbath breaking; and he advocates that America adopt the death penalty for these offenses as well (ibid., September 1988, p. 9). That sounds extreme to traditional American ears, but to a Christian right that's tired of America's plague of crime, it's beginning to sound like good news. Reconstructionist theology and philosophy are gaining increasing acceptance among conservative pastors and church leaders in America.

Reconstructionism is clearly the Christian version of Ayatollah Kohmeini's theology, and you may think there is little danger of that radical ideology gaining control of America's political system.

Don't be so sure.

For years the Christian Right has been working at the grass roots to take control of the political system in this country, and the payoff has begun. In California the Christian Right now controls the Republican Party's state board and half of its Central Committee. "In San Diego County the Christian Right fielded 90 candidates for local offices such as school board, water board and city council in November 1990. Sixty of them won" (ibid., October 1991, p. 4).

How do these people do it? Through disciplined voting blocks in sympathetic churches. The local church and its pastor are the key. Using what is known as the "shepherding/discipleship" model of church organization, the pastor trains a dozen laypersons to be his disciples, and these, in turn, train others. A nice-sounding idea. After all, didn't Jesus use that model?

Yes, but "shepherding/discipleship" means something far different to radical-right Christians than it does to you and me. In their model, each person who has been discipled is supposed to disciple other church members "to deepen their commitment and obedience to the church *and its political aims*" (ibid., p. 5, emphasis supplied).

And what is the ultimate goal? " 'Several national groups of [radical Christian right] strategists are looking now at 60 major cities in the U.S. and Canada' for long term influence. This would include 'Replace[ment] of anti-biblical elected officials with biblically oriented candidates' " (ibid).

Put with this the fact that Pat Robertson's *Christian American* newspaper recently claimed that "conservative and Christian forces control the Republican Party in California, Louisiana, Florida and a dozen other states" (ibid., p. 6), and you begin to get the picture.

Anti-abortionism truly is only the tip of the iceberg.

Secularists, and too many Adventists, do not understand the power that is locked up within radical right-wing Christianity in this country, nor do we understand how far these people have already gone toward taking over the nation. As long as we sniff at them, we actually refuse to take seriously what is in fact a mortal danger to our freedoms. As long as we sniff, these people will continue making gains, until one of these days, as it was in Iran, so it will be in America—radicals will have gained control. And by then it will be too late to stop them.

Roman Catholicism. The Catholic effort to gain political control is only slightly less obvious. For starters, in spite of Vatican II and the generous statements about religious freedom that followed, Rome's pontiffs have never abandoned their aversion to church-state separation. Malachi Martin made that clear in his book *The Keys of This Blood*:

> For John Paul, there is a basic human fallacy crippling the regnant secularism of the West and of Gorbachevism. The prevalent idea (erected into a principle nowadays) is that a wall is to be maintained at all costs—at the cost of liberty itself—between church and state, between religion and public life. The Wall—capitalized frequently in order to personify it as a legal entity much like America—is more sacred than motherhood and apple pie. But, the Pontiff argues, the idea that we can be related to the world and not related to God is as false as the idea that we can be related to God without being related to the world (p. 365).

In case those words don't persuade you that church-state separation is more than a luxury in this country, follow through with me on the logic of the following group of statements:

It is axiomatic for John Paul that no one has the right—democratic or otherwise—to a moral wrong; and no religion based on divine revelation has a moral right to teach such a moral wrong or abide by it (p. 287).

I don't know about you, but the question that jumps out at me when I read that statement is this: If no one has the right to believe, teach, or abide by a moral wrong, who is going to decide for the rest of us what's morally right and wrong? John Paul has the answer to that question too:

The Roman Catholic Church has always claimed—and, under John Paul II, claims today—to be the ultimate arbiter of what is morally good and morally bad in human actions (p. 157).

So what do John Paul and his church propose to do about people who choose to teach and abide by a moral wrong? Malachi Martin's answer and his church's answer to that question is sobering to contemplate:

The final prerequisite for georeligious capability [translation: religious domination of the world] is authority. The institution [Roman Catholic Church], in its organizational structures and undertakings, must have unique authority: an authority that is centralized; an authority that is *autonomous* vis-à-vis all other authority on the supranational plane; an authority that carries with it such *sanctions* as are effective in maintaining the unity and the aims of the institution *as it goes about its business of serving the greatest good of the community as a whole and in its every part* (p. 138, emphasis supplied).

Malachi Martin claims that for a religious entity to have global authority it must have autonomy—that is, it must be able to exercise its will without interference from any other nation; and it must be able to impose sanctions. Do you remember the sanctions imposed on Iraq following that nation's subjugation of Kuwait? Iraq was not allowed to buy or sell on the international market until she met the United Nations' demands.

According to Martin, it is John Paul's highest aim to see to it that his church controls not just America, but the one-world government that is coming. Once that goal is achieved, John Paul's key objective will be to impose moral order on the world, with whatever sanctions are necessary to achieve it. All this will be, of course, in the interest of "serving the greatest good of the community as a whole and in its various parts."

I am reminded of one of Roland Hegstad's favorite sayings: Persecution does not arise from bad people trying to make other people bad. It arises from good people trying to make others good.

That's why Americans do not want to give up church-state separation—or shouldn't. Religious intolerance can't happen here as long as that foundational principle of our constitution remains intact. But it *will* happen here once we give it up.

The question is, How soon will it happen? Since the fall of Communism in Eastern Europe we have become accustomed to seeing events in the world move very quickly. Ellen White's rapid final movements (see *Testimonies*, vol. 9, p. 11) seem to be upon us. Will an enforced moral authority with sanctions against buying and selling also come rapidly? Is that a part of the "rapid movements" we already appear to have entered upon?

Please read on.

John Paul does not expect to achieve control of the coming one-world government through force of arms, because the Vatican has no army. If you read Mr. Martin's book clear through, you will discover down near the end that John Paul expects political control of the world to fall into his hands through a natural catastrophe in the heavens:

> He [John Paul] is waiting . . . for an event that will fission human history, splitting the immediate past from the oncoming future. It will be an event on public view in the skies, in the oceans, and on the continental landmasses of this planet. It will particularly involve our human sun, which every day lights up and shines upon the valleys, the mountains and the plains of this earth for our eyes. . . .
>
> Fissioning it will be as an event, in John Paul's conviction of faith, for it will immediately nullify all the grand designs the nations are now forming and will introduce the

Grand Design of man's Maker. John Paul's waiting and watching time will then be over. His ministry as the servant of the Grand Design will then begin. His strength of will to hold on and continue, and then, when the fissioning event occurs, to assume that ministry, derives directly from the Petrine authority entrusted solely to him the day he became Pope, in October of 1978. That authority, that strength, is symbolized in the Keys of Peter, washed in the human blood of the God-Man, Jesus Christ. John Paul is and will be the sole possessor of the Keys of this Blood on that day (p. 639).

Ellen White was not the only one who predicted a season of calamity. Seventh-day Adventists are not the only ones anticipating a time of unprecedented natural disaster in the near future. John Paul understands what's coming too. Both sides understand what's ahead, and when it arrives, each side will offer its own explanation of its meaning.

In that terrible time, only the present high wall of separation between church and state can protect the American people and the world from the awesome religious power that is preparing to take charge. The present yielding by America's rulers and legislators to the popular demand to break down that wall, as predicted by Ellen White (see *The Great Controversy*, p. 592), is playing right into John Paul's hands. With that legal barrier out of the way, when the crisis comes, Roman Catholicism, with the support of America's right-wing Protestants, will step into the political vacuum to establish *"an authority that carries with it such sanctions as are effective in maintaining the unity and the aims of the institution as it goes about its business of serving the greatest good of the community as a whole and in its every part."*

For 150 years Seventh-day Adventists have taught that the first beast of Revelation 13 is the papacy and the second is the United States. According to that prophecy, the second beast will deceive the inhabitants of the earth into setting up "an image in honor of the beast who was wounded by the sword and yet lived" (Revelation 13:14). In other words, not only will the United States establish a form of church-state union within her own borders that is favorable to the papacy, she will also lead out in a campaign to do that all over the world.

Now that America is the world's only superpower, she is in a position to fulfill that prophecy. All it will take is the right circumstances—Ellen White's "season of calamity," John Paul's "fissioning event"—and it will happen.

The whole world was astonished [that the deadly wound had been healed] and followed the beast. Men worshiped the dragon because he had given authority to the beast, and they also worshiped the beast and asked, "Who is like the beast? Who can make war against him?" (Revelation 13:3, 4).

[And] no one could buy or sell unless he had the mark . . . of the beast (vs. 17).

CHAPTER

12

The Mark of the Beast

Adventists love to talk about Sunday laws, because to us they are among the clearest signs that the end is near. Unfortunately, some of us manage to get far more mileage out of the least shred of news about a Sunday law than the evidence justifies, and in the process we fail to realize that the mark of the beast encompasses much more than Sunday laws. Sunday laws, when they come, will simply be the outward, visible manifestation of a much deeper reality. We discussed Sunday laws a couple of chapters back, where I pointed out that throughout most of our history, Adventists have taught that the mark of the beast is the observance of Sunday when it is enforced by law. In this chapter we will discuss the spiritual implications of this end-time phenomenon.

One of the Bible's clearest teachings about the end time is that there will be just two classes of people in the world when Jesus comes: those who are loyal to God and those who are loyal to Satan. At the present time there are three classes of people: those who are loyal to God, those who are loyal to Satan, and those who have not made a decision either way. Since only God can read hearts, only He knows exactly who is in which camp. Many people who attend church faithfully think they are on God's side when, in reality, they are on Satan's side. Others who we think are sinners, God considers to be His children. And, of course, even those who are loyal to God now may change their loyalty before they die or before Jesus returns. As long as probation remains open, there is still the opportunity to change sides either way. But when the crisis of the end time comes, the whole world will be forced to choose one of two masters, and both sides will be clearly identified, in most cases even to human eyes.

Spiritual life of those with the mark of the beast

I pointed out in an earlier chapter that several of Jesus' parables clearly teach that there will be only two classes of people at the end of time. I won't repeat all of that evidence here. Rather, I want to examine with you the spiritual implications of these parables. Here are the parables we will examine:

The sower and the seed (Matthew 13:3-9, 18-23).
The faithful and unfaithful servants (Matthew 24:45-51).
The wise and foolish virgins (Matthew 25:1-13).
The men with the talents (Matthew 25:14-30).
The sheep and the goats (Matthew 25:31-46).

The sower and the seed. Jesus did not give the parable of the sower and the seed an end-time application, but I am including it because it divides people into two groups, and thus clearly defines the spiritual condition of those who reject God. At first glance, this parable appears to divide people into *four* groups. However, you will notice that the seed that falls on the path, on the rocks, and among weeds all describes non-Christians or backslidden Christians. Only the seed that falls on the good ground describes the truly righteous. Thus this parable, with its strong emphasis on those who reject God, is extremely useful in understanding the spiritual condition of those who will receive the mark of the beast.

Notice how Jesus applied these symbols:

- *The seed on the path.* These people are so indifferent to spiritual things that God's Holy Spirit can't even bring conviction to their hearts.
- *The seed among the rocks.* These people love the truth, but they fail to cultivate a deep relationship with Jesus, and when trouble comes they give up their faith.
- *The seed among the weeds.* These Christians may have established a close relationship with Jesus at one time, but earthly things gradually become more important to them.

It would be easy to suppose that the seed that falls on the hard path applies especially to secular people. However, those who receive the mark of the beast will be very religious people. They will be faithful churchgoers—every Sunday.

"Ah, but I keep the true Sabbath," you say.

Good! But watch out. You are one of the best candidates for receiving the mark of the beast. Remember the seed that fell on the path? It represents people who hear the Word but don't understand it. They hear the Holy Spirit's conviction, but they pay no attention to it. Often the Holy Spirit finds religious people among the hardest to convict because they don't think there is anything wrong with them. And often this is most true of those who think they have been especially called by God!

The seed that falls on the rocks and among the weeds represents Christians who fail to cultivate a deep relationship with Jesus. Life is so full of demands and important appointments; there just isn't time enough in the average day to study the Bible and pray. And then there are those who aren't terribly busy, but TV and sports and cars and making lots of money are so much more fun than reading the Bible. Surely going to church once a week is enough, isn't it?

If you see yourself in the first three kinds of seeds in Jesus' parable of the sower, you are in danger of receiving the mark of the beast someday.

The faithful and unfaithful servants. In this parable the servant is faithful for a while, but when the master delays his return, he becomes careless and abusive. He says to himself, " 'My master is staying away a long time,' and he then begins to beat his fellow servants and to eat and drink with drunkards" (Matthew 24:48, 49).

"But I don't abuse people," you say. Perhaps not physically, but how about emotionally? Paul warned the Galatians, "If you keep on biting and devouring each other, watch out or you will be destroyed by each other" (Galatians 5:15). Gossip and criticism are forms of "beating" your fellow Christians.

Notice, also, that Jesus said the unfaithful servant began to "eat and drink with drunkards." In the simplest sense, this refers to the use of alcohol. It is a fact that an increasing number of Seventh-day Adventist Christians are drinking alcohol, some moderately, perhaps, and some not so moderately. Has the delay in Christ's return caused this? If you are among those who have begun to use alcohol or street drugs even moderately, I urge you to read Matthew's parable of the faithful and unfaithful servants prayerfully.

I believe this parable applies to a variety of sins of self-indulgence and passion. It refers to violent and lustful movies at the theater and on TV. It refers to pornographic magazines and romance novels. And God only knows the number of Christians who are involved in extramarital affairs, incest, and other forms of sexual immorality—all the while attending church every Sabbath and often leading out in church activities. This parable applies to all of these.

The wise and foolish virgins. The parable of the ten virgins is a warning to Christians who think they are not in danger because they don't engage in sinful activities.

It's easy to suppose that in this parable "sleeping" refers to spiritual laziness. But notice that the wise girls slept too. I believe that in this parable sleeping represents a misuse of all the good things we ought to be doing each day. The point of Jesus' parable is not that the five foolish girls slept, but that they slept at the wrong time. They allowed the proper activities of life to get in the way of their relationship with Him.

There's nothing wrong with cleaning the house or mowing the lawn. There's nothing wrong with shopping or writing letters to friends or taking a vacation. There would be something terribly wrong if we *didn't* do these things. But it is an unwise use of our time when we allow all of these good things to get in the way of the one most important thing, which is establishing a relationship with Jesus.

The men with the talents. Jesus was very balanced. While it's important to spend time cultivating a relationship with Him, it's also very important to work. God expects us to work hard, and He expects us to work smart. To remind us of this, He told the story of the men with the talents.

I've always been intrigued by the reason the one-talent man gave for doing nothing: He was afraid (see Matthew 25:25). He allowed anxiety and depression to control his behavior. Maybe this parable is a warning to those who are prone to let emotions rule their lives. God wants us to take charge of our minds and not allow anxiety and depression to control us.

Some people refuse to accept a church office because they are afraid they cannot handle it. There is a legitimate place for recognizing our limitations and saying No to a request to do something for which we are not gifted. But if we have the ability and refuse to exercise it because of insecurity and fear, we are guilty of the sin of the one-talent man.

The sheep and the goats. In Jesus' final parable about the two classes of people at the end of time, He tells us that those on the wrong side are more interested in themselves than they are others. They are so busy taking care of their own affairs that they fail to notice the needs of the people around them. That's exactly what the people in the parable said: " 'Lord, when did we see you hungry or thirsty or a stranger or needing clothes or sick or in prison, and did not help you?' " (Matthew 25:44). They did not notice the obvious needs of others.

An impossible list?

"Wow!" you say, "I thought the people who received the mark of the beast would be really bad. I can understand about immoral people and people who reject the truth getting the mark. But people who are just a little neglectful of Bible study and prayer, and who gossip and fail to notice another person's needs—do you mean they will get the mark of the beast just for *that?*"

Please notice the following statement by Ellen White:

What are you doing, brethren, in the great work of preparation? Those who are uniting with the world are receiving the worldly mold and preparing for the mark of the beast (*Testimonies*, vol. 5, p. 216).

Notice that Ellen White uses a form of the word *prepare* twice in this statement. First, she suggests that we have to prepare to be among the righteous in the final conflict. Nobody will slide through that crisis on God's side. We must make the preparation now, during the delay, when there seems to be so little urgency about it.

And second, Ellen White points out that those who receive the mark of the beast will also prepare for that: "Those who are uniting with the world are receiving the worldly mold and *[are] preparing* for the mark of the beast."

Please read the italicized words in that statement again: "are preparing." That's present tense. If you thought the mark of the beast was a decision people will make by-and-by when the Sunday laws come, please think again. Check your lifestyle. Are you more interested in meeting your deadlines and making money and dressing fashionably and eating out and buying the latest gadget—and on and on—than you are in God? Do you spend so much time on these things that there's little or no time left each day for Him? *Then you are preparing right now to receive the mark of the beast.*

"But that list—it's impossible!" you say. "Look at all the things Jesus talked about in those parables—praying and working hard and paying attention to the needs of others, to say nothing of avoiding alcohol and immorality and watching how I use my time. It's enough to drive a person mad."

Slow down!

The list may be long, but God doesn't ask you to take a flying leap over all your sins at one time. Ask Him to show you what you need to concentrate on next. Remember that conviction is His business, not yours. Your part is to ask for conviction. So don't try to take on that whole list at once. In fact, *you* shouldn't try to take it on at all. Ask the Holy Spirit to show you the most important problem in your life, and give your attention to that for now. As long as you're on the way with Him, He'll help you deal with all your sins before the close of probation. And He won't close probation until you're ready. He won't let you receive the mark of the beast if you honestly want to be on His side in the final conflict and are doing your part to prepare.

Above all else, remember that the real issue is not your behavior but your heart, because the heart is where your deeds come from. Your greatest urgency and mine today is to cultivate our hearts. I've already talked a great deal about our conflict with sin (see especially chapter 7), but conflict with sin is not primarily the source of a changed heart. Conflict with sin is how we use a heart that has been changed, and the degree of our success in the conflict is directly related to the degree of heart change we have experienced. But the majority of the heart change must happen at times other than when we are in conflict with sin.

I'm sure you know as well as I what we can do to make heart change happen, but I think it's important to put it on paper anyway. Above all else, our hearts are changed through Bible study and prayer.

Do you read your Bible each day, or most days? I don't mean do you read the day's page in your morning watch book while you eat breakfast. I'm asking whether you spend time reading several chapters at a time and reflecting on what you read. Do you grapple with apparent contradictions in the Word until you find the answers? Do you study the hard parts until you understand them? Do you prayerfully search the Bible for insight into your own life, to better understand how God's plan of salvation works and how victory over sin happens? Do you memorize chapters from the Bible? These activities take time that too often we prefer to spend doing other things.

And about prayer—do you know how to pray longer than five minutes at a time? Have you ever prayed for half an hour or an hour and wished you didn't have to stop? Have you ever wished during the middle of the day that you could stop right where you were and talk to the Lord?

This is the kind of Bible study and prayer that transforms hearts. Please don't think I've got all this down pat myself and that I'm just preaching to you. I live in the real world with its pressures too, and I struggle with my priorities just as you do with yours. I don't always make the right choices either, but I have experienced enough of what I'm talking about to know that it's real and that I want more.

I also find that as I choose this devotional way of life, the desire to experience more of it grows within me, and making the time for it gets easier.

This is what it means to cultivate a relationship with Jesus. This is what it means to be preparing now to keep your relationship with Jesus in earth's darkest hour.

Maybe all this seems like quite a diversion in a chapter on the mark of the beast, but it isn't. The mark of the beast is nothing more than a mark God can read that says, "This person has not experienced a change of heart. This person does not have a relationship with Jesus."

The third angel's message

The *Comprehensive Index to the Writings of Ellen G. White* includes seven pages of references to the "third angel's message."

Obviously, she considered the subject to be important. Here are some of her more cryptic statements:

- "The most fearful threatening ever addressed to mortals is contained in the third angel's message" (*The Great Controversy*, p. 449).
- "[The third angel's message] is the last message. There are . . . no more invitations of mercy to be given" (*Testimonies*, vol. 5, pp. 206, 207).
- "The third angel's message is the gospel message for these last days" (ibid., vol. 6, p. 241).
- "The third angel's message is the great testing truth for this time" (ibid., p. 128).
- "This is a distinct, separating message" (ibid., vol. 7, p. 150).

After the controversial 1888 General Conference session on righteousness by faith in Minneapolis, someone asked Ellen White if justification by faith was a part of the third angel's message. Perhaps this person was looking for an excuse to make light of righteousness by faith. If so, he or she was severely disappointed, because Ellen White shot back the reply that justification by faith "is the third angel's message in verity" (*Selected Messages*, book 1, p. 372).

But when you read that message, you may wonder what it has to do with righteousness by faith. Look at what the third angel's message actually says:

A third angel followed them and said in a loud voice: "If anyone worships the beast and his image and receives his mark on the forehead or on the hand, he, too, will drink of the wine of God's fury, which has been poured full strength into the cup of his wrath. He will be tormented with burning sulfur in the presence of the holy angels and of the Lamb. And the smoke of their torment rises for ever and ever. There is no rest day or night for those who worship the beast and his image, or for anyone who receives the mark of his name." This calls for patient endurance on the part of the saints who obey God's commandments and remain faithful to Jesus (Revelation 14:9-12).

That sounds terrible, doesn't it? It's easy to understand why Ellen White said it was "the most fearful threatening ever addressed to mortals." What's not so easy to understand is why she called these words "justification by faith in verity," and "the gospel for these last days."

But she did, and with good reason. I'd like to conclude this chapter with a brief examination of this message, because it wraps up into one package everything we've discussed in this chapter.

God's people will be balanced in faith and works. Notice, first, that the third angel's message is not all bad news. The concluding verse says, "This calls for patient endurance on the part of the saints who obey God's commandments and remain faithful to Jesus" (verse 12). The King James Version says, "Here is the patience of the saints: here are they that keep the commandments of God, and the faith of Jesus." Usually, when Ellen White spoke about the third angel's message in the context of righteousness by faith, she had verse 12 in mind. It has three parts:

1. Patient endurance
2. Keeping God's commandments
3. Keeping faith in Jesus

Patience, especially under provocation, is one of the most difficult character traits to develop. God's people who live through the crisis of the end time will be tested more severely than any other group of His people has ever been tested. That's why God sets such a high standard of character development for them. There's no other way they can keep their relationship with Jesus during earth's darkest hour.

The last two parts of verse 12 go together: obedience and faith. Throughout Christian history God's people have struggled to understand the balance between faith and works. Some groups have placed a stronger emphasis on faith, while others emphasized works. Adventists during the latter part of the nineteenth century were so works oriented that Ellen White said some of us were "as destitute of the quickening influence of the Holy Spirit as the hills of Gilboa were destitute of dew and rain" (*Evangelism*, p. 170). During the last half of the twentieth century there has been a stronger emphasis on faith, and perhaps some of us have swung the pendulum too far in that direction. According to the third angel's message, God's end-time people will have a balanced understanding of faith and works, and I believe that applies not only to our theology but also to our experience.

The world in rebellion against God. The third angel's message pictures a stark contrast between the righteous and the wicked. God's people at that time will have a balanced understanding of righteousness by faith that will bring them into a very close relationship with Jesus. The wicked will refuse righteousness by faith. They will refuse to enter into a close relationship with Jesus. That's why they will be "the wicked." That's why they will receive the mark of the beast. That's why in one breath Ellen White can call the third angel's message "the gospel message for these last days" and "justification by faith in verity," and in the next breath she can call it "the most fearful threatening ever addressed to mortals." *The third angel's message is a fearful warning of the consequences of rejecting the message of righteousness by faith, of rejecting a transformed heart and a relationship with Jesus.*

But Adventists say the mark of the beast is the observance of Sunday when it is enforced by law. How can that have anything to do with righteousness by faith and a relationship with Jesus?

Actually, the whole point of the fourth commandment is a relationship with Jesus. Any relationship between intelligent beings takes time to develop. Young people who fall in love spend many hours learning to know each other. One of the reasons why so many people get divorced after a few years of marriage is that they become so busy with their work and other activities that they stop spending time together. They stop devoting time to their relationship.

It's the same with God. If we expect to have a close relationship with Him, we must spend time with Him. We must set aside significant amounts of time for a devotional life. The Sabbath sets apart one-seventh of our time exclusively for God's people to grow spiritually, to enter into a close relationship with Him and each other.

People who spend time with Jesus will be transformed on the inside. People who truly keep the Sabbath will discover that the harsh side of their nature is subdued. Rough people will become kind; hot-tempered people will become patient; lustful people will become pure. That's why God told the Israelites that the Sabbath was to be a sign "that I am the Lord, who makes you holy" (Exodus 31:13).

Notice that the Sabbath does not make us holy. The Sabbath is a sign that *God* makes us holy. Sanctification does not come from Sabbath keeping. Sanctification comes from knowing Jesus. The Sabbath simply provides an opportunity to know Him. It's an opportunity that He Himself gave us for knowing Him. Those who receive the mark of the beast are not just refusing to keep the Sabbath. They are refusing the opportunity to develop the transformed heart and the relationship with Jesus that the Sabbath makes possible.

Granted that there are other ways and other times besides the Sabbath for developing a relationship with Jesus. But the Sabbath is the one opportunity that God Himself gave us at the time He created our race, which He wrote into His Ten Commandment law. Those who refuse to keep the Sabbath refuse the greatest opportunity to develop a relationship with Jesus that God has to offer.

The simplest way to define the mark of the beast, then, is to say that it is a mark that God will place on those people during earth's darkest hour who have refused to enter into a relationship with Jesus.

Yet in another sense it's not something God will do *to* us at all. The doing is ours. The mark is simply His recognition of our choice. It's not something He will impose on us sometime in the future. It's a choice you and I are making right now. Anyone who will receive the mark of the beast tomorrow is creating that mark in his or her own heart today.

We create the mark of the beast in ourselves. No wonder God spends so much time in Revelation warning us about it!

And now please think about this: Seventh-day Adventists who are not developing transformed hearts and a relationship with Jesus today will not be protected from the mark of the beast during earth's darkest hour just because they have advance warning about Sunday laws. If you are not developing a close relationship with Jesus now, you may receive the mark of the beast even while professing to believe the Sabbath. I suspect that many of those who receive the mark of the beast "in the hand"

(Revelation 13:16) will be Seventh-day Adventists who still believe the Sabbath but yield to the pressure to conform.

Nothing is more important for God's people today than learning to know Jesus. If we don't, soon the consequences will be eternal—and terrible. We simply must not allow the delay to lull us to sleep till it's too late.

13

The Seal of God and the 144,000

After I write a letter, I fold it and put it in an envelope. Then I lick the flap of the envelope, fold it over, and run a finger across the edge. My letter is now safely sealed inside the envelope. Theoretically, nobody can change it before the person to whom it's addressed opens the envelope.

The New Testament tells us that God seals His people, and the word *seal* in this spiritual sense is similar in many respects to what happens when you and I seal an envelope. The word *seal* meant the same thing in Bible times that it does today. A letter was written on papyrus or parchment, and it was sealed with a drop of hot wax along the edge of the scroll, ensuring that it could not be altered or read by anyone except the one to whom it was addressed.

However, in Bible times a seal also meant something more. The sender pressed a small metal mold with his name on it into the hot wax, and the person receiving the letter knew who had sent it by the name in the seal. Christians who are sealed have God's name imprinted on their minds, His character written on their hearts; and He guarantees that nobody else can "open up" their lives and change them.

Ephesians and Revelation both mention the seal that God places on His people. Ephesians says:

You also were included in Christ when you heard the word of truth, the gospel of your salvation. Having believed,

135

you *were marked* in him with a seal, the promised Holy Spirit (Ephesians 1:13, emphasis supplied).

Do not grieve the Holy Spirit of God, with whom you *were sealed* for the day of redemption (Ephesians 4:30, emphasis supplied).

Notice two things about the seal Paul mentions in Ephesians:

- In both cases he used the past tense. Paul wrote his letter to the church in Ephesus around A.D. 60, and he told them that at that time they had already been sealed.
- Paul did not tell these Christians that only certain ones of them were sealed. Apparently all of them were sealed.

Compare this with what John said in Revelation about the seal of God:

After this I saw four angels standing at the four corners of the earth, holding back the four winds of the earth to prevent any wind from blowing on the land or on the sea or on any tree. Then I saw another angel coming up from the east, having the seal of the living God. He called out in a loud voice to the four angels who had been given power to harm the land and the sea: "Do not harm the land or the sea or the trees until we put a seal on the foreheads of the servants of our God." Then I heard the number of those who were sealed: 144,000 from all the tribes of Israel (Revelation 7:1-4).

If you look closely, you will see two significant differences between Paul's use of the seal and John's:

- John spoke of the sealing of God's people as a future event. That is, the 144,000 had not yet been sealed in A.D. 90 when he wrote.
- A specific number, not everyone in the church, receive the seal that is mentioned in Revelation.

The following comparison may help to make these differences more clear:

Paul's seal	**John's seal**
● Available to everyone	● Available to 144,000
● Already given	● Not yet given

From what Paul said, it seems reasonable to assume that from New Testament times to the present, any Christian who qualified has been sealed. But who are the 144,000 that John spoke about in Revelation? Is their seal different from the one Paul described? And were they sealed shortly after John wrote Revelation, or is their sealing still future?

In this chapter I'd like to discuss these and other technical aspects of the 144,000, and in the next chapter we'll examine the spiritual experience of the 144,000. We will be discussing Revelation 13 and 14 quite a bit, and I'm going to assume that you are familiar with the basic content of those chapters. If not, you may want to lay this book aside right now and read these two chapters in Revelation before continuing.

An end-time people

In addition to his description of the 144,000 in Revelation 7:1-4, John also mentions them in chapter 14:1-5. Notice the context of his description in chapter 14, and especially what he says just before and just after Revelation 14:1-5.

Revelation 13 describes Satan's people a short time before the close of probation, and Revelation 14:6-12 tells us the message that God's end-time people are to proclaim just before the close of probation. John's description of the 144,000 in chapter 14:1-5 is sandwiched in between these two descriptions of the end time. This point is so important that I have diagrammed it below:

Revelation 13	**Revelation 14:1-5**	**Revelation 14:6-12**
MARK OF THE BEAST	THE 144,000	THREE ANGELS' MESSAGES
Describes the wicked just before the close of probation	Describes the 144,000	Describes the righteous just before the close of probation

Since the passages before and after Revelation 14:1-5 describe events in the world just before the close of probation, it seems evident that the 144,000 in chapter 14:1-5 will live during that same time. They are an end-time people, which means that they will receive the seal during the end time. According to Revelation 7:1-4, the 144,000 will receive their seal just before the four winds blow, which is just before the time of trouble. If the 144,000 are sealed just *before* the time of trouble, then they will be alive on the earth *during* the time of trouble. Notice what Ellen White said:

> They sing "a new song" before the throne, a song which no man can learn save the one hundred and forty and four thousand. . . . "These are they which came out of great tribulation;" they have passed through the time of trouble such as never was since there was a nation; they have endured the anguish of the time of Jacob's trouble; they have stood without an intercessor through the final outpouring of God's judgments (*The Great Controversy*, pp. 648, 649).

> Soon we heard the voice of God like many waters, which gave us the day and hour of Jesus' coming. The living saints, 144,000 in number, knew and understood the voice (*Early Writings*, p. 15).

Putting all this evidence together, I think it is reasonable to conclude that the 144,000 have not yet been sealed. But what *is* the seal of God, and how is Paul's seal different from John's?

What is the seal of God?

A seal represents a closing up. It ensures the permanence of the thing that is sealed. Paul said that the Christians in Ephesus had been sealed "for the day of redemption" (Ephesians 4:30), which suggests that in some way their salvation was guaranteed. Scripture clearly affirms that Christians can be sure of their salvation (see John 10:27, 28; 1 John 5:12, 13). I believe this is what Paul meant when he spoke of God's people being sealed in his day. They were assured of salvation.

How is John's end-time seal different from that?

We know that Revelation 13 and 14 describe the countdown to

the close of probation, and in this context the seal and the mark mean the close of probation for those who receive them. Those who receive the seal of God are guaranteed a place in God's eternal kingdom, while those who receive the mark of the beast are doomed to eternal death. This is what Jesus means in Revelation 22:11:

> Let him who does wrong continue to do wrong; let him who is vile continue to be vile; let him who does right continue to do right; and let him who is holy continue to be holy.

The seal of God and the mark of the beast are the symbols of this close of probation. Paul's seal is God's assurance to Christians of all ages, before their probation closes, that so long as they are in a right relationship with Him, their salvation is assured. Since their probation has not closed, they could lose that salvation. But when the 144,000 are sealed, their probation will close at the same time, and their salvation will be assured for all eternity.

Is the number 144,000 literal or symbolic?

Adventists often ask whether the number 144,000 is literal or symbolic. Unfortunately, a lot of heat has been generated over this question, and each answer still has its loyal adherents. While I do have an opinion in this matter that I will share with you, I refuse to argue about it. I state my view. I do not push it. It's not worth losing one's temper over. I will give you the arguments on both sides, and you can decide which one makes more sense to you.

That the number is literal. Those who favor the literal interpretation point to two references, one in the Bible and one in Ellen White's writings. John said:

> *I heard the number* of those who were sealed: 144,000 from all the tribes of Israel (Revelation 7:4, emphasis supplied).

The fact that John actually heard the number suggests that it will be a literal number of people, and Ellen White appears to support that view in at least one statement:

Soon we heard the voice of God like many waters, which gave us the day and hour of Jesus' coming. The living saints, *144,000 in number,* knew and understood the voice (*Early Writings*, p. 15, emphasis supplied).

That the number is symbolic. Those who believe the number to be symbolic point out that John also said there would be exactly 12,000 sealed from every tribe of Israel. Those tribes do not exist today, so the number 12,000 has to be symbolic. Why should the total be literal when the fractions are symbolic?

If the 144,000 represent the sum total of all those who will be translated when Jesus comes, as some people believe (see the next section for a discussion of that issue), then I have a serious problem with interpreting the number literally. I don't believe God has said that just so many people and no more can live beyond the close of probation to see Jesus come. If, on the other hand, the 144,000 represent a special group *among* those who will live through the time of trouble (again, see the next section), then I am more willing to concede that the 144,000 may be a literal number.

The 144,000 and the great multitude

Revelation 7 discusses two groups of people. We have already discussed the 144,000. In verses 9-17 John also mentions a "great multitude." He says:

After this I looked and there before me was a great multitude that no one could count, from every nation, tribe, people and language (Revelation 7:9).

Notice that these people come from all over the world—"from every nation, tribe, people and language." Probably the easiest conclusion is that the great multitude will be the redeemed of all ages. However, there is a problem with that conclusion, for John said:

Then one of the elders asked me, "These in white robes [the great multitude]—who are they, and where did they come from?"

I answered, "Sir, you know."

And he said, "These are they who have come out of the great tribulation; they have washed their robes and made them white in the blood of the Lamb" (verses 13, 14, emphasis supplied).

The great multitude will apparently pass through the great time of trouble just like the 144,000. So the question is, Will one group or two experience the time of trouble? Adventists are divided on that question too, so again I will state the reasoning behind both views. In my opinion neither is conclusive.

That they are the same group. Probably the strongest evidence in favor of the view that the 144,000 and the great multitude are the same group is a statement by Ellen White:

None but the hundred and forty-four thousand can learn that song. . . . "These are they which came out of great tribulation." . . . They have "washed their robes, and made them white in the blood of the Lamb." "Therefore are they before the throne of God, and serve Him day and night in His temple: and He that sitteth on the throne shall dwell among them" (*The Great Controversy*, p. 649).

In this passage Ellen White described the 144,000 with the same language that Revelation uses to describe the great multitude. This suggests that they are really one group. But how do we make one group out of two? Those who believe in one group point out that John shows us the 144,000 on earth while the great multitude are in heaven. When the 144,000 get to heaven, they say, we discover that they are not a finite number of people after all, but a countless multitude. This view obviously requires understanding the number 144,000 to be symbolic.

That they are two groups. The strongest evidence in favor of two groups is the striking differences between them:

The 144,000
- A specific number
- From the tribes of Israel

The great multitude
- A countless number
- From all nations

These differences suggest that John intended us to understand them as two groups.

Another argument in favor of two groups is that Revelation 14:1-5 describes the 144,000 in heaven, and it gives us their number (see Revelation 14:1). Apparently the distinction between the great multitude and the 144,000 will be maintained in heaven.

In response to Ellen White's use of language about the great multitude to describe the 144,000, those who believe in two groups point out that she often used phrases from the Bible out of their regular context to express a point she was trying to make.

Those who believe the 144,000 and the great multitude are two groups also believe that the great multitude will be sealed before the close of probation just like the 144,000, even though Revelation 7:9-17 does not mention that. They would have to be sealed in order to live without a Mediator after the close of probation.

When will the 144,000 be sealed?

We already learned that the 144,000 will be sealed before the winds blow—before the time of trouble comes on the earth. Now we will focus more closely on exactly when that will be. I want to mention two points in particular.

We are being sealed now. The most important lesson you and I can learn about the timing of the seal of God is that we are being sealed right now. Ellen White said the seal is not:

[a] mark that can be seen, but a settling into the truth, both intellectually and spiritually, so that *they [God's people] cannot be moved* (Ellen G. White Comments, *SDA Bible Commentary*, vol. 4, p. 1161, emphasis supplied).

The seal of God is "a settling into the truth." When my wife and I "settle into" a new home, we unpack, put things away, and fix up the house the way we like it. That's a process that usually takes a year or two.

In the same way, it will take time for God's people to settle into the truth. The close of probation is a process as well as a point in time, and so is the seal of God. There will come a time when our probation will have closed and it can be said that we *are* sealed. But prior to that it can also be said that we are *being* sealed. And the sealing as a process is going on now. We cannot expect to wait until the time comes for the final seal to be applied and then get ready. The settling in has to be happening now. *The sealing process has to be happening now.* That is the only way to assure that we will keep our relationship with Jesus in earth's darkest hour.

Before the little or the great time of trouble? When John says that the four winds cannot blow until the 144,000 are sealed, he's talking about the time when the process is completed, when God's people are through *being* sealed and it can be said that they *are* sealed. And John says that the 144,000 will reach that point before the four winds blow.

Now here's a question for you: When John speaks of the four winds blowing, does he have in mind the little time of trouble or the great time of trouble? My answer to that question and my personal views that follow assume that the 144,000 and the great multitude are two groups.

You will recall that in an earlier chapter I said the final crisis will begin *before* the close of probation and continue *beyond* the close of probation to the second coming of Christ, like this:

Judgment of the living	Close of probation	Second coming
Little time of trouble	Great time of trouble	
Final crisis		

Notice the two arrows at the bottom of the diagram. The 144,000 will be sealed prior to the time of one of these arrows. Which one?

In the chapter on the close of probation, I pointed out that God's remnant people will be judged first—their probation will close first—while the door of mercy will still be open to those who have not had an opportunity to hear the truth. This being the case, the 144,000 should be the first ones sealed, because they will have achieved the highest level of character development among God's end-time people. Revelation says that they are "pure," "no lie was found in their mouths; they are blameless, (Revelation 14:4, 5). Perhaps Revelation 14:4 calls the 144,000 the "firstfruits" (verse 4) because they are the first ones sealed.

If this is true, then the 144,000 can't be sealed the day before Jesus ceases His ministry in the heavenly sanctuary (the final close of probation), or it would be impossible for them to be sealed first and many others after them. For that to happen, the 144,000 must be sealed near the beginning of the sealing process, some time before the final close of probation.

I would like to suggest that the four winds that will be released after the 144,000 are sealed will be God's judgments in the little time of trouble, and that the 144,000 will be sealed a short time before this season of calamity begins. Here is a diagram that outlines this view of the sealing of the 144,000:

144,000 sealed	Four winds released	Close of probation		Second coming
	Little time of trouble		Great time of trouble	
	Final crisis			

This conclusion is an educated guess, something I've arrived at by putting together the evidence a certain way. While I think I'm right, I may be wrong.

My personal view

I believe the number 144,000 is symbolic and that the 144,000 and the great multitude are two groups, not one. I also believe the four winds that will begin to blow after the 144,000 have been sealed represent the beginning of the final crisis—the little time of trouble, not the great time of trouble. I believe that the 144,000 will be sealed before the final crisis and the little time of trouble begin.

If so, what is the difference between the two groups, and why does God seal the 144,000 before the little time of trouble? You will recall that immediately following the description of the 144,000 who receive the seal of God, Revelation 14 announces the three angels' messages—God's final warning to the world.

I believe God wants us to understand that the 144,000 will be the leaders in the final warning to the world and that the great multitude will be those from all over the world who are won to the Lord at the last hour through their efforts.

This is consistent with the fact that the 144,000 are Israel—God's remnant church, while the great multitude are from all "nations"—all religious persuasions. The reason the 144,000 will be sealed *before* the little time of trouble is that they must proclaim the final warning *during* the little time of trouble.

However, the most important issue about the 144,000 is that they are *being* sealed right now. God's seal is simply His guarantee that whatever our relationship with Him is at the time our probation closes, that relationship will stay the same forever. If we don't have a relationship with Him when our probation closes, there's no way He can seal us with His seal for eternity. We must be "settling into" the truth now. We must be developing that relationship now if we expect to have it made permanent then.

The sad truth is that we may be members of the Seventh-day Adventist Church with all the correct theology that that implies, but our theology won't put us on the right side when probation closes if we have neglected to develop a relationship with Jesus.

I simply cannot stress enough that you and I must be developing a spiritual experience now that will enable us to be loyal then. And I don't believe we have a lot of time left in which to do it.

14

The Spiritual Experience of the 144,000

About twenty-five years ago I attended a youth rally in Texas. That was back when I was young enough to qualify for such events. I've forgotten the name of the town—it was probably close to Houston—but I remember very well that John Thurber was leading the singing. One of the young pastors in the Texas Conference was sitting beside me. Presently John asked us to sing "Shall We Gather at the River." That's always been one of my favorites, and as I sang it that morning, I thought of standing on the bank of the river of life, talking with my friends and sharing with them the joys of the New Jerusalem.

I was going through a difficult period in my life right then, and the thought of heaven was particularly meaningful to me. Suddenly the haunting melody and the meaning of the words washed over me, and I began to weep. I bowed my head, my body shook, and the tears ran down my cheeks. The young pastor reached over, put his arm around me, and hugged me tight.

I needed that. I needed his hug, and I needed to think about heaven that morning and weep.

That was holy joy.

Fifteen or twenty years later, my wife and I spent a weekend in Lincoln, Nebraska, visiting with my mother and stepfather. On Sabbath morning we attended the first service in the College View Adventist Church, where there is a marvelous pipe organ.

The opening hymn that morning was one of those magnificent songs that praises God for His love and majesty. I love to sing those hymns because they transport me to the heavenly sanctuary. I get a picture in my mind of God on His throne and millions of the redeemed standing before Him with all the holy angels. I imagine that I'm among them, my arms uplifted, praising God and Jesus Christ.

I've sung these hymns many times, but this particular morning was different. The glorious music from the pipe organ and the large congregation singing together made me feel as though I was praising God before His throne. Heaven seemed very real, very near at that moment. I choked up, the tears started running down my cheeks, and I had to stop singing. A few lines down I tried singing again, but I choked up and had to stop. So I just let the tears run down while I imagined that I was listening to the angels, the 144,000, and the vast multitude from every nation, tribe, and language praising God before His throne.

That was holy joy.

The whole experience was so marvelous that after Sabbath School I said to my wife, "You can go on back to Mom and Dad's place if you want, but I'm going to stay for the second service."

I just had to worship God again.

By now you're probably wondering what on earth all this has to do with the 144,000. Everything, as a matter of fact. Please read the story of the 144,000 as John tells it in Revelation 14:

> Then I looked, and there before me was the Lamb, standing on Mount Zion, and with him 144,000 who had his name and his Father's name written on their foreheads. And I heard a sound from heaven like the roar of rushing waters and like a loud peal of thunder. The sound I heard was like that of harpists playing their harps. And they sang a new song before the throne and before the four living creatures and the elders. No one could learn the song except the 144,000 who had been redeemed from the earth (Revelation 14:1-3).

A worshiping community

Adventists have traditionally defined the 144,000 in terms of their character. They will be perfect, conquerors in the battle with evil, ready for the close of probation, ready to live through the time of trouble without a Mediator.

All that is true, of course, and I'll have more to say about it later in this chapter. But we've failed to notice that when God tells us what the 144,000 will be like, a full two-thirds of the description is about how they will worship Him before His throne. John tells us about their worship before he tells us about their perfection. The 144,000 will be above all else a worshiping community! I'll go one step further and tell you that the 144,000 will never be a perfect people until they learn to be a worshiping people.

Isn't it too bad that for years and years in this church, whenever someone talked about worship, everyone else yawned? Books on worship gathered dust on the shelves in our ABCs.

That's sad!

I want to tell you something. I believe that those who proclaim the three angels' messages in earth's darkest hour will be a community of people who praise God in glorious, rapturous, joyful worship, and that until we learn to really worship, we won't really proclaim the message. The early rain came on the disciples *after* they had praised God in the temple and *after* they had spent ten days worshiping Him in their own small group in the upper room (see Luke 24:50-53; Acts 2:1-4). I believe the latter rain will come to us today only when we learn what it means to worship God. *Renewal of our worship services is essential if we are ever to experience the latter rain.*

If you have a concern about this, I recommend that you speak to your pastor about it. If you know of others in your church who share your concern, get together with your pastor to talk about it. But don't expect your pastor to bring about instant change in your congregation's worship service. It's nearly impossible for a pastor to change a worship service all by himself. He has to have the congregation's willingness to change and their willingness to commit significant chunks of time to the task.

The most essential thing your church can do to bring renewal to your services is to plan them ahead of time and then work hard at perfecting each part of the service each week. Each service needs a theme, and, insofar as possible, each part of the service should contribute to that theme. That's an important part of the planning.

You can't expect to have a dynamic worship service if those

who participate throw the whole thing together during the five minutes the elders and the pastor meet in the back room before going onto the platform. Neither can you expect to have a meaningful Sabbath School program if the superintendent throws the whole program together on Thursday evening and Friday. Each of these services needs to be planned several weeks in advance, and each person who participates must know of his or her part well in advance in order to plan it, and, where necessary, to practice it. For example, prayers need to be thought out ahead of time; Scripture readings need to be practiced.

One of the most spiritually invigorating experiences any Christian can have is to participate in a dynamic worship service with other Christians. Growing Christians need this experience every week. Once you've experienced it, you will want it every week. The reason most Adventist churches don't have such a service even every few months is that we are so busy with everyday life we don't commit the time it takes to make Sabbath School and church meaningful. Just as we must set aside the time for our personal devotional life, so we must set aside the time to make our Sabbath School and worship services spiritually meaningful.

Some Adventist churches are trying, and some are being criticized for trying. I am neither a wholehearted proponent nor an absolute critic of so-called "celebration worship" in the Adventist Church. I question some of the things I see going on, but I also affirm much of what those churches are doing.

Regardless of what you or I may think of celebration worship, I think we can agree that worship should be joyful, filled with praise to God, and spiritually invigorating. And I think we can agree that Revelation describes the 144,000 as praising God in song and worship.

The 144,000 will be a worshiping community, and Adventists who want to be among the 144,000 must commit major time and resources to corporate worship now, while there is still time.

A perfect community

Worship is the first characteristic Revelation mentions about the 144,000. Perfection is another.

From the very beginning of her ministry, Ellen White strongly emphasized the character that God's people must have who live through the end time. She said that those who receive the seal of God must be perfect. The following statements are typical of many that could be quoted:

Are we seeking for His fullness, ever pressing toward the mark set before us—the perfection of His character? When the Lord's people reach this mark, they will be sealed in their foreheads (Ellen G. White Comments, *SDA Bible Commentary*, vol. 6, p. 1118).

The seal of the living God will be placed upon those only who bear a likeness to Christ in character (ibid., vol. 7, p. 970).

All who receive the seal must be without spot before God—candidates for heaven (*Testimonies*, vol. 5, p. 216).

Some people don't like the fact that Ellen White stressed the perfection God's people must have in order to receive the seal of God and live after the close of probation without a Mediator. That smacks too much of righteousness by works, they say, and they stress forgiveness and justification as adequate for receiving the seal of God.

Others, holding rigidly to what Ellen White said, have developed an extreme perfectionism. To them it's essential that every Adventist believe in absolute sinlessness after the close of probation, and they have a hard time accepting the orthodoxy of anyone who disagrees with them. Unfortunately, even among those who have managed to avoid extreme perfectionism, I suspect that a majority still fear they may not or cannot be good enough.

Quite a controversy has developed between these two camps in the Adventist Church, and a great gulf is fixed between them.

Where lies the truth?

First, I think we need to understand that Ellen White was perfectly in harmony with Scripture when she said that those who receive the seal of God just before the close of probation must be perfect. Revelation 14:4, 5 mentions the following characteristics of the 144,000:

- They did not defile themselves with women
- They kept themselves pure
- No lie was found in their mouths
- They are blameless.

Those who criticize Ellen White for holding up such a high standard of character development for God's end-time people need to understand that their problem is not just with Ellen White. It's also with the Bible. And that means that the problem doesn't lie either in Ellen White or in the Bible. It lies with us. It's our misunderstanding of what the Bible and Ellen White are telling us that is the problem.

So how do we find our way out of this puzzle? How can Christians stress perfection as a qualification for receiving the seal of God without being perfectionistic and afraid?

The solution begins, I believe, with understanding that there are two kinds of perfection. One qualifies us to receive the assurance of salvation, and the other qualifies us to receive the seal of God. One happens at the beginning of the Christian life and the other at its end.

Perfection for the assurance of salvation. If the 1888 controversy over righteousness by faith did anything for the Adventist Church, especially since about 1950, it helped us to understand that we receive our assurance of salvation by grace through faith, not through character development. The determining factor is whether we have a relationship with Jesus—not how strong a relationship we have or the quality of the relationship—but just having one.

Why? Because faith, which is the basis of a relationship with Jesus, brings forgiveness of sins. It transforms the heart. And it brings us all the perfection God requires when He saves us. Ellen White described it like this:

> He lived a sinless life. He died for us, and now He offers to take our sins and give us His righteousness. If you give yourself to Him, and accept Him as your Saviour, then, sinful as your life may have been, for His sake you are accounted righteous. Christ's character stands in place of your character, and you are accepted before God just as if you had not sinned (*Steps to Christ*, p. 62).

That's perfection. However, it's not *character* perfection. We may still have many faults to overcome, but God counts us perfect because Christ has given His perfect character to us. His character covers ours, so that when God looks at us He sees Christ's perfect character, not our sinful one. We are not perfect in ourselves. We are perfect only through Christ.

This perfection is available instantly to every human being on planet Earth who accepts Jesus. It's called *justification*. The thief on the cross had almost no time to overcome sin and develop his own character to reflect Christ's character, but he was still perfect in God's sight because Christ's perfection covered his sinfulness.

This form of perfection is also called "the robe of Christ's righteousness." A robe is a garment that covers the body, and when we use it as a symbol of justification we mean that it covers our sins. It's important to understand, of course, that Christ's righteousness will not cover sins that we do not repent of and confess. But it's also important to understand that so long as we maintain our relationship with Jesus—and that assumes that we continue to repent of our sins and confess them—His robe continues to cover us.

Several stories in the Bible illustrate the lesson about the robe of Christ's righteousness. You will recall that the prodigal son's father called for "the best robe" to cover his son's clothes that were filthy from the pig pen (see Luke 15:22). In the Old Testament story of Joshua and Satan, the angel of the Lord removed Joshua's filthy garments and covered him with "rich garments" and a "clean turban" (see Zechariah 3:1-5).[1] Jesus' parable of the man who attended a wedding feast without a garment illustrates the fate of those who refuse the robe of Christ's righteousness to cover their sins (see Matthew 22:1-14).

The robe of Christ's righteousness, perfection of character through justification, is granted to every sinner the moment he accepts Jesus as his Saviour. Assuming that he maintains his

---

1. In the parable of the prodigal son, the father placed the family's "best robe" over his son's filthy garments, illustrating that God forgives and accepts sinners in the condition He finds them. We do not have to make ourselves perfect before we come to Jesus. In Zechariah's parable, Joshua's clothes were removed before the robe was put on him, illustrating that in addition to forgiving us, Christ also cleanses us (see 1 John 1:9). Zechariah does not mean that God refuses to accept us till we are cleaned up. Notice that Joshua did not remove his own dirty clothes. The command was given for someone else to "take off his filthy clothes" (Zechariah 3:4).

relationship with Jesus, this robe continues to cover him until the moment of his death or until Jesus returns, whichever comes first. We can diagram it like this:

Justification Christian life begins ASSURANCE		**Sanctification** Christian life ends
	The robe of Christ's righteousness	
	Christ's character in place of my character	
	The sanctification process	

My sins are covered;
Christ's character
given to me

You and I are assured of salvation the moment we accept Christ as our Saviour, confess our sins, and ask Him to forgive us. At that very moment we can know that we are saved. John says:

He who has the Son *has* life. . . . I write these things to you who believe in the name of the Son of God so that you may *know* that you *have* eternal life (1 John 5:12, 13, emphasis supplied).

Nobody will ever be saved without the perfection Christ gives us at the beginning of our Christian life. And that is as true of those who will live without a Mediator after the close of probation as it is for those who live before.

Perfection for the seal. However, as I read Ellen White's statements about the character that God will require in order to seal His people just before the close of probation, I find that she has in mind much more than Christ's character standing in place of our character. She means that we must overcome sin:

The seal of God will never be placed upon the forehead of an impure man or woman. It will never be placed on the forehead of the ambitious, world-loving man or woman. It will never be placed upon the forehead of men or women of false tongues or deceitful hearts. All who receive the seal must be *without spot before God*—candidates for heaven (*Testimonies*, vol. 5, p. 216, emphasis supplied).

Those that overcome the world, the flesh, and the devil, will be the favored ones who shall receive the seal of the living God (*Testimonies to Ministers*, p. 445).

Not even by a thought could our Saviour be brought to yield to the power of temptation. . . . There was no sin in Him that Satan could use to his advantage. This is the condition in which those must be found who shall stand in the time of trouble (*The Great Controversy*, p. 623).

This kind of character perfection comes only after a long life in relationship with Jesus. During that entire time, Christ's character continues to cover the imperfections in our characters, *even as we overcome those imperfections*. Those who are sealed will have overcome their imperfections. They will have attained full Christian maturity. We can diagram it like this:

Justification	Sanctification
Christian life begins	Christian life ends
ASSURANCE	MATURITY
The robe of Christ's righteousness Christ's character in place of my character	
Christ and I are developing my character	
My sins are covered; Christ's character given to me	My sins are conquered; Christ's character developed in me

Unfortunately, Ellen White's statements about the character perfection God's people will need in order to be sealed and live after the close of probation without a Mediator unsettles the assurance received through justification in the minds of many

Adventists. It shouldn't, but it does. Somehow we think that after probation closes, we will have to be completely good within ourselves, without any help from God. One woman told me she always thought we'd have to get along without the Holy Spirit after the close of probation!

That's tragic!

The character perfection we attain at the end of our Christian life does not do away with our need for the kind of perfection we received at the beginning. Justification will still be the only basis for our assurance of salvation during the time of trouble. Character perfection will also be important at that time, but it will not be the basis of our assurance then any more than it is now.

I'd like now to bring your mind back to the theme I stressed in the first part of this chapter—that the 144,000 who are sealed just before the close of probation will be joyful Christians who love to worship and praise God. Adventists are in danger of putting so much stress on perfection that we forget what it means to have joy and happiness in Jesus. Yet this very joy, this freedom in Jesus to worship joyfully, is one of the most important parts of what it means to be perfect!

Some critics of joyful worship point to Ellen White's statement that "the class who do not feel grieved over their own spiritual declension, nor mourn over the sins of others, will be left without the seal of God" (*Testimonies*, vol. 5, p. 211). They remind us that God told the Israelites to afflict themselves in preparation for the earthly day of atonement, and we should do the same during heaven's great day of atonement that began in 1844. Somehow, in their minds, mourning and afflicting one's self over sin are inconsistent with joyful worship.

Notice, however, that David was able to bring confession of sin and joyful praise together in the same prayer. In Psalm 51:3 he said, "I know my transgressions, and my sin is always before me," and in verse 12 he said, "Restore to me the joy of your salvation."

Psalm 51 and Psalm 150 do not contradict each other.

If my memory serves me correctly, Ellen White says that during the final crisis before the close of probation, multitudes will join this movement. If there is rejoicing in heaven over one sinner who repents (see Luke 15:7), think what a celebration there will be over multitudes coming in!

Now let me ask, Will God's people at that time sit on their hands with stoical faces because "it's the Day of Atonement, and we aren't supposed to celebrate"? Or will we join in heaven's praise for the thousands—perhaps millions—who are being saved?

One more thought, and a question. When the prodigal son returned home, the father threw a party, and the whole family celebrated, save one. Which member of the family objected, and whom, in the cast of characters around Jesus, did that family member represent?

We must not be so gloomy over perfection as we prepare for the seal of God and the close of probation that we have neither the time nor the heart for joyful praise and worship, for joy is part of what it means to be perfect, and we are in great danger of losing out on the perfection if we don't have the joy.

CHAPTER

15

The Latter Rain

On Monday morning, August 19, 1991, the headline on the front page of my morning newspaper said, "Gorbachev is out." For several days the world held its collective breath, wondering what would happen to Gorbachev and the budding democratic movement in Russia. Three days later television stations and newspapers all over the world announced, "Gorbachev is in!"

The next day I read a report in my newspaper of why the coup by the Communist hard-liners had failed, and the following week, the major news magazines in the United States ran in-depth analyses of that fiasco. I read that the hard-liners failed to arrest Boris Yeltsin immediately; they failed to cut communication with the outside world; they failed to disperse the mobs demonstrating on the streets. Because of these failures, the coup failed.

It is always possible to give a reasonable explanation from a human point of view for everything that happens on the earth. But the Christian who understands God's role in history, and who recognizes where we are today on the prophetic time clock, knows that there is a far deeper answer to why Communism fell in Eastern Europe during the latter half of 1989 and why the hard-liner coup in Russia failed during early August 1991. God is in control of world events. *He is preparing the world, and especially His people, for the final crisis.*

The Old Testament tells the story of Elisha's servant waking up one morning, going out on the roof of the house, and rushing back to his master with the news that the Syrian army had surrounded their city during the night. Elisha led his frightened servant back onto the roof and asked the Lord to open his eyes. Immediately the servant saw the hills around the city filled with heavenly chariots of fire (see 2 Kings 6:8-17).

You and I can't see them, but the Bible tells us that those same angels are holding back the winds of strife from blowing on our earth right now (see Revelation 7:1-4). They are working on the minds and hearts of men like Mikhail Gorbachev and Boris Yeltsin, and on the minds and hearts of the Russian people. God prevented the hard-liners from succeeding in their effort to abort the Russian launch into freedom, because He wants His work finished in that land.

And the work *is* being finished in the Soviet Union. With the demise of Communism, a spiritual hunger is erupting in that vast nation, accompanied by an explosion in church growth.

A couple of weeks prior to the aborted coup in Russia I heard a report on Russian evangelism given by Elder Richard Wilcox, the General Conference's Special Assistant for Soviet Development. Elder Wilcox reported that during the month of July 1991, Adventist baptisms in Moscow alone totaled 1,000, and during the same month nearly 3,000 were baptized across the Soviet Union. At the time of this writing, Adventist membership in that nation is about 41,000. According to former General Conference president Neal C. Wilson, who is now a special advisor for administrative affairs to the Adventist Church in the Soviet Union, leaders there anticipate that if present trends continue, membership in that division will reach the half-million mark by the 1995 General Conference session!

Satan doesn't want to see God's work finished in Russia, and in August 1991 he prompted the hard-liners to try to stop it. But God stepped in and said No.

Particularly in light of the other signs of the end that I've already discussed in this book, I believe the collapse of Communism in Eastern Europe and Russia, the explosive growth of the church that we are beginning to see in that part of the world, and the dramatic failure of the hard-liners' coup attempt are clear signs of the nearness of the end. They are evidence of the outpouring of the latter rain.

Perhaps you never thought of political events such as the fall of Communism as an evidence of the latter rain. Though in the strictest sense it is not, in a broad sense I believe it is, and in a moment I believe you will understand what I mean. I will begin my explanation by sharing with you what I believe is a Bible prophecy of the latter rain:

> I saw another mighty angel coming down from heaven. He was robed in a cloud, with a rainbow above his head; his face was like the sun, and his legs were like fiery pillars. He was holding a little scroll, which lay open in his hand. He planted his right foot on the sea and his left foot on the land, and he gave a loud shout like the roar of a lion (Revelation 10:1-3).

You may never have thought of this as a prophecy of the latter rain, so I would like to show you why I believe that it is. Ellen White said:

> The mighty angel who instructed John was no less a personage than Jesus Christ. Setting His right foot on the sea, and His left upon the dry land, shows the part which He is acting in the closing scenes of the great controversy with Satan. This position denotes His supreme power and authority over the whole earth (Ellen G. White Comments, *SDA Bible Commentary*, vol. 7, p. 971).

The message of Revelation 10—the entire chapter—is that at the very end of time Jesus Christ will take personal control of His work all over the world. Of course, since He left this earth, Jesus has always worked through the Holy Spirit (see John 16:5-7). Therefore, John's vision of Jesus' taking charge of His work at the very end of time is also a vision of the work of the Holy Spirit at the end of time, moving upon God's people to proclaim the final warning to the world.

The primary focus of Revelation 10 is the end-time preaching of the gospel. For that to happen and for God's work to be finished all over the world, those nations that are closed to the preaching of the gospel must open up. Thus, part of Christ's involvement with the world at this time has to be guiding the affairs of the nations so that His work can progress unimpeded everywhere.

It is no accident, in my opinion, that Mikhail Gorbachev has liberated Eastern Europe and Russia from Communist domination. I believe God raised him up for that very purpose. God has often used rulers who opposed Him to advance His purposes in the world. I believe the Holy Spirit has been at work in Mr. Gorbachev's mind and heart, and that in his own way, Mr. Gorbachev has been submissive to the Spirit's guidance. Thus, in a very real sense, we can say that the events in Russia and Eastern Europe since 1989 have been the result of the Holy Spirit's working in latter-rain power.

The vision of Revelation 10 actually began to be fulfilled in 1844, when God raised up a final remnant to finish His work on the earth. The closer we get to the end of time, the more relevant that vision becomes. Christ's most intense personal involvement in His work on earth through the Holy Spirit will come during the final crisis, when the need is the greatest.

You and I will not be left alone to fight the forces of evil during the crisis of the end time.

What are the early and latter rains?

For those who may be unfamiliar with the expression "latter rain," let's review briefly what it means.

The Bible uses a number of symbols to represent the work of the Holy Spirit, including wind, oil, fire, and water (see John 3:8; Matthew 25:1-13; Acts 2:1-4; John 7:38, 39). Since rain is water, the Bible often uses it as a symbol of the Holy Spirit. Water pours and rain falls, so it is only natural to speak of the Holy Spirit being "poured out" and "falling" on God's people.

In the Adventist Church, the expression "latter rain" refers to a special outpouring of the Holy Spirit at the very end of time. The idea comes from the Old Testament. In Israel the rain fell during two seasons—at planting time and shortly before the harvest. The Old Testament prophets said:

Ask the Lord for rain in the time of the latter rain (Zechariah 10:1, NKJV).

He [God] will come to us like the rain, like the latter and former [early] rain to the earth (Hosea 6:3, NKJV).

In Palestine during Bible times, the expression "early rain" referred to showers in the fall of the year that caused the seeds that farmers sowed in their fields to sprout and begin to grow. The latter rain, in the spring, completed the growth process and ripened the crop for harvest. Both the Bible and Ellen White use the early and latter rains as symbols of spiritual growth.

The latter rain in the life of the Christian. In the experience of the individual, the early rain represents the power of the Holy Spirit during the first part of his or her Christian experience, especially for conversion and the initial steps toward character transformation. The latter rain represents the power of the Holy Spirit in the life of the mature Christian that brings him or her to perfection.

> As the dew and the rain are given first to cause the seed to germinate, and then to ripen the harvest, so the Holy Spirit is given to carry forward, from one stage to another, the process of spiritual growth (*Testimonies to Ministers*, p. 506).

The Christian life requires the continual presence of the Holy Spirit from beginning to end. The early rain represents the presence of the Holy Spirit that begins with the new birth and continues throughout the Christian life. Ellen White said:

> At no point in our experience can we dispense with the assistance of that which enables us to make the first start. The blessings received under the former rain are needful to us to the end (ibid., p. 507).

The latter rain in the life of the church. Ellen White also used the early and latter rains to symbolize God's work on behalf of the entire church. She likened the early rain to the outpouring of the Holy Spirit at Pentecost and the latter rain to a similar manifestation of spiritual power shortly before the second coming of Christ:

> The outpouring of the Spirit in the days of the apostles was the beginning of the early, or former, rain, and glorious was the result (*The Acts of the Apostles*, pp. 54, 55).

In the time of the end, when God's work in the earth is closing, the earnest efforts put forth by consecrated believers under the guidance of the Holy Spirit are to be accompanied by special tokens of divine favor (ibid, p. 54).

The early rain is utterly essential in both the life of the individual and the church. However, from now on I will restrict my remarks to the latter rain, since that is our special interest in this chapter. Also, it would make my explanation unnecessarily complicated to keep distinguishing between the effect of the latter rain on the life of the individual and its effect on the church, so for the most part I will discuss them together without calling attention to the distinction.

Let's turn our attention now to the reasons God will pour out His Holy Spirit upon His people in the last days.

Purpose of the latter rain

The latter rain has two purposes. One is to give individual members and the church as a whole the power to witness. Ellen White said:

The disciples did not ask for a blessing for themselves. . . . The gospel was to be carried to the ends of the earth, and they claimed the endowment of power that Christ had promised. Then it was that the Holy Spirit was poured out, and thousands were converted in a day (*Testimonies*, vol. 8, p. 21).

What the Lord did for His people in that time [of the apostles], it is just as essential, and more so, that He do for His church today. All that the apostles did, every church member is to do. And we are to work with as much more fervor, to be accompanied by the Holy Spirit in as much greater measure, as the increase of wickedness demands a more decided call to repentance (ibid., vol. 7, p. 33).

Another purpose of the latter rain is to help Christians perfect character. One of the reasons why we do not need to worry about whether we will be "good enough" to pass through the time of trouble without a Mediator is that the Holy Spirit will fill us with special power at the time of the latter rain, and whatever final steps in perfection are *necessary* to prepare us for the close of probation will also be *possible* at that time.

The latter rain and the final crisis

One of the most comforting promises in all the Bible is found in 1 Corinthians 10:13:

> No temptation has seized you except what is common to man. And God is faithful; he will not let you be tempted beyond what you can bear. But when you are tempted, he will also provide a way out so that you can stand up under it.

God has promised to help us during our time of greatest temptation. Revelation speaks of "the hour of temptation, which shall come upon all the world" (Revelation 3:10, KJV). We will need help standing up to the persecution we are called upon to endure at that time, and we will need help responding to the questions that are hurled at us. That's why God has promised to send the latter rain at the time of the final crisis.

We will also need special help developing characters that can stand without a Mediator after the close of probation. In an earlier chapter I pointed out that following the 1844 Disappointment, God's people were not yet ready for His second coming, but after the Refiner's fire has purged them of their sins, they will be ready for the trying hour that is before them (see *The Great Controversy*, pp. 424, 425). The Holy Spirit, poured out in latter-rain power, will give us the final touch of character perfection during the final crisis.

When will the latter rain fall?

From what I have said about the latter rain so far, it is obvious that it will fall on God's people just before the close of probation. But exactly when will that happen? Again, let's use a little logic. If the seal of God is to be placed only on those people who have overcome sin, and if the final steps in that spiritual growth come under the power of the Holy Spirit during the latter rain, then obviously the latter rain has to fall before God's people are sealed. Ellen White said:

Before the work is closed up and the sealing of God's people is finished, we shall receive the outpouring of the Spirit of God (*Selected Messages*, book 1, p. 111).

Furthermore, if the 144,000 are sealed before the season of calamity, as I suggested in an earlier chapter, then the latter rain must begin falling on them prior to their sealing also. I believe that the latter rain will begin falling on different people at different times, according to their need. It will fall upon the 144,000 earlier than on others because they will need it earlier.

However, I do think we can speak of a time when the latter rain first begins to fall, and expect that it will continue falling clear through to the close of probation and even to the second coming of Christ. We can diagram it like this:

	Season of calamity begins	Close of probation	Second coming
Latter rain	. . . .	. . . .	
144,000 sealed	Little time of trouble	Great time of trouble	
	Final crisis		

If the explosive growth of the church in Eastern Europe and Russia is an evidence of the outpouring of the latter rain in that part of the world, and if the dramatic church growth we've seen in our church across Africa, Latin America, and certain parts of Asia in recent years is further evidence of the latter rain, then I believe we need to seriously ask ourselves two questions.

First, if this is indeed the beginning of the latter rain, then is the final crisis just around the corner? The entire premise of this book is that the answer to that question is Yes, absolutely.

Second, if the latter rain is being poured out in other parts of the world, when will we begin to see the same evidence—the same dramatic church growth—in North America, Western Europe, and Australia? And the answer is quite simple: When we ask for it. Jesus said that God will give the Holy Spirit to anyone who *asks* for it (see Luke 11:13), and Jeremiah said, "You will seek me and find me when you seek me with all your heart" (Jeremiah 29:13). Our own messenger for the end time has told us: "We should pray as earnestly for the descent of the Holy Spirit as the disciples prayed on the day of Pentecost" (*Review and Herald*, 25 August 1896).

Morning, evening, and during the day, we need to spend time asking God to send His Holy Spirit into our hearts and upon our church as a whole. I believe it's time God's people got on their knees and said, "Father, the time has come for the final crisis. The time has come for You to end the history of sin and take us home. Please send the latter rain into our hearts."

What do you think would happen if God's people all across North America and all over the world prayed that prayer day after day for a month, six months, a year?

I do not believe that God will delay Christ's return forever, waiting for a people who will not seek His Spirit or respond to His call to service. If we refuse, God will fill other willing hearts with His Spirit and give them our work.

I believe that in the near future, we will see amazing things happen in our part of the world too. The question is, Will we be a part of it?

16

Preparing to Receive the Latter Rain

Those who receive the latter rain must be spiritually prepared for it. If we drift along, making no spiritual preparation now, we will not receive the latter rain when it falls. In Bible times, if the early rain did not sprout the seed and start it on its growth, there was no way the latter rain could bring the seed to maturity. There would have been nothing to mature.

Similarly, our Christian character development must start under the early rain, or there will be nothing for the latter rain to mature. I quoted earlier a statement in which Ellen White said:

Unless the former rain has fallen, there will be no life; the green blade will not spring up. Unless the early showers have done their work, the latter rain can bring no seed to perfection (*Testimonies to Ministers*, p. 506).

I have discussed spiritual preparation in several other parts of this book, and everything I have said before is important as a preparation for the latter rain. In this chapter I will discuss three things that I have not discussed elsewhere, all of which are essential for receiving the latter rain.

Daily devotional life

The Holy Spirit comes into the hearts of Christians primarily through the study of the Bible and prayer. Signs in the world around us suggest that the end is very near, and this means that nothing is more important right now than Bible study and prayer every day. And I'm not talking about ten minutes in the morning and ten minutes in the evening. Each of us must find enough time for serious Bible study and prayer at a time that is most convenient for us.

My wife and I prefer taking our devotional time in the morning before we go to work. Our practice is to get up at five o'clock each morning, an hour earlier than we would otherwise have to. Personally, I try to spend about half an hour reading and studying my Bible and half an hour praying. Occasionally I spend more time reading the Bible, while other days I may spend more time in prayer. Overall, though, it averages about half and half. Each Christian needs to establish his own pattern for Bible study and prayer.

There are at least three ways to study the Bible. One is to simply read it the way you'd read any book. I've been doing a lot of that recently, and have found it very beneficial. Another way is to take a particular passage—perhaps even an entire book of the Bible—and study it in depth. I especially like to keep a journal with this kind of Bible study. I meditate on a particular verse, or even on a phrase or a single word, and write out the thoughts that come to me. The third way to study is to look up everything the Bible says on a particular subject or to trace a particular theme throughout the Bible. I especially like to do that when I'm wrestling with a problem. Looking up what the Bible says about that problem helps me to use the Bible as a guide in that area of my life.

Some Christians have a hard time praying silently for more than a few minutes. I can assure you, though, that once you learn how to do it, it becomes extremely meaningful. I spend a good bit of prayer time asking God to reveal to me what I need to know in order to live through the times that lie ahead, and I pray that He will transform my heart and take away my desire for evil.

I also like to pray about my family members and friends, my work, and the people I work with. I pray for my church—the congregation I attend, and also the worldwide Adventist Church. I know my church is far from perfect. Ellen White says we should "weep between the porch and the altar" for the sins in the church. I can't say that I've ever shed tears, but I do pray earnestly that God will bless our General Conference, division, union, and local conference leaders, and I often pray for them by name. I pray for our institutional leaders. And I pray that God will forgive us our sins as a church and the many ways we allow His work to fall short of the ideal.

Finally, I often pray earnestly that God will bring the latter rain and that the coming of Jesus will be soon.

When I learned how to pray for an hour, I found that it was easy!

Even though it doesn't happen every day, Sabbath keeping is an important part of our devotional life. We need the change of pace from the everyday affairs of life and the time the Sabbath provides for spiritual activities. We need the fellowship that comes from attending church on Sabbath morning, and we need the spiritual renewal that comes through joyful praise to God with a worshiping community. Sabbath must be an integral part of the preparation of every Seventh-day Adventist for receiving the latter rain.

If you're like me, you find the affairs of everyday life pressing in so hard that taking time for a meaningful devotional life is difficult. I've found that if I am going to be able to fit a devotional period into my schedule, I must set aside a regular time. For me, the morning hours are best, because in the evening I'm busy and I'd have to stop what I'm doing. It's easier to start the day with my devotional life than to end it that way. My wife and I each have our own private devotional time in the morning, and we have a shorter worship together in the evening.

One of the major barriers to a meaningful devotional life is lack of interest. Maybe it shouldn't be that way, but we humans, with our sinful nature, are materialistic, and the things we can see and hear and touch seem much more important to us than spiritual things that are invisible. For me, the solution to this problem is to ask God to change my heart, to help me develop a love of spiritual things. I've found that as I pray that prayer and discipline myself to take the time for a personal devotional life, my love for those hours with God keeps growing.

A personal devotional life that includes Bible study, prayer, and Sabbath keeping is utterly essential to receiving the Holy Spirit. We will not receive the latter rain unless we are actively engaged in a devotional life.

Unity in the church

Another requirement for the Holy Spirit to come on us as a church is unity. It will be impossible for us to receive the latter rain and proclaim the final warning to the world if we are still quarreling among ourselves the way so many of us do now. Local congregations in the Adventist Church are sometimes torn apart by internal strife. All such congregations must settle those differences, or as a congregation they will be passed by when the latter rain begins to fall. Also, as a denomination we must stop the contentions that now divide us. All divisive debate over celebration and non-celebration churches must stop. All divisive bickering over the nature of Christ must be put away. Some Adventists claim that it is essential to settle these fine points of theology and worship practice in order to receive the latter rain—and of course they are convinced that each argument must be settled their way. I don't think it is necessary to resolve all these differences, and even if it is, they must be settled in a spirit of kindness and unity, or we will miss receiving the power of the latter rain. *We will miss the very character perfection for which we claim that our theology is so necessary!* Ellen White wrote:

> Let Christians put away all dissension and give themselves to God for the saving of the lost. Let them ask in faith for the promised blessing [the latter rain], and it will come (*Testimonies for the Church*, vol. 8, p. 21).

After Jesus ascended to heaven, His disciples spent ten days together in the upper room. Ten days is not a lot of time, but it was enough for them to achieve the unity they needed in order to receive the early rain. Only a few weeks earlier, they had been quarreling over which one of them would be the greatest in God's kingdom. Now all of these differences had been put away.

I believe God's people today can experience a similar unity, and just as quickly, when we meet the conditions. And when we do, we will receive the Holy Spirit in latter rain power.

Confession of sin

What brought about the dramatic change in the lives of the apostles that made Pentecost possible? I could mention several things, but I would especially like to mention confession of sin, because that is one of the keys to both our individual spiritual health and our unity as a church. Without heartfelt confession of sins, especially those sins that have divided us, no unity can occur, and the Holy Spirit cannot be poured out. Confession makes us honest. It cleanses our hearts. It breaks down the barriers that keep us apart.

Confession is, at the same time, one of the most wonderful and one of the most difficult of the Christian disciplines. It is wonderful because it brings such release of tensions. It heals wounds and breaks down barriers. It is difficult because it cuts across the pride of the natural heart.

I could have brought up confession in some other part of this book. I can think of a number of places where such a discussion would have fit. However, it especially fits here because I believe that the latter rain will come only upon those who are willing to be completely honest with themselves, with others, and with God. If we are holding back from confessing any known sin, God cannot pour out His latter rain upon us.

I know that what I have just said will be distressing to many. Confession exposes our darkest secrets. Some people find that confession is just about impossible under any circumstances. Others are willing to confess the more socially acceptable sins—cheating on a test, shoplifting, a sudden burst of anger. However, many Christians have dark secrets in the deepest recesses of their minds that are so unacceptable to polite society, perhaps even criminal in the eyes of the law, that they would rather die than admit the facts to another person, especially the one they have wronged.

Some Christians are haunted with these secrets for years and years. Nobody else knows. After all, they go to church every week; they pray and smile and praise the Lord; many even hold church office. Some are ministers who preach hope and salvation every Sabbath, yet they know and God knows that somewhere in the past is a detestable act that they desperately wish had never happened. Oh, for a chance to live life over again! Oh, for the courage to make that sin right! The way things are, they feel utterly hypocritical.

Often the disputes and quarrels that break out in our congregations have their roots in deep, dark, unconfessed sins. I suspect that some of the most divisive arguments within our denomination in North America also arise from the guilty consciences of the critics.

If you have been plagued by an unconfessed sin, please keep reading, because I have wonderful news for you.

First, I want to assure you that God loves you. You also need to know that God wants nothing more than to see you cleansed, free, and happy again. That's His goal for your life, and He is anxious to make it real.

Second, I want to assure you that the fact you have not found the courage to confess all these years is not an indication that you are not a Christian. There are a couple of exceptions to this general principle. If you have made a conscious decision that you absolutely will not confess, or if you are continuing to practice this sin and are making no effort to quit, then you need to think seriously about whether you are a Christian, even if you claim to be one. But if you have been struggling to figure out how to deal with this sin, God accepts that as the best you have had to offer up to the present time. I find the following statement by Ellen White particularly meaningful:

> When it is in the heart to obey God, when efforts are put forth to this end, Jesus accepts this disposition and effort as man's best service, and He makes up for the deficiency with His own divine merit (*My Life Today*, p. 250).

You must be honest with God and not play games. But if you genuinely want freedom from your sin and simply do not know how to bring yourself to the point of confession, then you are a Christian, and there is a way out.

The reason I can speak so positively is that I have had sins in my life that I thought I could never confess, but I found a way, and I know that God was with me during the growth process toward confession. In fact, only genuine Christians can come to the point of confessing these dark sins, because it takes God's help to do that, and you have to be a Christian to get that kind of help.

Unfortunately, some Christians don't understand this. I

talked with a man once who told me he believed that a person was lost from the time he committed a sin until he confessed it. That is absolutely false. All of us are assured of salvation when we accept Jesus as our Saviour, and at that point none of us are mature Christians. God assures us of salvation at every step during the growth process, not just at the end of it. Coming to the point of confession is a growth process like anything else in the Christian life.

I would like to share with you the solution that I found for confessing a sin in my life when it seemed impossible to do so.

Years ago, while I was a student in college, I did something wrong against a fellow student whose room was down the hall from mine in the dormitory. This person never knew that I had done this thing, but I knew at the time that what I had done to him was not right. However, as time passed by, I hardly ever thought about it. Twenty-five years later I still did not feel particularly conscience-stricken over the matter.

But then I began praying the prayer that a few chapters back I suggested you pray. I said, "Lord, show me what I need to know in order to be ready for the close of probation." "Show me what I need to know in order to reflect the image of Jesus fully."

A couple of years went by, during which God showed me several problems. I dealt with these. Then one day the thought struck me that I ought to confess to this person what I had done years before. Unfortunately, I felt the way many of you feel— that I would rather die than confess this sin. So I dismissed the thought for the moment.

However, God wasn't through with me. He kept telling me that I needed to make this thing right. Finally one day I said, "OK, Lord, I'm willing to confess this sin, but You know that the way I feel about it right now, I am completely unable to do that. If You know that I need to confess this sin in order to be right with You, then please bring me to the place that I am willing to talk to the individual I wronged about it."

Several months passed, and God led me through other incidents that strengthened the conviction I ought to make this thing right. Finally one day I decided that I would do it. I had an appointment to meet with this individual in a few weeks anyway, so in a phone conversation with him ahead of time, I said, "There is something specific I want to discuss with you when we get together." I set myself up not to back down on my decision.

I had to drive several hours to meet the appointment, and I can still remember that the closer I got to the place where we were to meet, the better I felt about following through with my decision.

When the moment came that we actually met, I knew that not only was I *willing* to talk about it—*I actually wanted to confess this sin.*

And I did.

Unbelievable! But it actually happened.

Please analyze this experience with me for a moment.

In a previous chapter I spoke about the fact that God transforms our hearts, taking away the desire for sin. The pride that keeps us from wanting to confess is simply another of those sins that God has to transform. The transformation process went so far in me that I was not only willing but anxious to confess. I believe God will do the same for you.

Now let me ask, If you were struggling with a bad temper, do you think you would be in a saved condition during the transformation process? Of course. Rest assured, you are also in a saved condition during the time it takes to get rid of the pride that is keeping you from confessing.

Other principles of confession. Before concluding this chapter, we need to discuss several other principles of confession.

First, it is important to confess specific sins. If you stole something, you must go to the person you stole from and confess exactly what you took. If you were dishonest or angry, you must confess that specific sin. It is not enough to confess sin in general. An exception might be when your confession would reveal confidential information about someone else or when the individual to whom you need to confess is emotionally incapable of handling the information. It's usually best, in such a situation, to seek the advice of a pastor or a mature Christian friend whose judgment you trust before going to the person you wronged.

Whenever possible, I prefer a face-to-face conversation when I confess and ask for forgiveness. However, if my home is across the country from the person I need to talk to, I accept a telephone conversation as next best. Sometimes a letter is the most appropriate way to handle the situation. However, I won't write a letter unless I'm sure that I wouldn't mind someone else reading what I wrote. Written communications have a way of falling into the wrong hands, even when the one in possession of them doesn't intend for them to.

For a face-to-face conversation, I recommend that you choose a specific time when you will go to the one you wronged. You may need to make an appointment and ask God to help you keep it. When the time comes and you are in the person's presence, tell him or her exactly what you did. Don't excuse your sin or make light of it, and don't try to hide the worst part of it. Tell everything, just the way it happened, regardless of how embarrassing it may be. If God does for you what He did for me, you will *want* to do this.

Acknowledge that what you did was sinful, and ask the person to forgive you. I try to conclude a confession by saying, "I know that what I did was sinful, and I want to ask you to forgive me." It is very important to *ask* for forgiveness. Even if the person refuses to grant forgiveness, you have done your part by asking.

If the person you wronged suffered some loss or damage as a result of your sin, you must make restitution insofar as possible. If you took property that did not belong to you, you must return it. If that is not possible (maybe it wore out or got lost), you must replace it or pay for its replacement. If you damaged someone's reputation, you must, insofar as possible, inform those who hold a misconception because of what you said or did.

You should confess to as many people as were wronged by what you did, but no more. That may be one person, or it may be a whole churchful of people. A few people may even need to confess a particular sin to an entire denomination or an entire nation. Generally speaking, the most satisfactory way to do that is in print.

When someone confesses to you. From time to time someone will come to you with a confession. You may or may not have known about the sin beforehand, but you have two responsibilities when someone confesses to you.

First, you must forgive. You must say, "I forgive you." This sounds easy, but in some cases it can be bitterly hard, particularly when that sin caused you great loss or pain. If you knew before the person confessed that he or she had wronged you, you may already have granted forgiveness in your heart. Many Christians are able to do that. However, you may have been struggling with an inability to forgive just as long as the person who wronged you has been struggling with the inability to confess. If so, once that person confesses, you are confronted with a double need to forgive. You need to forgive for the sake of your own conscience—something you've needed all along; and you need to forgive for the sake of the wrongdoer. He or she needs to receive your forgiveness.

If the information about the wrong against you was unknown to you until you heard the confession, and if you are suddenly confronted with a terrible shock, you may feel very angry and find immediate forgiveness difficult or even impossible to grant, at least from the heart.

Just as the person who confessed may have needed considerable time to receive the transformation of heart necessary to confess, so you may need time to receive the transformation necessary to forgive. I suggest that you handle such a situation by saying something like this: "Thank you for making this confession. I appreciate your honesty. However, I must be honest in return and tell you that I feel very angry right now, and it is not possible for me to say 'I forgive you' from my heart. Please give me time to process this with the Lord."

You now have an obligation to take this matter to the Lord in prayer and ask Him to transform your heart so that you can truly forgive. If you do not do this, *your* eternal salvation is in jeopardy.

Your second responsibility to the person who wronged you is to keep the information confidential. In the case of sensitive information that you were unaware of before, the person who confessed to you may have gone to a considerable risk to share with you the facts. Under no circumstances must you jeopardize that person's reputation or his other interests by revealing to others what you know. The only exception is in a case where someone else is being harmed or at risk of being harmed if you don't tell, as in the case of ongoing child or spouse abuse. Even here, I believe you should handle the situation in such a way that damage to the one who confessed to you is kept to a minimum, and he or she is supported in the effort to grow spiritually.

The very worst thing you can do is to use that person's confession as a way to gain revenge. Included in revenge is condemnation. If the person who confessed to you had to thrust a knife into his or her heart in order to make things right, you should not twist the knife for personal satisfaction. Confession and forgiveness must always be redemptive. Those who use another's confession to gain revenge have an obligation to make a confession in return.

Sometimes both parties in a wrong need to confess to each other. Often, in a large church split, the people on both sides need to confess. Where hostilities have run high, no healing can come until both sides humble their hearts and confess. Often, when one person initiates a confession like this, others will follow. One person can lead an entire church into a profound spiritual renewal.

Among the most difficult church splits to resolve through confession are those involving differences over theology and lifestyle. The people on each side feel absolutely certain that they are right and the opposition is wrong. To confess would be to deny the truth! This is especially a problem for Christians who adopt a very strict lifestyle. It seems so right to condemn those who are less strict, and our feelings against them seem so justified. But often behind these feelings is a spiritual pride that must be confessed and gotten rid of.

Sometimes it is particularly difficult for pastors to initiate a confession like this, because, after all, the pastor is supposed to be above pride and anger. However, pastors must recognize that they too are human, and their congregations must allow them to be human. Maybe the pastor needs to be the first one to confess, even if he thinks he is not in the wrong. A good principle to follow is for the one who thinks he or she is least to blame in a conflict to take the first step toward making things right.

Back to the latter rain

There are two reasons why confession of sin is essential in the context of the latter rain. First, God's people need the latter rain in order to achieve the full perfection of character that will be necessary for the close of probation, but it is impossible to receive the Holy Spirit in full latter-rain power while we have a known, unconfessed sin in our lives.

But didn't we just learn that God continues to work with us while we grow to the point that we can confess those especially difficult sins? Yes. That's what the early rain is for.

The second reason why confession is essential in order to receive the latter rain is that we cannot experience unity in our families and in our churches without it. The latter rain cannot fall on people who are still divided because of unconfessed sin, much less unite them, especially when those very sins are the cause of the discord. There must exist among God's people a sweet harmony through heartfelt confession and forgiveness, through humbling of our hearts before each other. Then as families, as churches, and as a denomination, God will unite us through the power of the latter rain.

CHAPTER
17
The Shaking

Imagine, if you can, what will happen when Los Angeles gets hit by "the big one" that everybody has been expecting for the last twenty or thirty years. Say it registers an unprecedented 9.4 on the Richter scale. An estimated 800,000 people are presumed dead, and twice that many are injured, at least a fourth of them badly enough to require hospitalization. But there is no hospitalization. Most hospitals in the L.A. basin have been destroyed. Nearly all modes of ground transportation into the area have been rendered useless, to a great extent because of damaged bridges. All the major airports have been destroyed, including LAX, Burbank, and Ontario. About the only way into the scene of the disaster is by helicopter.

The president has ordered all branches of the military into the area, especially medical units and field hospitals. Several major foreign nations have offered massive aid, including Britain, France, Germany, and Japan.

A week later a massive earthquake strikes Japan, leaving Tokyo in far worse shape than Los Angeles; five days later a third quake hits Western Europe, severely damaging Berlin. Those two sources of aid to the United States are eliminated. From now on it's every nation for itself.

On top of all this, a small asteroid has plunged into the heart of Brazil, setting fire to most of the Amazon jungle, and several volcanoes have erupted around the Pacific Rim. As a result of these disasters, weather patterns around the world are disrupted, causing an unprecedented number of tornadoes, hurricanes, and typhoons.

Early in the morning after the asteroid impact, you're watching the news on TV when suddenly the reporter interrupts his coverage of the earthquakes and the asteroid impact to inform his listeners that "the president of the United States will make a statement to the nation at ten o'clock this morning, Eastern Standard Time." Nobody knows the subject of the president's speech, the reporter says, but most observers speculate that he will call for an international conference to deal with the terrible calamities that have devastated the world in recent weeks.

Nobody, however, is prepared for the announcement the president actually makes:

"Good morning, Americans. As you know, during the past few weeks a series of devastating natural disasters has crippled our planet beyond anything we would have imagined possible even six months ago. The world is becoming paralyzed economically, politically, religiously, and environmentally. But our worst paralysis is, quite frankly, fear. For who knows whether the worst is still ahead? I must be honest and tell you that the impact on our planet of these disasters has been so severe that if others of equal or greater magnitude occur in the near future, the survival of the human race will be at stake. I believe it is time that this nation—and the world—seriously asked itself one question above all others: Is God angry with us? Is God trying to tell us something?

"The situation is so serious that I have sent a message to the secretary general of the United Nations, urging him to call an emergency session of that body two days from now. I am recommending that the heads of state of the member bodies of the Security Council be present at that meeting. And because of the extremely significant spiritual implications of these disasters, I am also urging the general secretary to invite the pope to join the world's political leaders at that conference, along with representatives from all of the major religions of the world.

"I am sure that some of you will feel this last initiative is a compromise of the time-honored American principle of church-state separation. However, in a time of international crisis of this magnitude, we must pursue all options. Fortunately, recent Supreme Court decisions have been considerably more flexible in their interpretation of the religion clause of the first amendment than in the past. In any case, even though its headquarters is on our soil, the United Nations is not an American body, and therefore is not subject to American law.

"I thank each of you for your support, not only of this nation but of the world, as together we strive to cope with these disasters that threaten our civilization."

That story was made up, of course. But when the season of calamity comes, *I believe something of that nature will happen.* We have seen repeatedly in this book that the Bible and Ellen White have predicted tremendous calamities that will fall on the earth without warning at the end time—natural disasters that will bring the world to the brink of collapse. As severe as these things will be, however, they will not be the great final test. The test will come as a result of the world's effort to cope with these disasters. Because the world's leaders will recognize the spiritual dimensions of what is happening, they will seek a spiritual solution. But you know as well as I do that any spiritual solution the world seeks is likely to be the wrong one. The test will come when God's people refuse to cooperate with the world's spiritual solution to the crisis.

That is what will bring the great final "shaking" that Seventh-day Adventists have talked about for nearly 150 years. This will also be the beginning of the final crisis that forces the entire world into two camps so probation can close and Jesus can come.

What is the shaking?

In the Adventist tradition, "the shaking" refers to a time when those who are not genuine Christians will be shaken out of the church. Right now there are two kinds of people in the church—genuine Christians and those who profess to be Christians but are actually unconverted. The shaking will change all that. Ellen White said:

> Soon God's people will be tested by fiery trials, and the great proportion of those who now appear to be genuine and true will prove to be base metal (*Testimonies*, vol. 5, p. 136).

Notice the cause of this shaking: "fiery trials." Ellen White tells us exactly when those fiery trials will come upon the church: "When the law of God is made void the church will be sifted by fiery trials" (*Selected Messages*, book 2, p. 368). Ellen White often referred to a time when the law of God will be made void, and, as far as I can tell, she always meant just one thing: Sunday laws. This does not mean that other laws in opposition to the law of God have not and will not be enacted. But America's great sin, by which she will close her national probation, will be the enactment of a law that recognizes Sunday as the Sabbath. And under America's leadership, the entire world will cooperate in enforcing this day of worship.

I believe that some form of Sunday law will probably be enacted prior to the final crisis and the season of calamity, especially in the United States. However, Sunday laws that are enacted prior to that time will probably not produce much of a shaking among God's people. If anything, they may have the opposite effect. They will probably cause us to pull together.

But Sunday laws that are passed in the United States and other countries after the crisis of the end time begins, in response to the season of calamity, will be a part of the world's effort to appease God. Anyone who refuses to cooperate with those laws will be considered a traitor, not only to his or her own country, but to the best interests of the entire human race. When that time comes, it will seem reasonable to go along with the majority for the sake of saving humanity. To most people it will also seem reasonable to punish with fines, imprisonment, and ultimately death those who refuse to seek the Lord in the way the majority is seeking Him.

Ellen White does not say exactly when during the final crisis Satan will appear as Christ. However, we know that spiritualism will be one of the powerful religious forces leading out in the effort to save the human race from the terrible effects of the judgments that God is sending on the world. I think it is reasonable, therefore, to suppose that if not Satan himself, then certainly some of his subordinates will appear, probably introducing themselves as extraterrestrials interested in helping the human race to save itself from annihilation.

I suspect that in order to create an appearance of legitimacy, these demons will not actually present themselves visibly to human beings, without first "making contact" through radio telescopes and some of the other sophisticated technology that scientists are accustomed to using. They may even make an advance "appointment" so that the world's leaders will be expecting them. Because scientists will have "verified" this communication in advance with their instruments, they will fall for the deception. And because scientists, who are the high priests of our society, believe it, so will everyone else.

Except, of course, a few "radicals" who have the audacity to call this a deception of Satan, when the whole world knows that the entire human race needs every bit of help it can get from whatever source.

I cannot stress enough that when the final crisis comes, most people will think that the laws against God's people are reasonable. Those who refuse to go along with the majority will be called fanatical and disloyal. Ellen White said that "conscientious obedience to the word of God will be treated as rebellion" (*The Great Controversy*, p. 608). Many Seventh-day Adventists will abandon their faith at this time:

> As the storm approaches, a large class who have professed faith in the third angel's message, but have not been sanctified through obedience to the truth, abandon their position and join the ranks of the opposition (*The Great Controversy*, p. 608).

> At that time [of persecution] the superficial, conservative class, whose influence has steadily retarded the progress of the work, will renounce the faith (*Testimonies*, vol. 5, p. 463).

> Those who have had great light and precious privileges, but have not improved them, will, under one pretext or another, go out from us (ibid., vol. 6, p. 400).

> When the law of God is made void the church will be sifted by fiery trials, and a larger proportion than we now anticipate, will give heed to seducing spirits and doctrines of devils (*Selected Messages*, book 2, p. 368).

In the last statement above, Ellen White said that "a larger proportion than we now anticipate, will give heed to seducing spirits and doctrines of devils." Jesus said that during the end time, false Christs will "deceive even the elect—if that were possible" (Matthew 24:25). With some of God's elect, it *will* be possible.

The question is, Which ones?

Who will survive the shaking?

I think it is reasonable to say that all of God's people today expect to be among the faithful at that time. But if a larger number than we now anticipate will join with the opposition, we need to ask, Who will these people be? Who will come through the shaking on God's side, and who will fall away and join the enemy? Is there a way to guarantee that we will not yield when the pressure becomes intense?

Jesus answered that question in His parables of the end time. In Matthew 24:37-39, He compared the end time with the period just preceding Noah's Flood. He said:

> As it was in the days of Noah, so it will be at the coming of the Son of Man. For in the days before the flood, people were eating and drinking, marrying and giving in marriage, up to the day Noah entered the ark; and they knew nothing about what would happen until the flood came and took them all away. That is how it will be at the coming of the Son of Man.

There is nothing wrong with eating, drinking, and marrying. Jesus' point is that the people before the Flood were preoccupied with everyday life to the neglect of spiritual preparation for the crisis ahead. They scoffed at the idea that such a crisis was even coming. The parable of the ten virgins has the same lesson. The foolish girls frittered away the time they should have spent getting oil.

However, we are not to spend all of our time in devotional exercises. The parable of the talents shows us that preparation for the final crisis includes faithfulness in the duties of life, and in the parable of the sheep and the goats, Jesus tells us that preparation includes helping to meet the needs of others.

The following statements by Ellen White provide insight into what is needed to be ready for the shaking and what will be the spiritual condition of those who are not ready. I have quoted eight statements, not so much to prove a point as to provide a broad understanding of the reasons why so many people will abandon their faith during the shaking. I urge you to read them all.

The superficial, conservative class, whose influence has steadily retarded the progress of the work, will renounce the faith (*Testimonies*, vol. 5, p. 463).

Those who have had great light and precious privileges, but have not improved them, will, under one pretext or another, go out from us (ibid., vol. 6, p. 400).

When the shaking comes, by the introduction of false theories, these surface readers, anchored nowhere, are like shifting sand. They slide into any position to suit the tenor of their feelings of bitterness (*Testimonies to Ministers*, p. 112).

All will be shaken out who are not willing to take a bold and unyielding stand for the truth and to sacrifice for God and His cause (*Early Writings*, p. 50).

Those who have step by step yielded to worldly demands and conformed to worldly customs will not find it a hard matter to yield to the powers that be, rather than subject themselves to derision, insult, threatened imprisonment, and death (*Testimonies*, vol. 5, p. 81).

Not having a love of the truth, they will be taken in [by] the delusions of the enemy; they will give heed to seducing spirits and doctrines of devils, and will depart from the faith (ibid., vol. 6, p. 401).

The careless and indifferent, who did not join with those who prized victory and salvation enough to perseveringly plead and agonize for it, did not obtain it, and they were left behind in darkness (*Early Writings*, p. 271).

We are coming to a crisis which, more than any previous time since the world began, will demand the entire consecration of every one who has named the name of Christ (*Gospel Workers*, p. 323).

Keeping your relationship with Jesus

In several places throughout this book I have discussed various aspects of the spiritual experience God's people must have in order to keep their relationship with Jesus during earth's darkest hour, but nowhere have I put everything together. Now seems a good time to do that.

Justification. The Christian's relationship with Jesus begins at conversion, when his sins are forgiven and he is justified. Justification means that God forgives our sins and accepts us just as though we had not done them. Placing His own perfect righteousness to our account, He declares us to be righteous even though our characters may still have many flaws in them. At that moment we are guaranteed salvation in His eternal kingdom. This guarantee is conditional, of course, but it is not conditional on our performance. It is conditional on our continuing to maintain a relationship with Jesus. He will never break His relationship with us, but He allows us the freedom to break our relationship with Him.

It is extremely important to understand that Christians are in a saved condition from the moment they accept Jesus as their Saviour. Salvation is not an on-off switch that we turn on by saying Yes to Jesus and turn off by every little sin we commit. God knows when He first accepts us that our characters are flawed and that there is a lot of "repair work" to be done. He also knows that the repair work will take time and that He can perform it only on converted Christians.

There is a reason why God's end-time people especially need to understand justification.

One of the most common traps Christians fall into is doubting the genuineness of their relationship with Jesus. During the peaceful times in which we now live, most of us do not lose our Christian experience over these doubts. But the trials of the end time will demand that we have implicit faith in God and Christ. Those who allow their minds to question whether God accepts them will be in great danger of being overwhelmed by the trials of the little time of trouble, to say nothing of the difficulties of the great time of trouble.

Now is the time to learn to trust God's love for sinners. Now is the time for each of us to learn that "God loves me in spite of my imperfections." This is an utterly essential preparation for the shaking and the trials associated with it.

Sanctification. However, a level of character development that few of us today possess will also be necessary for those who go through the final crisis. The demands on us at that time will be similar to those Christ experienced during His final crisis. As the Roman soldiers nailed Jesus to the cross, He said, "Father, forgive them, for they do not know what they are doing" (Luke 23:34). Only a person with a transformed heart can say that. Unconverted people curse their tormentors. Unconverted people curse God when trouble comes their way.

Resisting pride, bitterness, and injustice is tough business. It's tough to ask God to change our wrong desires, and it's tough saying No to them. However, if we don't learn these lessons now, we will not handle the trials of the end time successfully. Those who endure the trials of the little time of trouble will need a relationship and a depth of character that few possess today. People who all their lives have excused the defects in their characters instead of seeking God's transforming power to change them will find that those defects will cause them to yield under pressure. When the shaking comes, they will go out. Ellen White makes it clear that the shaking will test our character, especially our motives:

> God is now sifting His people, testing their purposes and their motives. Many will be but as chaff—no wheat, no value in them (*Testimonies*, vol. 4, p. 51).

> Soon God's people will be tested by fiery trials, and the great proportion of those who now appear to be genuine and true will prove to be base metal (ibid., vol. 5, p. 136).

> Let opposition arise, let bigotry and intolerance again bear sway, let persecution be kindled, and the halfhearted and hypocritical will waver and yield the faith; but the true Christian will stand firm as a rock, his faith stronger, his

hope brighter, than in days of prosperity (*The Great Controversy*, p. 602).

When the storm of persecution really breaks upon us, the true sheep will hear the true Shepherd's voice. . . . In view of the common peril, strife for supremacy will cease; there will be no disputing as to who shall be accounted greatest (*Testimonies*, vol. 6, p. 401).

One reason why we should now be overcoming sin and developing a character that reflects Christ's character is so we can live after the close of probation without a Mediator. Another reason is so we can remain true to God during the shaking. Because our relationship with Jesus is the only thing that will get us through.

18

The Loud Cry

Herb Ford, a friend of mine, has spent his entire life serving the Seventh-day Adventist Church in communications. He is one of the finest public relations people I know. The story I want to tell you happened to Herb one day while he was assisting in the newsroom during the 1990 General Conference session in Indianapolis.

One day toward the end of the session, the religion editor from the *Indianapolis Star* walked in, threw down a pamphlet with a picture of a beast from Revelation on the front, and demanded to know whether the Seventh-day Adventist Church "is responsible for the mass distribution of this paper around town."

Herb examined the pamphlet briefly. The picture on the front looked quite awful—both the artwork and the quality of the printing. (It's rather difficult to get good quality printing on newsprint.) Herb told me later that "it just didn't look like something from one of our publishing houses."

Herb leafed through the paper and discovered that it had been published by an independent ministry, so he said to the editor, "No, our church organization did not publish this pamphlet, and neither did we distribute it."

She had more questions, though. "The bishop brought this to my attention," she said. "Someone is distributing it all over town. It says that anyone who does not keep your Sabbath is going to hell and that the pope is a bad person."

Herb said, "I can assure you, this is not the way we like to approach people. Have you seen the material that our church *does* put out?"

"Yes," the woman said, "and it looks quite nice. But I still want to know if your church *believes* what that pamphlet says."

Before I tell you Herb Ford's answer to that last question, I want you to put yourself in his shoes. An irate religion editor is about to rush into print with whatever answer you give, and you have two seconds to think before you start talking. What words of wisdom would you have given Herb to share with the lady?

Before I tell you what Herb said, I also want to tell you that Herb believes the Adventist message as much as you and I do. And he not only believes it, he loves it. Furthermore, he's smart enough to know that the majority of Adventists in this country believe it and love it too.

I also want to tell you that what Herb *said* and what he *meant* were two different things.

Herb *said*, "Probably not one one-thousandth of our people believe this way."

Herb *meant*, "Probably not one one-thousandth of our people believe *in approaching the public* this way."

The article in the newspaper the next day quoted Herb as saying that "not one thousand of our people believe this way," when Herb had said "not one one-thousandth." We can forgive the religion editor of the *Indianapolis Star* for hearing "one thousand" instead of "one one-thousandth."

Unfortunately, the radical Adventist press picked up this statement and spread it all across the North American Adventist Church, and probably as far as possible overseas. They used the statement Herb made under pressure to excoriate the church, especially the General Conference—yes, always the General Conference—for abandoning the faith.

The tragedy is that not one of these people called Herb Ford to ask him *his* side of the story before they printed it. Some of the publications I read almost seemed to publish the newspaper's account of Herb's words with glee.[1]

---

1. One man did call Shirley Burton the next day to talk about it. Shirley was the communication director of the General Conference at the time and participated in Herb's discussion with the religion editor of the *Indianapolis Star*. Shirley made an appointment to speak personally with this man the next day, but fifteen minutes before the appointment, she was called into a conference to discuss a critical matter that could not be postponed. The man's wife called to keep the appointment, and when Herb Ford told her Shirley was in conference and would speak to her and her husband as soon as she got out, the woman said, "This just proves that the church doesn't want to talk to us," and hung up.

That's sad!

It's sad when we have so little confidence in each other, and so little Christianity about us, that we will tear down a brother's reputation and weaken people's confidence in the church without even asking the brother his side of the story. And it's even more sad when we get emotional satisfaction out of doing it.

This is just one example I could give you of the fallacious reporting I've read in pamphlets and seen on videotapes, lambasting the church for its unfaithfulness. And all, of course, in an effort to win Adventists over to the critic's cause. It's the *National Enquirer* mentality, and unfortunately there are Adventists who breathe in that kind of trash the way a fish breathes water.

I could easily write a small book on this point, but that's not why I told you this story about my friend Herb Ford. I want you to think, rather, about the implications of this story for our Adventist witness during the final crisis, before the close of probation, when terrible judgments from God will be falling all over the world, and the world's leaders will be desperately seeking spiritual and practical solutions to the crisis.

For 150 years we've been trying very hard to convince as many people as possible that our message is biblically sound. During the past forty or fifty years, our church has made amazing progress in breaking down prejudice. We are more widely accepted and better understood today than at any other time since our movement began back in the mid-1800s. I'm thankful that people trust us, that they've learned to like us, that they recognize we are not the cult they once thought we were.

Unfortunately, the critics like to thrash the church for this also, apparently forgetting Ellen White's advice:

> So should the followers of Christ, as they approach the time of trouble, make every exertion *to place themselves in a proper light before the people, to disarm prejudice,* and to avert the danger which threatens liberty of conscience (*The Great Controversy,* p. 616, emphasis supplied).

But now think of this. When the season of calamity comes, and the Roman Catholic Church makes a bid to regain the political control over the whole world that it once had over Europe, are you going to tell your neighbors that "this is the beast that John foretold in Revelation 13"?

Will you go on public record—in an evangelistic meeting perhaps, or over the air—unmasking "the stealthy but rapid progress of the papal power"? (*The Great Controversy*, p. 606).

What will you say then, when a news reporter throws down *The Great Controversy* and spits the words at you, "Does your church believe *that*"?

Several years ago I heard a preacher exclaim to a congregation one Sabbath morning, "The day is coming when this church will be so packed there will be standing room only!"

And I thought to myself, "Yes, and do you understand the bitter adversity we'll have to go through to make that happen?"

When the whole world is worshiping that glorious being who claims to be Christ, will you point your finger and say, "That's Satan"?

That's what "the loud cry" and "the final warning" will *really* be like. Most of us don't realize that, but it's true.

Which is why I told you the story about Herb Ford.

Frankly, if I'd been in Herb's shoes that morning at the General Conference session, I doubt I'd have performed as well as he did. And neither, I suspect, would the critics who landed on him so hard.

The point for all of us is that we need to be thinking now about what we'll say then. I realize that the Holy Spirit will tell us what to say when the time comes (see Matthew 10:19, 20), but if we aren't careful, today's warm climate will make us so public-relations conscious that we'll be reluctant to take a stand when the world turns against us. We'll think we have to protect our good image.

There won't be a good image during the final crisis. That's why it will be a crisis. Nothing is more clear from *The Great Controversy* than that.

I don't mean to suggest that we ought to throw away all tact when the final crisis comes. If anything, we'll need more tact than ever. I mean that the issues we face and the questions we are asked will require that we choose between telling the truth and denying our faith. For a people who have spent a lifetime cultivating a correct image of the church (which we all ought to be doing right now) and who have succeeded in gaining fairly wide acceptance, the temptation to preserve that good image by suppressing the truth will be very great.

Purpose of the loud cry

Now that we have looked at the great difficulty of proclaiming the message during that time, I would like to focus on the purpose of the loud cry, and then I'd like you to think with me for a moment about its success—for it will be a phenomenal success.

The expression "loud cry" comes from Revelation 18:1, 2, where John says:

> After these things I saw another angel come down from heaven, having great power; and the earth was lightened with his glory. And *he cried mightily* with a strong voice, saying, Babylon the great is fallen, is fallen, and is become the habitation of devils, and the hold of every foul spirit, and a cage of every unclean and hateful bird (KJV, emphasis supplied).

Strange as it may seem, those terrible words of condemnation are actually for the purpose of redemption. Ellen White said that "the last message of mercy to be given to the world, is a revelation of His character of love" (*Christ's Object Lessons*, p. 415).

We have to understand the context of John's awful words in order to understand how they will be a revelation of God's character of love. Christ's second coming will take place in the darkest hour of this earth's history, when the sinfulness of the human race will be so great that God can endure it no longer. Rebellion against God will have reached its zenith. The world will be enamored with a New Age god that tells them they are little gods, that the truth lies within themselves, and that they can do anything they please as long as it feels good. Yet the world will be on a slide straight to hell.

How do you tell people like that that God loves them and wants them to repent of their sins, not revel in them? How do you tell people like that that their probation is about to close and the choices they make right now are crucial because they are final? And how do you say these things with the threat of imprisonment and death hanging over your head for saying them?

Yes, we'll talk about God's love. But we'll also tell the world what the Bible says about sin and righteousness and judgment. Anything less than that would fall short of being a full revelation of God's love.

The very devastation in the world that creates the final crisis will be God's last effort to reach the world with His love. In spite of its length, please read the entire quote below, and notice especially the italicized words:

> Calamities will come—calamities most awful, most unexpected; and these destructions will follow one after another. . . . If men who have been deceived continue in the same way in which they have been walking, disregarding the law of God and presenting falsehoods before the people, God allows them to suffer calamity, *that their senses may be awakened.* . . .
>
> The Lord will not suddenly cast off all transgressors or destroy entire nations; but He will punish cities and places where men have given themselves up to the possession of Satanic agencies. Strictly will the cities of the nations be dealt with, and yet they will not be visited in the extreme of God's indignation, because *some souls will yet break away from the delusions of the enemy, and will repent and be converted,* while the mass will be treasuring up wrath against the day of wrath (*Evangelism*, p. 27, emphasis supplied).

The point is that some people will respond to God's judgments and to our explanation of what's actually going on. Some people will heed the words that seem to be so harsh, and these will take the place of those who abandoned their faith and left us. To them, our message of warning will also be a message of God's love.

Power of the loud cry

I'd like to share with you a passage from Revelation that I believe describes what it will be like for God's people to proclaim the loud cry:[2]

2. The fact that Revelation 11:1-6 follows immediately after Revelation 10, which describes the latter rain (see chapter 15), suggests to me that it probably describes the loud cry. The forces that were born at the time of the French Revolution will have reached their full maturity just before the close of probation, when they will mount a fierce opposition to the loud cry and the final warning.

"I will give power to my two witnesses, and they will prophesy for 1,260 days, clothed in sackcloth." . . . If anyone tries to harm them, fire comes from their mouths and devours their enemies. This is how anyone who wants to harm them must die. These men have power to shut up the sky so that it will not rain during the time they are prophesying; and they have power to turn the waters into blood and to strike the earth with every kind of plague as often as they want (Revelation 11:3-6).

Please notice two things about these two witnesses: (1) they proclaim their message in sackcloth—a symbol of mourning, and (2) nobody can stop them.

That, to me, illustrates the tremendous power that will accompany the loud cry. Given the savage opposition to their message, only people with that kind of power could succeed. However, this power will not be their own, but the power of the latter rain. Notice in the statement below the nature of the final message and the power with which it will be proclaimed:

In every generation God has sent His servants to rebuke sin, both in the world and in the church. But the people desire smooth things spoken to them, and the pure, unvarnished truth is not acceptable. Many reformers, in entering upon their work, determined to exercise great prudence in attacking the sins of the church and the nation. . . . But the Spirit of God came upon them as it came upon Elijah, moving him to rebuke the sins of a wicked king and an apostate people; they could not refrain from preaching the plain utterances of the Bible—doctrines which they had been reluctant to present. They were impelled to zealously declare the truth and the danger which threatened souls. The words which the Lord gave them they uttered, fearless of the consequences, and the people were compelled to hear the warning (*The Great Controversy*, p. 606).

That statement says it all—the love of God, the sinfulness of man, and the power with which those two ideas will be combined in the final warning that God's people will carry to the whole world under the power of the latter rain. The task will not be easy:

In this time of persecution the faith of the Lord's servants will be tried. They have faithfully given the warning, looking to God and to His word alone. God's Spirit, moving upon their hearts, has constrained them to speak. Stimulated with holy zeal, and with the divine impulse strong upon them, they entered upon the performance of their duties without coldly calculating the consequences of speaking to the people the word which the Lord had given them. They have not consulted their temporal interests, nor sought to preserve their reputation or their lives. Yet when the storm of opposition and reproach bursts upon them, some, overwhelmed with consternation, will be ready to exclaim: "Had we foreseen the consequences of our words, we would have held our peace." They are hedged in with difficulties. Satan assails them with fierce temptations. The work which they have undertaken seems far beyond their ability to accomplish. They are threatened with destruction. The enthusiasm which animated them is gone; yet they cannot turn back. Then, feeling their utter helplessness, they flee to the Mighty One for strength. They remember that the words which they have spoken were not theirs, but His who bade them give the warning. God put the truth into their hearts, and they could not forbear to proclaim it (ibid., pp. 608, 609).

The only way you and I will ever do that is with the Holy Spirit filling our hearts in latter-rain power.

But do not think that you can come up to that time and *then* get the power. The season of calamity that lies ahead will be the beginning of earth's darkest hour, and the only way to be prepared then is to be preparing now.

Success of the loud cry

Seventh-day Adventists believe that God called us to warn the world about the very things we've talked about so far in this book and to prepare people for them. However, this is more than just warning people about trouble. The trouble ahead will be for a purpose—to awaken people to the fact that human history is near its end and that anyone who wants eternal life has only a short time to get it. That is to be our message right now as well as then. Ellen White calls this "the last message of mercy to a perishing world" (*Testimonies to Ministers*, p. 313).

Think of it for a moment. The message of salvation has gone to the world for 6,000 years, but quite possibly it will all be over in just a few years from the time you are reading this book! And when the season of calamity comes, there will be only a short time left in which to be saved.

That's why the loud cry will be the most powerful spiritual message that has ever been given to the world. I pointed out earlier in this chapter that it will be powerful in the sense that it can't be stopped by its enemies, but it will also be powerful because it will be accompanied by the latter rain. Thousands and perhaps millions of people will understand the truths we've been talking about, and "a large number [will] take their stand upon the Lord's side" (*The Great Controversy*, p. 612).

Two factors will account for the power of the Adventist message during the time of the loud cry: the Holy Spirit and events in the world.

The Holy Spirit. In spite of the more positive attitude toward our church among American Protestants during the last half of the twentieth century, there is still a great deal of skepticism out there. People are friendly to us and respect us as genuine Christians, but many of them think we are a little odd, just the same. The human mind cannot understand truth, especially unpopular truth, without the help of the Holy Spirit. However, under the power of the latter rain, minds that have been closed will be opened:

> The message will be carried not so much by argument as by the deep conviction of the Spirit of God. The arguments have been presented. The seed has been sown, and now it will spring up and bear fruit. The publications distributed by missionary workers have exerted their influence, yet many whose minds were impressed have been prevented from fully comprehending the truth or from yielding obedience. Now the rays of light penetrate everywhere, the truth is seen in its clearness, and the honest children of God sever the bands which have held them. Family connections, church relations, are powerless to stay them now. Truth is more precious than all besides (ibid., p. 612).

In chapter 15 I expressed my belief that the latter rain will begin to fall before the season of calamity starts and that it will continue with increasing power to the close of probation. I believe that even in North America and the other developed countries of the world, where so little evangelism is happening today, we can expect to see the Holy Spirit bring unusual numbers of people into God's final message even before the final crisis begins. The same may happen in Moslem countries.

Events in the world. One reason, I suspect, why our message is rejected by so many people at the present time is that it seems too sensational. Our interpretation of prophecy seems impossible of fulfillment. But when the things we've been predicting actually come to pass, many people will see our message in a new light.

> By reading it [*The Great Controversy*], some souls will be aroused, and will have courage to unite themselves at once with those who keep the commandments of God. But a much larger number who read it will not take their position until they see the very events taking place that are foretold in it (*Colporteur Ministry*, p. 128).

> As the question of enforcing Sunday observance is widely agitated, the event so long doubted and disbelieved is seen to be approaching, and the third [angel's] message will produce an effect which it could not have had before (*The Great Controversy*, p. 606).

Do you remember, during the last few months of 1989 when Eastern Europe was falling out of the Communist orbit, saying to yourself (or hearing others say), "God has taken charge of events"? That's how it will be during the time of the loud cry:

> Let me tell you that the Lord will work in this last work in a manner very much out of the common order of things, and in a way that will be contrary to human planning. There will be those among us who will always want to control the work of God, to dictate even what movements shall be made when the work goes forward under the direction of

the angel who joins the third angel in the message to be given to the world. *God will use ways and means by which it will be seen that He is taking the reins in His own hands.* The workers will be surprised by the simple means that He will use to bring about and perfect His work of righteousness (*Testimonies to Ministers*, p. 300, emphasis supplied).

What will happen when God takes charge of His work in the earth?

When divine power is combined with human effort, the work will spread like fire in the stubble (*Review and Herald*, 15 December 1885).

I believe that the latter rain and the loud cry will be the glorious climax of the work that, as of this writing, Seventh-day Adventists have been doing around the world for almost 150 years. Often it seems that we are making very little progress. In fact it's easy to get discouraged when we compare our small numbers with the world's total population. But I don't think God is worried about that at all. And I don't think we need to be either. Rather, we need to understand God's purpose for us during the latter rain and the loud cry.

Have you ever strung lights on a Christmas tree? First you plug several strings together and wind them in and out among the branches. When the tree is covered with lights, you flip off the wall switch and darken the whole room. Then you plug the Christmas-tree lights into a socket in the wall. Instantly every one of those lights flashes on, and the tree is covered with tiny pinpoints of light.

For 150 years Seventh-day Adventists have been "stringing lights" all over the world, and all the while it has seemed as though we were accomplishing so very little. But when the latter-rain power of the Holy Spirit energizes God's church, suddenly pinpoints of light will flash on all over the world, and these little lights will rapidly increase until the world is flooded with light.

The church's missionary thrust during the five years between the 1990 and 1995 General Conference sessions is called Global Mission, and the objective is to establish a presence in as many people groups of a million or more as possible. *I can't think of anything that is more in harmony with God's purpose for this church than that.* Let's keep stringing the lights, because even if it seems as though we're accomplishing very little, the more "lights" we string now, the brighter the Holy Spirit can lighten the world when the time comes for the latter rain and the loud cry.

CHAPTER

19

The Time of Trouble

Revelation 17 begins with a description of a fearful beast on which a harlot is sitting:

> One of the seven angels who had the seven bowls came and said to me, "Come, I will show you the punishment of the great prostitute, who sits on many waters. With her the kings of the earth committed adultery and the inhabitants of the earth were intoxicated with the wine of her adulteries."
>
> Then the angel carried me away in the Spirit into a desert. There I saw a woman sitting on a scarlet beast that was covered with blasphemous names and had seven heads and ten horns. The woman was dressed in purple and scarlet, and was glittering with gold, precious stones and pearls. She held a golden cup in her hand, filled with abominable things and the filth of her adulteries. This title was written on her forehead:
>
> MYSTERY
> BABYLON THE GREAT
> THE MOTHER OF PROSTITUTES
> AND OF THE ABOMINATIONS OF THE EARTH.
>
> I saw that the woman was drunk with the blood of the saints, the blood of those who bore testimony to Jesus (Revelation 17:1-6).

Let's analyze this passage. First, notice that the one who showed John this woman was one of the angels who had the seven bowls (or plagues). This suggests that the vision of chapter 17 either coincides with or follows the seven last plagues. Since the seven last plagues conclude with the second coming of Christ, the vision of chapter 17 must coincide with the plagues as an additional description of that time. Thus the passage quoted above describes the final crisis after the close of probation.

The beast John saw is similar to the first beast of Revelation 13, which Adventists have always understood to be the Roman Catholic Church. Personally, I am more inclined to understand the first beast of Revelation 13 as representing a coalition of world religions (seven heads) under the leadership of Roman Catholicism (the wounded head). Revelation 13 clearly describes the final conflict before the close of probation, during the time when human beings are choosing to receive the mark of the beast or the seal of God. I understand the beast of Revelation 17 to be the same as the first beast of Revelation 13, but representing a later phase of its work. Thus Revelation 17 is describing the world's religious apostasy at its peak.

Adventists have always understood a woman in Bible prophecy to symbolize the church. A pure woman represents God's true church, and an impure woman represents an apostate church. We have concluded that the harlot of Revelation 17 symbolizes the height of Christian apostasy at the end of time. Notice that this woman—this church—committed adultery with the kings of the earth (verse 2). This refers to an illicit union of church and state. The woman was also "drunk with the blood of the saints" (verse 6). In other words, through her illicit union with the state, she will persecute God's people.

That is exactly how Seventh-day Adventists have always described events in the world after the close of probation, except that we have been more specific and said that under the combined leadership of the United States government and the Roman Catholic Church, the world will issue a death decree against those who refuse to bow to a universal Sunday law.

I have pointed out in previous chapters that this universal coalition of religion and government will be the world's response to the judgments of God during the little time of trouble. The world's political leaders, desperate for a solution, will join with the world's religious leaders to find a solution.

Before the close of probation, the world will blame God's people for these calamities and will bring intense pressure on us to give up our peculiar faith and join in seeking God the way the majority is seeking Him. Cooperation will seem so reasonable. Those who refuse to cooperate will be called bigots and traitors, and, in many parts of the world, they will be threatened with death. There will be martyrs before the close of probation (see *Selected Messages, book 3, p. 397*).

Judgments after the close of probation

However, the judgments of God before the close of probation will just be the beginning. Sent in mercy to warn the world of the close of probation and the coming of Jesus, these judgments will be restrained to some degree. But when probation closes, God's protecting hand will be completely removed. The world will suffer His complete wrath unmixed with mercy (see Revelation 14:9-11), and His final judgments, called seven last plagues (see Revelation 16), will be poured out. Ellen White wrote:

> When He [Jesus] leaves the sanctuary, darkness covers the inhabitants of the earth. . . . The restraint which has been upon the wicked is removed, and Satan has entire control of the finally impenitent. God's long-suffering has ended. The world has rejected His mercy, despised His love, and trampled upon His law. The wicked have passed the boundary of their probation; the Spirit of God, persistently resisted, has been at last withdrawn. Unsheltered by divine grace, they have no protection from the wicked one. Satan will then plunge the inhabitants of the earth into one great, final trouble. As the angels of God cease to hold in check the fierce winds of human passion, all the elements of strife will be let loose. The whole world will be involved in ruin more terrible than that which came upon Jerusalem of old (*The Great Controversy*, p. 614).

And notice who will get the blame:

> Those who honor the law of God have been accused of bringing judgments upon the world [the judgments of God

before the close of probation], and they will be regarded as the cause of the fearful convulsions of nature and the strife and bloodshed among men that are filling the earth with woe [the judgments of God *after* the close of probation]. The power attending the last warning has enraged the wicked; their anger is kindled against all who have received the message, and Satan will excite to still greater intensity the spirit of hatred and persecution (ibid., pp. 614, 615).

At this time, in their effort to find relief from the seven last plagues, the wicked will enact a worldwide death decree against God's people. Even before the close of probation, there may be laws in some nations condemning God's people to death, but the death decree after the close of probation will be universal. Understanding our own time as we do, we can say what Ellen White could not—that this death decree may well be passed by the United Nations itself.

I can also tell you with some certainty that this universal death decree will be passed prior to the third plague that turns fresh water supplies into blood. Commenting on the third plague, Ellen White said that "by condemning the people of God to death, they have as truly incurred the guilt of their blood as if it had been shed by their hands" (ibid., p. 628). Therefore I conclude that at the very latest, the death decree will be enacted by the end of the second plague. It will be the world's last desperate attempt to appease an offended God and stop His judgments.

Spiritualism during the time of trouble

Satan's major strategy during the final days of earth's history will be deception, and one of his most successful methods for deceiving people will be spiritualism. The Bible is very clear about the role of Satan in last-day events. Paul said:

The coming of the lawless one will be in accordance with the work of Satan displayed in all kinds of counterfeit miracles, signs and wonders, and in every sort of evil that deceives those who are perishing (2 Thessalonians 2:9, 10).

Then I saw three evil spirits that looked like frogs; they came out of the mouth of the dragon, out of the mouth of the beast and out of the mouth of the false prophet. They are spirits of demons performing miraculous signs, and they go out to the kings of the whole world, to gather them for the battle on the great day of God Almighty (Revelation 16:13, 14).

In *The Great Controversy* Ellen White makes several statements in her chapter on "The Time of Trouble" about the role of spiritualism during the time of trouble. Satan may appear as Christ before the close of probation; it is certain that he will appear after:

As the crowning act in the great drama of deception, Satan himself will personate Christ. . . . In different parts of the earth, Satan will manifest himself among men as a majestic being of dazzling brightness, resembling the description of the Son of God given by John in the Revelation (*The Great Controversy*, p. 624).

Two other statements in the chapter on "The Time of Trouble" are very significant:

Fearful sights of a supernatural character will soon be revealed in the heavens, in token of the power of miracle-working demons (ibid.).

To all the testing time will come. By the sifting of temptation the genuine Christian will be revealed. Are the people of God now so firmly established upon His word that they would not yield to the evidence of their senses? (ibid., p. 625).

Ellen White does not elaborate on either of these statements. What fearful, supernatural sights will appear in the heavens "in token of the power of miracle-working demons"? She does not give us further details. Will this be the evidence that presents itself so powerfully to our senses that we will have to deny the evidence in order to hold fast our faith in the Word of God? Again, she does not say.

However, I believe we are in a position today to make some fairly good educated guesses about what Ellen White meant. Our culture is saturated with novels and motion pictures based on space travel and wars between fictional intergalactic enemies. I pointed out in an earlier chapter that scientists are spending millions of dollars each year to find out whether intelligent beings exist in outer space. One of these days those efforts will be rewarded, except that the beings who introduce themselves to the human race at that time will not be aliens from other planets. They will be demons. And these demons may very well put on some very impressive signs in the heavens to "prove" that they are genuine.

Of course, evidence of the senses is exactly what science requires to prove a point. And Satan will give scientists what they need in order to believe in him. Revelation says that he will even cause fire to come down from heaven (see Revelation 13:13). He will do things in the presence of earth's scientists that they simply cannot deny. The Bible calls them "miracles" (see 2 Thessalonians 2:9; Revelation 13:13; 16:14).

It is that very evidence of the senses that God's people will have to deny. We will have to go against everything our rational, scientifically minded culture stands for in order to reject spiritualism. No wonder Ellen White said that "so closely will the counterfeit resemble the true that it will be impossible to distinguish between them except by the Holy Scriptures" (*The Great Controversy*, p. 593).

Fleeing to the solitary places

At this time it will be impossible for God's people to live a normal life in human society. Many of us will escape to the solitary places of the earth:

> As the decree issued by the various rulers of Christendom against commandment keepers shall withdraw the protection of the government and abandon them to those who desire their destruction, the people of God will flee from the cities and villages and associate together in companies, dwelling in the most desolate and solitary places (ibid., p. 626).

Those of us who do not make our escape to these solitary places will be thrown into prison. Ellen White said:

Many of all nations and of all classes, high and low, rich and poor, black and white, will be cast into the most unjust and cruel bondage. The beloved of God pass weary days, bound in chains, shut in by prison bars, sentenced to be slain, some apparently left to die of starvation in dark and loathsome dungeons (ibid., p. 626).

It is difficult for us to imagine what it will be like to leave our homes and flee to the solitary places. It is certainly realistic to suppose, however, that the day will come when each of us will have to walk out of our homes, lock the door, and never return. Will you be able to walk away from all the things you've accumulated over the years and not look back? You and I will have to do that someday, if what we believe is true. I don't know about you, but suddenly I have a lot more sympathy for Lot's wife (see Genesis 19:26).

Actually, if a vision Ellen White had in 1868 has anything to do with the time of trouble, we won't walk away from everything all at one time. In her vision she saw God's people loading wagons and leaving on a journey. As the road got narrower and narrower, they had to get rid of first one thing and then the other, until they were walking barefoot along a narrow ledge on a high cliff, hanging onto ropes for support (see *Testimonies*, vol. 2, pp. 594-597). According to this account, we will dispose of our earthly possessions gradually. We will come to depend more and more on the Lord and less and less on the security offered by the world, until finally, our entire dependance will be on God.

God's people will see "every earthly support cut off" (*The Desire of Ages*, p. 121). We won't be able to spend so much as a dime for the bare necessities of life—food, clothing, and a roof over our heads. Because of the decree against buying and selling (see Revelation 13:17), our money will be worthless. We won't have the protection of the law. Our communities will become unsafe places for us to live. To the world it will appear that our situation is hopeless. And, from a human point of view, that will be true. I believe that the language of a short phrase in Daniel 12:7 describes the circumstances of God's people at that critical time: "When the power of the holy people has been finally broken, all these things will be completed."

Yet God will not leave us alone:

One who sees their every weakness, who is acquainted with every trial, is above all earthly powers; and angels will come to them in lonely cells, bringing light and peace from heaven. The prison will be as a palace; for the rich in faith dwell there, and the gloomy walls will be lighted up with heavenly light as when Paul and Silas prayed and sang praises at midnight in the Philippian dungeon (*The Great Controversy*, p. 627).

That God who cared for Elijah will not pass by one of His self-sacrificing children. He who numbers the hairs of their head will care for them, and in time of famine they shall be satisfied. While the wicked are dying from hunger and pestilence, angels will shield the righteous and supply their wants (ibid., p. 629).

How shall we stand?

I believe that peer pressure will be our greatest temptation in that day when the world is ridiculing us and threatening us with death. When all the world scoffs at this little band of people who think they are the only ones who are right, the only ones who have God's favor, it will be extremely easy to believe that the majority is right and that we really are quite foolish to maintain such an extreme, independent stand.

So how will we stand under those circumstances? The same way Jesus did.

Several years ago I spent the better part of six months studying the closing hours of Christ's life on this earth, beginning with His arrest in Gethsemane. Time after time I was struck with the fact that Christ had a completely different understanding of what was really going on than any of the people around Him. I'd like to examine briefly with you the two views of "reality" as seen by different people in the judgment halls of Caiaphas and Pilate and at the cross.

The majority view. The Jewish leaders had been trying for months to bring Christ under their control, and now they had Him in their grasp. They had the upper hand, and they were determined to keep it.

The Roman officials, including the soldiers, saw Jesus as a pitiful human being who found Himself in the wrong place at the wrong time. It was patently clear who was going to win this power struggle—and who was going to lose. The Jewish leaders were quite willing to sacrifice Christ to protect their own power.

As the world saw it, Jesus was a fool. He was wrong, and soon He would literally be "dead" wrong. They had won; He had lost. From a human point of view, that was reality.

Christ's view. But Jesus didn't look at matters from a human point of view. Jesus recognized issues that were invisible to human eyes. Jesus understood that a greater battle was going on than could be seen with the eyes and heard with the ears. Jesus knew of a vast universe out there of which human beings had no notion whatsoever. And to Him, that universal view was far more important than the visible conflict taking place around Him in Jerusalem.

Even more important, Jesus understood His role in that universal conflict. He knew who He was—the Saviour of the world, the One who would vindicate God against Satan's charges, the One who would establish the universal government of God throughout eternity.

Several times during those dark hours, Jesus said things that give us a glimpse into His understanding of the issues. When the mob came to arrest Him, one of the disciples raised his sword. But Jesus said, "Put your sword back in its place. . . . Do you think I cannot call on my Father, and he will at once put at my disposal more than twelve legions of angels? But how then would the Scriptures be fulfilled that say it must happen this way?" (Matthew 26:52-54).

When the high priest placed Jesus under oath and demanded to know whether He claimed to be the Son of God, Jesus replied, "Yes, it is as you say. . . . But I say to all of you: In the future you will see the Son of Man sitting at the right hand of the Mighty One and coming on the clouds of heaven" (Matthew 26:64).

Twice Jesus revealed to Pilate His understanding of the universal nature of the conflict in which they were both engaged. On one occasion Pilate said to Him, "Are you the king of the Jews?"

Jesus said, "My kingdom is not of this world. If it were, my servants would fight to prevent my arrest by the Jews. But now my kingdom is from another place" (John 18:33, 36).

Later, when Jesus refused to talk, Pilate said, "Don't you realize that I have power either to free you or to crucify you?"

Pilate was speaking from his point of view, from the human point of view that said, "I'm in charge here. This Man is under my control. He's one against the crowd, and the crowd will win" (see John 19:10).

But Jesus revealed the broader issue to the Roman governor. "You would have no power over me," He said, "if it were not given to you from above" (verse 11).

The time of trouble will be for you and me what Christ's trial before the Sanhedrin and Pilate was to Him. It will be a time when we will be involved in a universal conflict that far transcends the conflict on earth that we can see and hear and feel. And the same thing that gave Jesus the victory will give us the victory: absolute certainty regarding that wider conflict and our role in it.

Jesus knew beyond a shadow of a doubt that He was the Son of God, the Saviour of the world, and the One whom God had appointed to establish the government of heaven throughout the universe for all eternity. He revealed a small bit of this information to the high priest, but the Jewish leader absolutely rejected Christ's interpretation of who He was and what was going on. He rent his clothes, scoffed at what Jesus said, and proclaimed Him a blasphemer.

To all human appearances, the high priest was right and Jesus was wrong. Jesus had only His faith to go on—faith in whom God had told Him He was and what His mission was.

During the time of trouble, you and I will be on God's side in earth's final battle against the universe. But that won't be obvious to human eyes and ears and skin. The world will say, "We're in control here. We've got these people under our thumb, and we aren't about to let them go."

For us, the issue at that time will be whether to believe the obvious or to believe what God has revealed to us about ourselves:

The dragon was wroth with the woman, and went to make war with the remnant of her seed, which keep the commandments of God, and have the testimony of Jesus Christ (Revelation 12:17, KJV).

When the whole visible world shouts us down, jeers at us, and tells us we're stupid religious bigots, will we continue to believe that we are God's remnant? In spite of appearances, will we keep uppermost in our minds that a great controversy is going on between Christ and Satan, between Christ's followers and Satan's followers, and that Christ has called us to be on His side even though for a brief moment we seem to be pawns in the hands of His enemies?

Believe me, at that time a merciless world is going to shove the 1844 Disappointment down our throats the same way a merciless crowd shoved Christ's virgin birth down His throat. And the issue will be, Do we believe them, or do we believe that we are who God through Scripture and His modern-day prophet has told us we are—heaven's end-time people with an end-time mission akin to that of Elijah and John the Baptist?

I would like to remind you of a statement Ellen White made early in her ministry:

> While I was praying at the family altar, the Holy Ghost fell upon me, and I seemed to be rising higher and higher, far above the dark world. I turned to look for the Advent people in the world, but could not find them, when a voice said to me, "Look again, and look a little higher." At this I raised my eyes, and saw a straight and narrow path, cast up high above the world. On this path the Advent people were traveling to the city, which was at the farther end of the path. They had a bright light set up behind them at the beginning of the path, which an angel told me was the midnight cry. This light shone all along the path and gave light for their feet so that they might not stumble. *If they kept their eyes fixed on Jesus, who was just before them, leading them to the city, they were safe.* But soon some grew weary, and said the city was a great way off, and they expected to have entered it before. Then Jesus would encourage them by raising His glorious right arm, and from His arm came a light which waved over the Advent band, and they shouted, "Alleluia!" Others rashly denied the light behind them and said that it was not God that had led them out so far. The light behind them went out, leaving their feet in perfect darkness, and they stumbled and lost sight of

the mark and of Jesus, and fell off the path down into the dark and wicked world below (*Early Writings*, pp. 14, 15, emphasis supplied).

The people on the path represent God's final movement on earth, and the light behind them represents the midnight cry—the movement that led up to the 1844 Disappointment. The issue for the people in Ellen White's day was whether to believe that Jesus had led in the movement that appeared to have ended so disastrously on October 22, 1844. If they kept their eyes on Jesus as the leader in that movement, then the light of the movement illuminated the path all the way to the city—to the second coming of Christ. But if they took their eyes off Jesus, if they lost sight of who He had called them to be and their mission to the world, then the light behind them went out, and they fell from the path to the dark world below.

The issue for you and me in earth's darkest hour will be exactly the same. Will we keep our eyes on Jesus? Will we believe that we really are His end-time people? Will we view the conflict from the perspective of the visible or the invisible?

Keeping our relationship with Jesus in earth's darkest hour will mean keeping in our minds the universal point of view that Jesus held in His mind during His darkest hour. That kind of confidence will not suddenly appear in our minds at the moment we need it. We must be developing it now, cultivating it now, and teaching it now. Then we will have it in earth's darkest hour, and it will give us the victory God has promised over the beast and his image, over those who worship the beast, receive his mark, and take his name (see Revelation 15:2).

20

The Time of Jacob's Trouble

Even God's people will not know when probation closes. However, I believe that shortly after it closes, we will begin to suspect that it has happened, because we will see the seven last plagues falling. When a disease—the Bible says it will be a skin sore (see Revelation 16:2)—begins to afflict the entire world except for us, I am sure we will ask ourselves, "Has probation closed?" And when the universal death decree goes forth, we will know that probation has indeed closed. That will also mark the beginning of the time of Jacob's trouble:

A decree will finally be issued against those who hallow the Sabbath of the fourth commandment, denouncing them as deserving of the severest punishment and giving the people liberty, after a certain time, to put them to death. Romanism in the Old World and apostate Protestantism in the New will pursue a similar course toward those who honor all the divine precepts.

The people of God will then be plunged into those scenes of affliction and distress described by the prophet as the time of Jacob's trouble (*The Great Controversy*, pp. 615, 616).

Adventists have always distinguished between the great time of trouble and the time of Jacob's trouble. The whole world will experience the time of trouble, including God's people (though

215

the seven last plagues will afflict only the wicked). However, the time of Jacob's trouble will be a unique experience for God's people only. It will be our spiritual experience after the close of probation.

Before we get into a discussion of that experience, perhaps we should identify as precisely as possible when it will occur. In the statement quoted above Ellen White says that the universal death decree will precipitate the time of Jacob's trouble. The death decree will be enacted prior to the third plague, since the third plague will be a punishment for the death decree. Here is the evidence for that conclusion:

> Terrible as these inflictions are [the first and second plagues], God's justice stands fully vindicated. The angel of God declares: "Thou art righteous, O Lord, . . . because Thou hast judged thus. For they have shed the blood of saints and prophets, and Thou hast given them blood to drink; for they are worthy." Revelation 16:2-6. By condemning the people of God to death, they have as truly incurred the guilt of their blood as if it had been shed by their own hands (ibid., p. 628).

From this I conclude that the death decree will be proclaimed no later than at the end of the second plague, and the time of Jacob's trouble will begin immediately after that. Since Christ's second coming will deliver God's people from the power of the wicked, the time of Jacob's trouble will end at that time.[1] We can diagram it like this:

Close of probation		Death decree	Time of Jacob's trouble				Second coming
1	2	3	4	5	6	7	
TIME OF TROUBLE							

---

1. See appendix at the end of this chapter.

Notice that, according to this diagram, the time of Jacob's trouble ends at the beginning of the seventh plague. That's because I believe the seventh plague is the second coming of Christ and that the deliverance of God's people from the power of the wicked will take place at the beginning of that plague. I will explain this further in the chapter on the second coming.

Adventists did not invent the expression "the time of Jacob's trouble." It comes from the Old Testament prophet Jeremiah. Jeremiah probably had in mind the impending destruction of Jerusalem when he wrote the following words, yet there is a clear end-time ring to them. The destruction of Jerusalem by the Babylonians is one of the most common biblical types of the end of the world, particularly in Revelation. Here are the words the Lord spoke to Jeremiah:

> Cries of fear are heard—terror, not peace.
> Ask and see: Can a man bear children?
> Then why do I see every strong man with his hands
>   on his stomach like a woman in labor, every face
>   turned deathly pale?
> How awful that day will be!
> None will be like it.
> It will be a time of trouble for Jacob,
>   but he will be saved out of it (Jeremiah 30:5-7).

Jacob was one of God's most famous patriarchs in the Old Testament. Of all people, we would certainly expect that he, along with Abraham and Isaac, will be saved in God's eternal kingdom. In this passage Jeremiah makes Jacob a type of God's people who will pass through the final time of trouble at the end of the world. The most important words in the passage above, at least as far as God's people are concerned, are found in the phrase, "But he will be saved out of it." God's people will have to live through the time of Jacob's trouble, but they will not be destroyed by it. They will be "saved out of it."

That's good news!

Why the time of *Jacob's* trouble?

But why call it "the time of *Jacob's* trouble"?

Ellen White compares Jacob's experience when he wrestled

with the angel on the bank of the Jabbok River with the experience of God's people during the time of trouble:

> Jacob's night of anguish, when he wrestled in prayer for deliverance from the hand of Esau (Genesis 32:24-30), represents the experience of God's people in the time of trouble (*The Great Controversy*, p. 616).

You will recall that many years earlier Jacob had obtained the birthright from his brother by fraud, and now, on his trip back to his homeland, he received word that Esau was coming after him with a band of armed men. Esau's anger at his brother for deceiving him still burned hot in his breast, and he intended to kill him.

Terrified, Jacob crossed the Jabbok River after dark the night before Esau was due to arrive and spent the entire night in prayer. Ellen White describes the scene:

> He confesses his sin and gratefully acknowledges the mercy of God toward him while with deep humiliation he pleads the covenant made with his fathers and the promises to himself in the night vision at Bethel and in the land of his exile. The crisis of his life has come; everything is at stake. In the darkness and solitude he continues praying and humbling himself before God (ibid., pp. 616, 617).

Jacob was under a death threat from Esau, just as we will be under a death threat from the enemies of God. And just as Jacob was conscious of his sin against his brother, so we will be conscious of the sinfulness of our lives, particularly in view of the fact that we will know probation has closed and there is no Mediator in the heavenly sanctuary.

Furthermore, Satan, always "the accuser of our brethren" (Revelation 12:10, KJV), will be on hand to make our feeling of unworthiness even greater:

> As Satan accuses the people of God on account of their sins, the Lord permits him to try them to the uttermost. . . . They are fully conscious of their weakness and unworthiness. Satan endeavors to terrify them with the thought that

their cases are hopeless, that the stain of their defilement will never be washed away. He hopes so to destroy their faith that they will yield to his temptations and turn from their allegiance to God (ibid., pp. 618, 619).

Preparing for the time of Jacob's trouble

This brings us to one of the most crucial aspects of Adventist eschatology—an issue we simply *must* understand correctly as we anticipate earth's darkest hour between the close of probation and the second coming of Christ. I believe God has given us advance information about that time so that we can begin preparing for it now. I see two primary ways in which we need to be preparing.

Confession of sin. The first is confession of sin. Earlier in this book, in the chapter "Preparing to Receive the Latter Rain," I took several pages to discuss confession—both its importance and how to do it. If you skipped that chapter, I urge you to go back and read it now.

Known sin cannot be forgiven until it is confessed. The apostle John wrote, "If we *confess* our sins, he is faithful and just and will forgive us our sins and purify us from all unrighteousness" (1 John 1:9, emphasis supplied). Furthermore, no sin can be forgiven unless Jesus, our Mediator in the heavenly sanctuary, is on hand to grant that forgiveness. John said, "My dear children, I write this to you so that you will not sin. But if anybody does sin, we have one who speaks to the Father in our defense—Jesus Christ, the Righteous One" (1 John 2:1).

That's why it's so important that we confess all our sins now, while there is still a Mediator in the heavenly sanctuary. If we postpone confession until after the close of probation, forgiveness will be impossible to obtain:

> All who endeavor to excuse or conceal their sins, and permit them to remain upon the books of heaven, unconfessed and unforgiven, will be overcome by Satan. . . . Those who delay a preparation for the day of God cannot obtain it in the time of trouble or at any subsequent time. The case of all such is hopeless (ibid., p. 620).

Please note that these warnings refer to known sins that we have been unwilling to acknowledge and confess. This does not mean that we will be lost if we cannot recall every instance of wrongdoing.

Understanding righteousness by faith. During the time of Jacob's trouble it will also be absolutely essential that we have a clear understanding of the difference between justification and sanctification. If you read the chapter "The Spiritual Experience of the 144,000," you will recall the following chart:

Christian life begins ASSURANCE		Christian life ends MATURITY
	The robe of Christ's righteousness Christ's character in place of my character	
	Christ and I are developing my character	
My sins are covered; Christ's character given to me		My sins are conquered; Christ's character developed in me

It is crucial to understand that our standing with God after the close of probation—our assurance of salvation during the time of trouble—will be grounded on exactly the same foundation as it is today: justification, not sanctification. I have said a great deal in this book about the importance of Christians developing a perfect character in order to live without a Mediator during the time of trouble. Ellen White is very emphatic on this point. And here, unfortunately, is where many Seventh-day Adventists have gotten themselves off track. They think that justification provides our standing with God *before* probation closes, but that sanctification—a perfect character—must provide our standing with God *after* probation closes.

That is totally false! It is a deception that will cause you untold grief and unnecessary spiritual anguish during the time of trouble. Satan would like nothing better than for you to believe that lie.

I urge you to read through the chapter "The Time of Trouble" in *The Great Controversy* and notice that not once does Ellen White say that character perfection will be the basis for our assurance of salvation during that time. The basis for assurance then will be exactly what it is now: repentance and confession of sin, and faith in the blood of Jesus to forgive those sins. Please notice:

> Had not Jacob previously repented of his sin in obtaining the birthright by fraud, God would not have heard his prayer and mercifully preserved his life. So, in the time of trouble, if the people of God had unconfessed sins to appear before them while tortured with fear and anguish, they would be overwhelmed; despair would cut off their faith, and they could not have confidence to plead with God for deliverance. But while they have a deep sense of their unworthiness, *they have no concealed wrongs to reveal.* Their sins have gone beforehand to judgment and have been blotted out, and they cannot bring them to remembrance (*The Great Controversy*, p. 620, emphasis supplied).

When we stand before God during the time of Jacob's trouble, we must plead His righteousness to cover our confessed sins the same way we do now, and that will be our assurance of salvation then just as it is now.

Then why perfection?

Why, then, you may wonder, do both Ellen White and Scripture stress perfection of character so emphatically as a preparation for the end time?

That's a good question, and I will give two answers.

First, the time of trouble will be the most traumatic period ever to take place in earth's history. The judgments of God will be in the land, but even more important for God's people, Satan and the wicked will be doing their very best to destroy us. The wicked will be trying to destroy us physically, and Satan will be trying to destroy us spiritually. Every earthly support will be cut off. We will have to depend on God to provide the very food we put in our mouths and the shelter over our heads. Such a time will require a faith that cannot faint the way the faith of the children of Israel fainted in the wilderness. And that will require an extremely high level of character development.

Second, after the close of probation there will be no Mediator in the heavenly sanctuary to forgive sins that we might commit during the time of trouble. At first, this may seem to be the same thing as saying that our standing with God will depend on our good character rather than on our faith in Christ's righteousness to cover our sins. However, please keep a couple of things in mind.

First, for myself, I do not intend to waste time worrying whether I'm "good enough" during the time of trouble any more than I'm going to waste time worrying about it now. Earlier in this book, the chapter "Preparing for the Close of Probation" made it very clear that we have no way of knowing whether we are "good enough" for the close of probation, and therefore we should not worry about it now. Once we do our part—and I explained very clearly what that is—then making sure we are ready for the close of probation is God's problem, not ours. *He will not close probation until each of His children is ready.* That is a confidence we should maintain just as much after the close of probation as before.

Second, the seal of God, whatever it is, will "close up" our characters so that they cannot be changed. The seal of God will protect us from committing any act during that time that would jeopardize our standing with God. Remember that at the close of probation Jesus will say, "He that is righteous, let him be righteous still: and he that is holy, let him be holy still" (Revelation 22:11, KJV). That's a promise. If you're sealed, *you will not sin during that time*, so don't worry about it.

Ellen White points out that the great struggle in the minds of God's people during the time of Jacob's trouble will be whether they have confessed every sin, not whether they are perfect (see the quotation from *The Great Controversy*, p. 620, given earlier in this chapter).

And that, of course, brings us to another great fear that Adventists have today about the close of probation and living during the time of trouble without a Mediator: Suppose that probation closes and *then* I discover a sin that I have failed to confess. What then? Let me assure you, there is a perfectly good answer to that question.

Right now, before the close of probation, the Holy Spirit knows every sin that you and I need to confess. Furthermore, it's His business to convict us of them. If we've forgotten some sin, He has ways of which we know nothing for bringing it to our attention. As long as you and I faithfully maintain our relationship with Jesus now, we can rest assured that He will not allow probation to close without convicting us of every sin that needs confessing, and doing so in time for us to make it right long before probation closes. If He doesn't reveal it before the close of probation, then you and I don't need to know it. For those who are truly God's children, there will be no such thing as discovering an unconfessed sin after the close of probation.

If the people of God had unconfessed sins to appear before them while tortured with fear and anguish, they would be overwhelmed. . . . But while they have a deep sense of their unworthiness, *they have no concealed wrongs to reveal*. Their sins have gone beforehand to judgment and have been blotted out, and they cannot bring them to remembrance (*The Great Controversy*, p. 620, emphasis supplied).

Notice that God's people will "have no concealed wrongs to reveal." Why? Because God revealed all those sins to them before probation closed and they confessed them—"sent them beforehand to judgment." God will see to it that you and I have that experience, and He will see to it that we have it in time.

A demonstration of perfection?

Before closing this chapter on the spiritual struggle of God's people during the time of trouble, I want to bring up one more point that I believe has caused some Seventh-day Adventists undue concern. I am aware that what I say next will challenge an idea that some of us cherish deeply, but I am convinced that we cherish it dangerously, if not wrongly.

I refer to what I call the "demonstration model" of the time of Jacob's trouble.

By "demonstration model," I mean the idea that during the time of trouble, God's people will be models of absolute perfection to the universe. During the entire history of the world, no human being other than Christ has ever lived a perfect life. No one but

Jesus has ever kept the law of God absolutely perfectly over an extended period of time, particularly under severe duress. But Jesus cannot return, so this line of reasoning goes, until He has a whole community of saints so absolutely perfect that they can demonstrate to the universe that God's law can be kept, even during the greatest time of trouble the world has ever known. The integrity of God's law is at stake, we are told. The question is: Can humanity keep the law or can't they? God says Yes. Satan says No. The saints during the time of trouble vindicate God by proving that His law can be kept, even by sinful human beings.

I have three problems with this theology. First, I believe it can very easily lead to spiritual pride, an attitude that says, "Hey, everybody out there, look at me. *I'm* going to vindicate God! *I'm* going to prove to the universe that *I* can keep His law."

I'm not saying that God's people won't in some way be a demonstration to the universe. We probably will be. I just don't think we'll be all that conscious of it. Satan challenged God about Job, and Job demonstrated to the universe that God was right and Satan was wrong, *but Job had no idea that that was the issue in his suffering*.

My second problem has to do with the strong emphasis on absolute perfection that almost invariably goes along with the demonstration model. Some people almost become angry with anyone who does not believe in absolute perfection after the close of probation. I used to cringe whenever I was asked if I believed absolute perfection is possible, because I knew that if I said No, my questioiner would think I was a heretic. However, I am no longer afraid of that question, because it has such a simple answer. The answer comes from an earlier chapter in this book called "Preparing for the Close of Probation." In that chapter I put the following words in boldface type: "We don't know what perfection is or how to get there, but when we do our part, God is responsible for getting us there."

My answer now, whenever I'm asked if I believe in absolute perfection after the close of probation, is this: I don't know what absolute perfection is. I can't define it. Even if absolute perfection is God's desire for me, there is no way I or any other human being can know when we've reached that state. Therefore, it's not a question any of us should be concerned about, and it's certainly not a question we should use as a test of orthdoxy.

If God has absolute perfection planned for you and me during the time of trouble, that's fine with me. He will make us absolutely perfect, and He'll do it on time. If God doesn't have absolute perfection planned for us during that time, that's His business. All I know is that once you and I are willing to let God control our lives, getting us to whatever level of perfection He knows we need is up to Him. He'll know when we're good enough, and He won't close probation on any of us until we are ready. Whether our readiness for the close of probation means absolute or partial perfection is a problem for God to settle, not you or me. I refuse to debate the issue, because it's impossible to debate something no one can define.

My third problem with the "demonstration model" of God's people during the time of trouble is theological. I thought *Jesus* proved to the universe that God's law can be kept. I thought *Jesus* proved false Satan's claim that fallen humanity cannot keep it. In fact, if I'm not mistaken, the same people who believe in the "demonstration model" of the time of trouble also insist that Jesus had a sinful nature identical to yours and mine in order that He could demonstrate that sinful human flesh can keep God's law. But if Jesus has already demonstrated the point, why will God's people have to do so again during the time of trouble? Or was Jesus not quite enough like you and me to demonstrate the point adequately?

It seems to me that the "demonstration model," at least as I've heard it explained, transfers to you and me the work that Christ has already accomplished. I have a real problem with that.

God called the Israelites out of Egypt and told them that they were His unique people with a special mission to the world. That was easy to believe when the plagues delivered them from Egypt and tough to believe when they had the Red Sea before them, mountains on either side, and an Egyptian army bent on vengeance behind them. But God delivered them.

Yet only a few days later, when they were faced with the threat of perishing from thirst, they forgot all about God and started complaining. And a few days after that, when they seemed about to die of starvation, they complained about that. Every time the Israelites encountered another trial, they completely lost their faith in who God had called them to be. God led them through the wilderness on the way to the promised land, but when the going got tough, they accused Moses of bringing the unfortunate circumstances and wished they were back in Egypt (see Numbers 14:1-4; 21:5).

God will lead us through "the wilderness" too, on the way to our "promised land." The trials in our wilderness, after the close of probation, will be far more severe than anything Israel ever thought about, but we must have patience and a strength of faith that they did not have. We cannot, during that time, allow impatience to cause us to complain, nor can we allow our faith to grow weary, regardless of the intensity of our suffering. That's why God's people at that time will need a strength of character that is rarely seen in the world today. We must learn to overcome all complaining now, before the close of probation, or we will never make it through the time of trouble then.

The chief issue in the final conflict, it seems to me, will be faith, not obedience. If we have the faith, we will have the obedience. The Israelites disobeyed because they disbelieved. I don't think we'll feel much like models of anything during that time. Yet when we get to heaven we may well discover that we were models of everything.

I believe that two questions confront you and me as we look forward to the time of trouble:

1. Are we developing a relationship with Jesus now that can endure weariness and pain and delay during earth's darkest hour? Are we developing a faith in Him now that can stay intact even when every visible, human means for supporting life is removed?
2. Are we maintaining our experience of justification? Are we coming to Him day by day, asking Him to convict us of the sins we need to confess? And when He reveals them to us, are we coming to Him for the transformation of heart that is required to confess even the ones we think we can't possibly confess?

I can assure you that those who develop this kind of relationship with Jesus will be "good enough" to live beyond the close of probation in earth's darkest hour.

Appendix to chapter 20

Some Adventists have said that the time of Jacob's trouble extends only through the third and fourth plagues and ends at the beginning of the fifth. You will recall that the fifth plague is a great darkness that falls on the seat of the beast (see Revelation 16:10). The conclusion that the fifth plague marks the end of the time of Jacob's trouble is based on the following statement in *The Great Controversy* from the chapter, "God's People Delivered":

When the protection of human laws shall be withdrawn from those who honor the law of God, there will be, in different lands, a simultaneous movement for their destruction. As the time appointed in the decree draws near, the people will conspire to root out the hated sect. It will be determined to strike in one night a decisive blow, which shall utterly silence the voice of dissent and reproof.

The people of God—some in prison cells, some hidden in solitary retreats in the forests and mountains—still plead for divine protection, while in every quarter companies of armed men, urged on by hosts of evil angels, are preparing for the work of death. It is now, in the hour of utmost extremity, that the God of Israel will interpose for the deliverance of His chosen. . . .

With shouts of triumph, jeering, and imprecation, throngs of evil men are about to rush upon their prey, when, lo, a dense blackness, deeper than the darkness of the night, falls upon the earth. Then a rainbow, shining with the glory from the throne of God, spans the heavens and seems to encircle each praying company. The angry multitudes are suddenly arrested. Their mocking cries die away. The objects of their murderous rage are forgotten. With fearful forebodings they gaze upon the symbol of God's covenant and long to be shielded from its overpowering brightness (*The Great Controversy*, pp. 635, 636).

I agree that this statement shows us the end of the time of Jacob's trouble, for it begins with the wicked threatening to destroy the righteous and God's people pleading with Him for divine protection. Those who see this as the time of the fifth plague call attention to the words "A dense blackness, deeper than the darkness of the night, falls upon the earth." They associate this darkness with the darkness of the fifth plague.

I disagree with this view for two reasons. First, the darkness under the fifth plague falls only on the seat of the beast, whereas the darkness Ellen White describes covers the whole earth. Even more significant is the fact that Ellen White's darkness arrests the multitudes. "The objects of their murderous rage are forgotten. With fearful forebodings they gaze upon the symbol of God's covenant and long to be shielded from its overpowering brightness." From this point on in *The Great Controversy*, there is not the slightest hint that the wicked continue to fight against God. But in Revelation 16, earth's final battle between God and the wicked world has yet to occur when the fifth plague is poured out.

21

The Battle of Armageddon

Few biblical images are more widely known in today's secular culture than the Battle of Armageddon. Few images from the Bible stir the Christian imagination more. And few subjects have created more controversy over a longer time in the 150-year history of the Seventh-day Adventist Church than Armageddon.

Most Adventists today probably do not realize that during the first seventy years of our church's existence, most of our pastors, administrators, evangelists, and Bible teachers believed that the fall of Turkey, or the Ottoman Empire, as it was then called, would be the great sign that Christ's second coming was near. Most believed that Armageddon would be a physical battle between Turkey and the Christian nations of the world. To the day of his death, Uriah Smith was the foremost champion of this view in our church.

While the majority of Adventist leaders held to Smith's view, a minority, including James White (until his death in 1881), taught that Armageddon would be a spiritual battle between the forces of good and evil in the world. And that's what caused the controversy. Would Armageddon be a physical battle or a spiritual battle? Most insisted that it would be a physical battle. A few insisted it would be a spiritual battle.

Those who insisted on the "physical battle" model of Armageddon believed it would be a battle between opposing nations on the earth. The difficulty was to figure out which nations would be on one side and which would be on the other.

Smith can be glad he was not alive in the years during and after World War I. At that time the Ottoman Empire was dismantled, but of course there was no Battle of Armageddon, and Christ failed to return. Smith was spared the agony of attending the burial of his interpretation.

You'd think the demise of Smith's view would have meant the resurgence of the "spiritual battle" point of view regarding Armageddon. Instead, a new slant on the "physical battle" interpretation came to the front. Along about the turn of the century, as Japan became a force to reckon with in the world, the notion spread through Adventism that Armageddon would be a battle between the East and the West. After all, didn't Revelation 16:12 say that the Euphrates river would dry up "to prepare the way for the kings of the East"? Suddenly a new flash of "light" burst upon Adventist theology: If the kings of the East will be on one side, the "kings of the West" must be on the other side.

The only thing new about this view, of course, was a change in which nations would be on each side. The idea that Armageddon would be a physical battle between nations on earth was stronger than ever. You can well imagine that Armageddon fever reached another peak when Japan attacked Pearl Harbor. (Though, to their credit, with the memory fairly fresh in their minds of the embarrassing fall of the Ottoman Empire without the anticipated Battle of Armageddon, Adventist evangelists during World War II were more restrained in their proclamations about the future of Japan.)

The fall of Japan in 1945 finally laid to rest the "physical battle" view of Armageddon. Today, fifty years later, it is little more than a relic in the museum of Adventist theological history.

The Bible and Armageddon

What does the Bible say about Armageddon? Does Scripture suggest that it will be a battle between opposing forces on the earth? To reach that conclusion, one has to restrict his search to Revelation 16:12-16, which describes the sixth plague. When we extend our search for evidence about earth's final battle to chapters 17 and 19 we see a much different picture.

Revelation 17. I pointed out in a previous chapter that Revelation 17 describes the religious and political forces of evil in the world after the close of probation. Revelation 17 opens with a description of a harlot sitting on a scarlet-colored beast, symbolizing an illicit union of church and state. We have already seen that there is a clear trend in the United States today toward church-state union. Revelation 17 shows us that trend in its completed form all over the world.

The beast has ten horns, and verse 12 says these horns are ten kings. Some people speculate that the horns represent the nations of Western Europe, which as of this writing are planning an economic union in 1992, with the hope of eventually establishing a political union. I am more inclined to think that the ten horns represent all the major political powers of the world, and that we need not look for exactly ten nations. Their number is not as important as their prominence in world affairs.

Revelation 17 says that these ten horns will join the beast in a battle:

> The ten horns you saw are ten kings who have not yet received a kingdom, but who for one hour will receive authority as kings along with the beast. They have one purpose and will give their power and authority to the beast. They will make war against the Lamb, but the Lamb will overcome them because he is Lord of lords and King of kings—and with him will be his called, chosen and faithful followers (Revelation 17:12-14).

Since this is a description of earth's final battle, it must refer to Armageddon, even if it doesn't call it by that name.

Now let's identify the forces on each side in this battle. Revelation 17:13 says that the ten horns "have one purpose and will give their power and authority to the beast." Obviously, the ten horns are not fighting among themselves, because they "have one purpose." And they will not fight against the beast, because they "give their power and authority to the beast." So the ten horns and the beast, representing earth's combined religious and military might, will unite to "make war against the Lamb." Since the Lamb's "called, chosen and faithful followers" will be "with him" (verse 14), we know that Christ's people on earth, and also the angels in heaven, will be a part of His great army.

Now let me ask you, according to Revelation 17, will Armageddon be a physical battle between opposing nations on earth, or will all of the world's nations be lined up on one side against Christ and His people on the other?

And whom does Revelation say will win this battle? "The Lamb will overcome them because he is Lord of lords and King of kings" (verse 14).

Revelation 19. Revelation 19 also describes earth's final battle. This time we see Jesus riding out of heaven on a white horse, and with Him are the armies of heaven, also riding white horses (see verses 11-14). And who does Revelation say Jesus will engage in battle?

> Out of his mouth comes a sharp sword with which to strike down the nations. "He will rule them with an iron scepter." . . . On his robe and on his thigh he has this name written: KING OF KINGS AND LORD OF LORDS (Revelation 19:15, 16).

Again, we see that earth's final battle—the Battle of Armageddon—will be fought between heaven's forces on one side and all of earth's nations united against Him on the other.

To underscore the point, when the battle is over, an angel stands in the sun and cries to the birds of prey:

> Come, gather together for the great supper of God, so that you may eat the flesh of kings, generals, and mighty men, of horses and their riders, and the flesh of all people, free and slave, small and great (Revelation 19:17, 18).

Notice that the angel calls the birds of prey to devour the flesh of military leaders and horses. This is battle. Earth's final battle. Armageddon.

And that isn't all. Please read on:

> Then I saw the beast and the kings of the earth and their armies gathered together to make war against the rider on the horse and his army. But the beast was captured, and with him the false prophet. . . . The two of them were thrown alive into the fiery lake of burning sulphur. The rest of them [the kings and military leaders] were killed with the sword that came out of the mouth of the rider on the

horse, and all the birds gorged themselves on their flesh (verses 19-21).

Words simply could not be more plain. The two sides in earth's final battle will not be opposing nations on earth. Armageddon will be God and His people on one side against the entire world—Satan and his people—on the other. And the world will be defeated. Revelation says that all evil human powers will either be "thrown alive into the fiery lake of burning sulphur" or "killed with the sword" (Revelation 19:20, 21). Satan will be bound in the Abyss for 1,000 years (see Revelation 20:1-3), after which he too will be thrown into the lake of fire (see Revelation 20:10).

This is the broad view of the universal conflict between good and evil that you and I must understand in order to keep our relationship with Jesus in earth's darkest hour, when to everyone else's eyes and ears it will appear that God's people are a tiny, bigoted minority that are doomed to lose.

Ellen White and Armageddon

The *Comprehensive Index to the Writings of Ellen G. White* gives only five references under the heading "Armageddon," and in one of these she refers to the battle without using the word. However, this does not mean that she had little to say about Armageddon. She just didn't always refer to it by that name. She more often spoke of it as "the final conflict," "the battle of the great day of God Almighty," "the last struggle," etc. The question is, did Ellen White understand Armageddon to be a battle between nations on earth, with half the world's nations lined up on one side against the other half on the other side? Or did she think of it as a battle between good and evil?

A spiritual battle. The following statement is typical of many that she made about the Battle of Armageddon and the final conflict:

Every form of evil is to spring into intense activity. Evil angels unite their powers with evil men, and as they have been in constant conflict and attained an experience in the best modes of deception and battle, and have been strengthening for centuries, they will not yield *the last great final contest* without a desperate struggle. All the world will be on one side or the other of the question. *The battle of Armageddon* will be fought, and that day must find none of us sleeping. Wide awake we must be, as wise virgins having oil in our vessels with our lamps. . . .

The power of the Holy Ghost must be upon us, and the Captain of the Lord's host will stand at the head of the angels of heaven to direct the battle (Ellen G. White Comments, *SDA Bible Commentary,* vol. 7, p. 982, emphasis supplied).

Ellen White wrote these words in 1890, when the notion that Armageddon would be a physical battle between Turkey and the world's Christian nations was at a fever pitch in Adventism. Yet she clearly ignored all of this and stated that it will be a spiritual battle between good and evil. In the first part of the statement she speaks of "every form of evil," "evil angels," and "evil men," and then she says that "they will not yield the last great final contest without a desperate struggle. . . . The battle of Armageddon will be fought." Near the end of the statement she says that "that day must find none of us [the righteous] sleeping," "the power of the Holy Ghost must be upon us," and "the Captain of the Lord's host will . . . direct the battle."

Clearly, the two sides in the conflict will be God's people and Satan's people, and "all the world will be on one side or the other of the question." There will be no fence sitters. The following two statements are equally unequivocal. One appears in *The Great Controversy*, which was first published in 1888, and the other was written in 1901:

The spirits of devils will go forth to the kings of the earth and to the whole world, to fasten them in deception, and urge them to unite with Satan in *his last struggle against the government of heaven* (*The Great Controversy*, p. 624, emphasis supplied).

Two great opposing powers are revealed in the last great battle. On one side stands the Creator of heaven and earth. All on His side bear His signet. They are obedient to His commandments. On the other side stands the prince of darkness, with those who have chosen apostasy and rebellion (Ellen G. White Comments, *SDA Bible Commentary,* vol. 7, pp. 982, 983).

Notice, in the first statement, that the conflict will be, not between nations on earth, but between Satan and his armies and the government of heaven. And in the second statement Ellen White clearly identifies the "two great opposing powers . . . in the last great battle." On one side "stands the Creator of heaven and earth," and on the other side, "the prince of darkness."

A battle of the nations. Some of Ellen White's statements seem to suggest that the nations of the world will play a part in the Battle of Armageddon:

> We are to see in history the fulfillment of prophecy, to study the workings of Providence in the great reformatory movements and to understand the progress of events in the marshaling of the nations for the final conflict of the great controversy (*The Ministry of Healing,* pp. 441, 442).

> The nations of the world are eager for conflict; but they are held in check by the angels. When this restraining power is removed, there will come a time of trouble and anguish. . . . All who have not the spirit of truth will unite under the leadership of satanic agencies. But they are to be kept under control till the time shall come for the great battle of Armageddon (Ellen G. White Comments, *SDA Bible Commentary,* vol. 7, p. 967).

> As yet the four winds are held until the servants of God shall be sealed in their foreheads. Then the powers of earth will marshal their forces for the last great battle (*Testimonies,* vol. 6, p. 14).

If we interpret these statements in light of the century-long Adventist controversy over whether Armageddon will be a physical battle between various nations of earth or a spiritual battle between good and evil, then in these statements Ellen White appears to support the physical battle point of view. However, when we understand what she said will be the role of the nations in the final conflict, the apparent contradiction disappears.

She does not mean that this will be a physical battle *between* nations, with half the world's nations lined up on one side against the other half on the other side. Rather, *all* of the world's nations will be on one side, against God's people, who are on the other side.

Where will Armageddon be fought? One of the questions that has kept students of Bible prophecy busy over the years is the location of the Battle of Armageddon. Where will it be fought? The answer depends on which view one adopts regarding the nature of the battle. And among those who espoused the "physical battle" point of view, the location depended on which nation or group of nations they thought would be involved. The favorite choice, of course, was the Valley of Megiddo in Israel, but other locations have had their day in Adventist history, including Jerusalem (Uriah Smith's view) and the United States (William Miller's view).

Ellen White made at least one statement about the location of the Battle of Armageddon that is entirely consistent with her view that it will be exclusively a spiritual battle, with the nations of the world against God's people:

> The earth is to be the battlefield—the scene of the final contest and the final victory (*My Life Today*, p. 308).

If Armageddon is to be a battle between the world's nations, then it would not make much sense to say that the entire world will be the battlefield. Nations usually fight over territory, and they usually gather for battle at the spot on earth over which they are fighting.

However, if Armageddon is to be a spiritual battle between all the world's nations on one side and God and His people on the other side, then Ellen White's statement that "the earth is to be the battlefield—the scene of the final conflict" makes good sense. God's people at that time will be found in every country of the world. Every nation will oppose God's people within its territory.

Why did we ignore Ellen White?

Adventists believe that Ellen White received the gift of prophecy, and during the entire century that we interpreted Armageddon primarily as a physical battle between nations, we followed her leadership in most areas of our church's life and teaching. Why, then, did we fail to recognize the obvious difference between what she said about Armageddon and what we were saying? Why did we ignore Ellen White—to say nothing of Scripture—for so long?

People who expect Jesus to come "very soon," as Adventists have since 1844, look anxiously for signs that His coming is near. Ever since William Miller, we have charted the history of the world through the rise and fall of nations in Daniel's prophecies, so it is only natural that we should try to chart our way through earth's end-time events by the rise and fall of modern nations. After all, this provides something quite visible on which to hang our hopes. And hope—anxiety might be a better word—we have had aplenty.

Spiritual realities, on the other hand, are not very visible. The "spiritual battle" view does not provide much of a "map" by which to locate our own day in the lineup of events leading to the second coming. Be the evidence ever so flimsy, and in retrospect ever so foolish, we are loath to give it up for the truth. It took us 100 years and the demise of two "physical battle" scenarios of Armageddon to give up that hook on which to hang our hopes.

I can't help but wonder if that may not be one of the changes God has been waiting for in order that He can come. Ellen White made it so clear that spiritual preparation *now* is absolutely essential if God's people are to survive the overwhelming challenges of the Battle of Armageddon. But people whose whole attention is fastened on evidences of a physical battle between nations are not nearly so likely to be making the necessary preparation for a spiritual battle.

Now that we have divested ourselves of the "physical battle" interpretation, the challenge for contemporary Adventists is not only to understand that Armageddon is a spiritual battle, but to prepare ourselves spiritually for it.

The real issue

Every Seventh-day Adventist understands the basic plot of the great controversy between Christ and Satan. Several millennia ago, when he was still in heaven, Satan refused to acknowledge that Jesus was the divine Son of God who rightfully held a higher position, closer to the Father, than he (Satan) did. In the first chapter of her book *Patriarchs and Prophets*, Ellen White describes the conflict that took place in heaven over this issue. Among other things, she said that God the Father called a meeting of all the created, intelligent beings in the universe. Here is her description of that meeting:

> The King of the universe summoned the heavenly hosts before Him, that in their presence He might set forth the true position of His Son and show the relation He sustained to all created beings. . . . Before the assembled inhabitants of heaven the King declared that none but Christ, the Only Begotten of God, could fully enter into His purposes, and to Him it was committed to execute the mighty counsels of His will. . . .
>
> The angels joyfully acknowledged the supremacy of Christ, and prostrating themselves before Him, poured out their love and adoration. Lucifer bowed with them, but in his heart there was a strange, fierce conflict (*Patriarchs and Prophets*, pp. 36, 37).

You know the story. Yielding to pride, Lucifer intensified his campaign against Christ. "Leaving His place in the immediate presence of the Father, Lucifer went forth to diffuse the spirit of discontent among the angels" (ibid., p. 37). The angels, and Christ Himself, tried to show Lucifer his error, but he refused to listen. Instead, "he persistently defended his own course, and fully committed himself to the great controversy against his Maker" (ibid., p. 40).

Cast into the earth, Satan succeeded in winning Adam and Eve to his side, and through them the entire human race. "Now I have a beachhead," he said to himself, "I will win the whole world to my side, and from this earth I can spread my rebellion to the entire universe." Satan assumed that Adam and Eve and their descendants were his assured followers forever.

However, God had a surprise in store for Satan. He intervened on behalf of the human race in a way that Satan had not anticipated. Jesus offered personally to pay the penalty for our sins and restore us to favor with God. In order to do that, He came to this earth to live and die as a man. Christ's encounter with Satan in the wilderness following His forty days of fasting and prayer was simply another face-to-face confrontation with His old foe in heaven. *The issue on the cross was who would win in the universal conflict between good and evil that had been going on for at least four thousand years.* That is the universal point of view that Jesus understood during His trial and crucifixion. He realized that yielding to the pressure of the visible conflict on this earth meant losing the conflict throughout the universe.

Now please notice the following statement by Ellen White about earth's final battle:

It is the purpose of Satan to cause them [God's people] to be blotted from the earth, in order that his supremacy of the world may not be disputed. (*Testimonies to Ministers*, p. 37).

That's what the battle of Armageddon is all about. It will be Satan's final effort before the second coming of Christ to keep the world in his clutches so that he can spread his rebellion to the rest of the universe. Already, science, with its advanced technology, is talking about space travel to other parts of the universe. If God were to allow it, today's human race would as literally try to build "a tower that reaches to the heavens, so that we may make a name for ourselves" (Genesis 11:4), as did the people shortly after the Flood. Our "tower," however, is not made of bricks and mortar, but of aluminum and steel, with engines to carry human beings to the distant planets and eventually to other galaxies.

That is the goal of today's modern space scientist. It is Satan's goal. But at the conclusion of the Battle of Armageddon (at which time Christ will come), God will put a stop to those plans as surely as lightning and the confusion of languages put a stop to the building of the tower of Babel (see Genesis 11:5-7; *Patriarchs and Prophets*, pp. 119, 120).

Reality of the final battle

While earth's final battle will be over spiritual issues, we must understand that it will be physical in a very real sense. Ellen White said that "the battles waging between the two armies are as real as those fought by the armies of this world" (*Prophets and Kings*, p. 176). Here is how she describes that reality:

I saw writing, copies of which were scattered in different parts of the land, giving orders that unless the saints should yield their peculiar faith, give up the Sabbath, and observe the first day of the week, the people were at liberty after a certain time to put them to death (*Early Writings*, pp. 282, 283).

I saw the saints suffering great mental anguish. They seemed to be surrounded by the wicked inhabitants of the earth. . . . Next came the multitude of the angry wicked . . . to slay the saints (ibid., p. 283).

The people of God—some in prison cells, some hidden in solitary retreats in the forests and the mountains—still plead for divine protection, while in every quarter companies of armed men, urged on by hosts of evil angels, are preparing for the work of death (*The Great Controversy*, p. 635).

That's real guns and bullets Ellen White is talking about. Armageddon may be a spiritual battle, but it's not going to be a public debate. I believe that Satan's forces will use the same kind of weapons in the Battle of Armageddon that the coalition of nations used against Iraq during Operation Desert Storm.

"Oh, come on," you say. "The coalition used battleships and tanks and laser-guided missiles during that war. Ellen White never said anything about that kind of weapons."

True enough. That kind of military hardware didn't exist in her day. So what weapons can we expect the world to use in its effort to enforce the death decree? Their bare hands? Given the space age in which we live, it is entirely plausible to imagine that when God's people are hiding in the rocks and the mountains, the enemy will use all of its spy satellites and heat-sensing technology to find us. I can also imagine that after locating each praying company, they will aim a guided missile straight at each one.

Am I being extreme, or am I merely interpreting the Battle of Armageddon in terms of today's military capability?

I'm sure you are aware of the space science fiction prevalent in today's motion picture and television films. You are also no doubt aware that today's scientists are spending millions of dollars each year in an effort to find out whether intelligent beings exist in other parts of the universe. I spoke about that earlier in this book.

I am convinced that before the end of time, scientists will establish that contact, and when Satan and his angels appear on this earth, they will present themselves as beings from another galaxy. You can call that high-tech spiritualism. These beings will be foremost in urging the world to destroy God's people, and I would like to suggest that as the end approaches, they will warn the world of an invasion from a "hostile alien race."

> I saw three evil spirits that looked like frogs; they came out of the mouth of the dragon, out of the mouth of the beast and out of the mouth of the false prophet. They are spirits of demons performing miraculous signs, *and they go out to the kings of the whole world, to gather them for the battle on the great day of God Almighty* (Revelation 16:13, 14, emphasis supplied).

Not only will Satan and his angels warn the world of a coming invasion from a hostile alien race; they will also help the world to prepare for the invasion. I find it entirely plausible to suppose that as Christ and His angels approach the earth, the world's military leaders will train their most sophisticated missiles with nuclear warheads toward the heavens in an effort to prevent His second coming.

Does that sound preposterous? The Bible tells us that "the kings of the earth and their armies gathered together to make war against the rider on the horse and his army" (Revelation 19:19). And where did the rider on the horse come from? "I saw heaven standing open and there before me was a white horse, whose rider is called Faithful and True" (Revelation 19:11).

Scripture literally says it: When Jesus comes from heaven to earth the second time, the world's kings and generals and their armies will go to war against Him. You don't think they'll use bows and arrows, do you? Or Civil War cannons? Believe me, they'll use the same sophisticated military hardware that we are familiar with today, along with whatever else Satan and his angels can help them to build.

Armageddon will be the star war of all star wars—Satan's last stand.

This will truly be earth's darkest hour. Far greater firepower than the world's nations brought against Iraq will be arrayed against God and His people. From a human point of view, our circumstances will be as hopeless as Christ's appeared to be at His trial and crucifixion. In one of the last verses describing the sixth plague, Revelation tells us what our only hope will be at that time:

> Behold, I come like a thief! Blessed is he who stays awake and keeps his clothes with him, so that he may not go naked and be shamefully exposed (Revelation 16:15).

In Jesus' darkest hour, when He hung on the cross, hope did not assure Him that He would rise from the tomb (see *The Desire of Ages*, p. 753). He simply *believed* that His Father would bring Him through. He cast His entire trust on His Father. That's all He could do.

Our only hope in earth's darkest hour will be to keep our relationship with Jesus. When our circumstances appear to be the most desperate, we must believe that He is on our side even though everything we see and hear tells us we are doomed. We must keep in view the wider conflict in the universe—the conflict going on beyond our eyes and ears. We must cling to our faith that God is in control of events and that He will soon deliver us. We must believe that against the God of the universe, all the sophisticated human instruments of warfare will be less bothersome than a toy gun. In Satan's final battle against Christ and His people, you and I can rest absolutely assured of victory, regardless of how impossible our situation may appear to be from a human point of view.

Maybe in heaven someday God will ask the author of Hebrews to update his faith chapter (see Hebrews 11). If He does, I'm sure it will include the names of those who kept their relationship with Jesus in earth's darkest hour.

I'd like to be a part of that list, wouldn't you?

CHAPTER
22
The Second Coming of Christ

I'm glad I wasn't an Iraqi soldier in Kuwait during Operation Desert Storm. American firepower was awesome. War means two sides throwing everything they've got against each other, and technology in the last fifty years has made "everything they've got" appalling.

Not only was American capability overwhelming; it was incessant. For the better part of a month, the coalition forces pounded the Iraqis on the ground every two hours. Those who survived wished they hadn't. The Iraqis found it extremely difficult to get food and water to their troops, and rest was next to impossible. Whenever a soldier did fall asleep, he was awakened within two hours by another barrage of bombing.

Deception was another strategy. Before their ground attack, the coalition allied against Iraq feigned a sea invasion that never happened, but which drew large chunks of the Iraqi military forces east to the gulf coast. The allied forces then penetrated Iraq by land west of Kuwait under cover of darkness.

These strategies worked. Awesome firepower, wearing down the enemy, and deception won the war with a minimum of coalition casualties.

Satan will use these same strategies in the Battle of Armageddon. During the time of trouble, he will apply his most cunning deceptions in his effort to seduce God's people. But we will have something the Iraqis did not—advance information about his falsehoods. Our advance information is found in the Bible. "So closely will the counterfeit resemble the true that it will be impossible to distinguish between them except by the Holy Scriptures" (*The Great Controversy*, p. 593).

Satan will also try to wear God's people down:

The beloved of God [will] pass weary days, bound in chains, shut in by prison bars, sentenced to be slain, some apparently left to die of starvation in dark and loathsome dungeons. No human ear is open to hear their moans; no human hand is ready to lend them help (ibid., p. 626).

Again, God's people will have something the Iraqi soldiers did not have: faith in One who has promised to deliver them. For "as they endeavor to wait trustingly for the Lord to work they are led to exercise faith, hope, and patience" (ibid., p. 631).

Finally, Satan will try to overwhelm God's people with his superior power:

When the protection of human laws shall be withdrawn from those who honor the law of God, there will be, in different lands, a simultaneous movement for their destruction. As the time appointed in the decree draws near, the people will conspire to root out the hated sect. It will be determined to strike in one night a decisive blow, which shall utterly silence the voice of dissent and reproof. . . .

In every quarter companies of armed men, urged on by hosts of evil angels, are preparing for the work of death (ibid., p. 635).

But again, God's people will have protection that was unavailable to the Iraqi soldiers hunkered down in Kuwait, for "if their eyes [the eyes of God's people] could have been opened, they would have seen themselves surrounded by angels of God" (*Early Writings*, p. 283).

The second coming begins

Christ's coming will be the second phase of the Battle of Armageddon. During the first phase, the battle will be restricted to a conflict between the human forces of good and evil on the earth. That's the part of the battle we discussed in the previous chapter, and which I've described so far in this chapter. During this phase of the battle, vastly superior numbers, the law of the land, and the help of demons will give the wicked the appearance of an overwhelming advantage. The issues will be spiritual, but the massive physical force brought against God's people will be very, very real. "To human sight it will appear that the people of God must soon seal their testimony with their blood" (*The Great Controversy*, p. 630).

However, the second coming of Christ will quickly turn the tide. If Armageddon is a power struggle, as wars always are, God will demonstrate who *really* has the power at the second coming.

I used to think the second coming of Christ would take place in a single day, but after carefully reading Ellen White's description in *The Great Controversy*, I have the distinct impression that it may take several days. And it will not happen instantly.

The description of the second coming of Christ that we will look at in the rest of this chapter is roughly in the order Ellen White gives it in *The Great Controversy*. I'm not sure she intended her description to be an exact chronological account of events, but neither am I in a position to put them in a more proper sequence.

When Christ comes to intervene on behalf of His people, He will use "massive firepower," but it will not be the power of human military technology. Often, when God intervened in human conflicts in the Old Testament, He used the forces of nature to defeat Israel's enemies. That is what Christ will do at the second coming.

However, the first warning the wicked will have that the tide is turning against them will not be this display of "massive firepower." It will be an awesome—though silent—natural phenomenon:

> With shouts of triumph, jeering, and imprecation, throngs of evil men are about to rush upon their prey, when, lo, a dense blackness, deeper than the darkness of the night, falls upon the earth. Then a rainbow, shining with the glory from the throne of God, spans the heavens and seems to encircle each praying company. The angry multitudes are suddenly arrested. Their mocking cries die

away. The objects of their murderous rage are forgotten. With fearful forebodings they gaze upon the symbol of God's covenant and long to be shielded from its overpowering brightness (*The Great Controversy*, pp. 635, 636).

Notice that the second coming of Christ has not yet occurred, but the wicked are abruptly stopped in their attack on God's people. A passage in Revelation suggests that just before Christ comes, the wicked will turn on each other, in much the same way that, on several occasions, the enemies of God's people turned on each other during Israel's Old Testament wars (see for example Judges 7:22; 2 Chronicles 20:23):

> The ten horns you saw are ten kings. . . . They . . . will give their power and authority to the beast. They will make war against the Lamb. . . . [But] the beast and the ten horns you saw will hate the prostitute. They will bring her to ruin and leave her naked; they will eat her flesh and burn her with fire. For God has put it into their hearts to accomplish his purpose by agreeing to give the beast their power to rule, until God's words are fulfilled (Revelation 17:12-17).

Earlier in the Battle of Armageddon the woman was riding on the beast quite safely, and the ten horns gave their full support to this arrangement. However, toward the end, the ten horns and the beast will attack the harlot. The wicked will turn on each other. This is when the balance of power will shift, and it will be God's turn to bring His "massive firepower" against the wicked. The wicked may have thought they had God's people in their clutches, but God's power will far surpass anything they have imagined in their most awesome "star wars" movies.

The following list of quotations, both from Scripture and Ellen White, is quite long, but by bringing them together we see a vivid picture of God's "massive firepower" and the reaction of the wicked to it:

> The seventh angel poured out his bowl into the air, and . . . there came flashes of lightning, rumblings, peals of thunder and a severe earthquake. No earthquake like it has

ever occurred since man has been on earth, so tremendous was the quake. . . . Every island fled away and the mountains could not be found. From the sky huge hailstones of about a hundred pounds each fell upon men (Revelation 16:17-21).

The sun appears, shining in its strength. Signs and wonders follow in quick succession. The wicked look with terror and amazement upon the scene, while the righteous behold with solemn joy the tokens of their deliverance. Everything in nature seems turned out of its course. The streams cease to flow. Dark, heavy clouds come up and clash against each other. In the midst of the angry heavens is one clear space of indescribable glory, whence comes the voice of God like the sound of many waters, saying: "It is done." Revelation 16:17.

That voice shakes the heavens and the earth. There is a mighty earthquake, "such as was not since men were upon the earth, so mighty an earthquake, and so great." Verses 17, 18. The firmament appears to open and shut. The glory from the throne of God seems flashing through. The mountains shake like a reed in the wind, and ragged rocks are scattered on every side. There is a roar as of a coming tempest. The sea is lashed into fury. There is heard the shriek of a hurricane like the voice of demons upon a mission of destruction. The whole earth heaves and swells like the waves of the sea. Its surface is breaking up. Its very foundations seem to be giving way. Mountain chains are sinking. Inhabited islands disappear. The seaports that have become like Sodom for wickedness are swallowed up by the angry waters. . . . The proudest cities of the earth are laid low. The lordly palaces, upon which the world's great men have lavished their wealth in order to glorify themselves, are crumbling to ruin before their eyes (*The Great Controversy*, pp. 636, 637).

"Every sea captain, and all who travel by ship, the sailors, and all who earn their living from the sea, will stand far off. . . . They will throw dust on their heads, and with weeping and mourning cry out: 'Woe! Woe, O great city, where all who had ships on the sea became rich through her wealth! In one hour she has been brought to ruin!' " (Revelation 18:17-19).

Thick clouds still cover the sky; yet the sun now and then breaks through, appearing like the avenging eye of Jehovah. Fierce lightnings leap from the heavens, enveloping the earth in a sheet of flame. Above the terrific roar of thunder, voices, mysterious and awful, declare the doom of the wicked. The words spoken are not comprehended by all; but they are distinctly understood by the false teachers. Those who a little before were so reckless, so boastful and defiant, so exultant in their cruelty to God's commandment-keeping people, are now overwhelmed with consternation and shuddering in fear. Their wails are heard above the sound of the elements. Demons acknowledge the deity of Christ and tremble before His power, while men are supplicating for mercy and groveling in abject terror (*The Great Controversy*, pp. 637, 638).

God's firepower will be truly awesome. I would not want to be in the shoes of the wicked at that time!

This description of the terrible destruction associated with the second coming of Christ teaches us an important lesson about the millennium.

According to popular Protestant theology, the millennial reign of Christ will take place on earth, where the righteous will rule over the wicked for a thousand years. However, the passages just quoted provide us with a very good reason why that cannot be true. By the time the judgments of God in the little and great times of trouble have devastated the earth's ecology, and by the time the second coming of Christ has broken up the surface of the earth and further devastated the ecology, I suspect that the planet will be incapable of supporting human life. It may take the better part of the millennium for the earth to recover from the shock of nature's convulsions during the final conflict and the return of Christ. It may take a thousand years to make the world habitable even for the short time when the wicked will inhabit the earth following the millennium.

The resurrection

There will be two resurrections—a special resurrection for all those who died between 1844 and the second coming, and a general resurrection for those who died during the ages prior to 1844 (see *The Great Controversy*, pp. 637, 644).

The special resurrection will occur shortly before the second coming of Christ, and the general resurrection will occur at His actual appearing. Among those raised in the special resurrection will be a select few from among the wicked, including those who participated in the death of Christ. Jesus promised the high priest that he would "see the Son of Man sitting at the right hand of the Mighty One and coming on the clouds of heaven," and John said that "every eye will see him," including "those who pierced him" (Matthew 26:64; Revelation 1:7). According to Ellen White the wicked raised to life at this time will also include "the most violent opposers of His truth and His people" (*The Great Controversy*, p. 637).

In two ways, the second coming of Christ will be a great revelation to both the righteous and the wicked, but especially to the wicked. Their first revelation will be moral, and it will occur between the special and the general resurrections, when God displays the Ten Commandments in the sky:

> There appears against the sky a hand holding two tables of stone folded together. . . . The hand opens the tables, and there are seen the precepts of the Decalogue, traced as with a pen of fire. The words are so plain that all can read them. Memory is aroused, the darkness of superstition and heresy is swept from every mind, and God's ten words, brief, comprehensive, and authoritative, are presented to the view of all the inhabitants of the earth (Ibid., p. 639).

Right now it is very difficult for Christians to get nonchristians to understand that the things we believe are true, that they are reality. Adventists also have a very hard time helping other Christians to understand our special truths. However, this shroud will be stripped away at the second coming of Christ. Following is another description, fairly long, but very vivid, of the tearing away of the veil that today blinds the eyes of the wicked to the truth:

It is impossible to describe the horror and despair of those who have trampled upon God's holy requirements. The Lord gave them His law; they might have compared their characters with it and learned their defects while there was yet opportunity for repentance and reform; but in order to secure the favor of the world, they set aside its precepts and taught others to transgress. They have endeavored to compel God's people to profane His Sabbath. Now they are condemned by that law which they have despised. With awful distinctness they see that they are without excuse. . . .

The enemies of God's law, from the ministers down to the least among them, have a new conception of truth and duty. . . . Too late they see the true nature of the spurious sabbath and the sandy foundation upon which they have been building. They find that they have been fighting against God (ibid., pp. 639, 640).

The appearance of Christ
In addition to being a moral revelation, the second coming of Christ will be a physical revelation to the wicked, for they will see Deity with their own eyes. "Soon there appears in the east a small black cloud, about half the size of a man's hand. . . . The people of God know this to be the sign of the Son of man" (ibid., p. 640). As the cloud approaches the earth it becomes "lighter and more glorious, until it is a great white cloud, its base a glory like consuming fire, and above it the rainbow of the covenant" (ibid., p. 641).

For 6,000 years God has concealed Himself from human sight so completely that many people have refused to believe in Him. "Let me see Him," the atheist says, "then I'll believe in Him." The second coming of Christ will be a grand revelation in which for the first time divinity will expose itself to all humanity in a full blaze of indescribable glory. God will say, in effect, "You wanted to see Me to believe in Me? Here I am." And the wicked will understand why God did not reveal Himself to sinful human beings any earlier in earth's history. For they will call in terror "to the mountains and rocks, 'Fall on us and hide us from the face of him who sits on the throne and from the wrath of the Lamb' " (Revelation 6:16).

Now comes the general resurrection, and the righteous of all ages will come to life.

> The Lord himself will come down from heaven, with a loud command, with the voice of the archangel and with the trumpet call of God, and *the dead in Christ will rise first* (1 Thessalonians 4:16, emphasis supplied).

> Amid the reeling of the earth, the flash of lightning, and the roar of thunder, the voice of the Son of God calls forth the sleeping saints. . . .
> All come forth from their graves the same in stature as they entered the tomb. Adam, who stands among the risen throng, is of lofty height and majestic form, in stature but little below the Son of God. He presents a marked contrast to the people of later generations; in this one respect is shown the great degeneracy of the race. But all arise with the freshness and vigor of eternal youth (*The Great Controversy*, p. 644).

Ellen White suggests that the bodies of the righteous who are alive on the earth at the time Christ returns will be invigorated with immortality just prior to the time they are caught up to meet the Lord in the air (see *The Great Controversy*, p. 645).

Ascending to the cloud

Then all of God's people, those who lived to see Him come and those who were raised to life in the two resurrections, will ascend to meet Jesus in the clouds. This is how Ellen White described the scene after the translated saints reach the clouds:

> On each side of the cloudy chariot were wings, and beneath it were living wheels; and as the chariot rolled upward, the wheels cried, "Holy," and the wings, as they moved, cried, "Holy," and the retinue of holy angels around the cloud cried, "Holy, holy, holy, Lord God Almighty!" And the saints in the cloud cried, "Glory! Alleluia!" And the chariot rolled upward to the Holy City. Before entering the city, the saints were arranged in a perfect square, with Jesus in the midst. . . .

Then I saw a very great number of angels bring from the city glorious crowns—a crown for every saint, with his name written thereon. As Jesus called for the crowns, angels presented them to Him, and with His own right hand, the lovely Jesus placed the crowns on the heads of the saints (*Early Writings*, pp. 287, 288).

Then Jesus will open the gate to heaven, and His people will take possession of the city.

Language is altogether too feeble to attempt a description of heaven. As the scene rises before me, I am lost in amazement. Carried away with the surpassing splendor and excellent glory, I lay down the pen, and exclaim, "Oh, what love! what wondrous love!" The most exalted language fails to describe the glory of heaven or the matchless depths of a Saviour's love (ibid., p. 289).

For 6,000 years Satan has held the world in his clutches. The "god of this world" has degraded God's creation and persecuted His followers. The wars he has inspired have caused untold human suffering and death. Millions of martyrs have given their lives through the cruel inventions he devised. And all to satisfy the pride of one who was offended that Christ held a higher position than he; all to satisfy the ambition of one who thought he had a better plan for governing the universe than God.

The crisis of the end time has been the final burst of Satan's pride and ambition. Into these last few months, he has poured every ounce of his energy, the full force of his wrath, to defeat God by crushing His people (see Revelation 12:12).

But God's faithful people have demonstrated to a breathless universe that in earth's darkest hour, in a darkness deeper than the darkest midnight, nothing can cause them to break their relationship with Jesus. Nothing can cause them to abandon their loyalty to Him or their faith in Him.

Now the crisis is over. As God's people step through those gates of pearl into the New Jerusalem, the scene of that conflict is trillions of miles behind them. A new life, which until this moment has been only a promise and a hope, now bursts upon their senses.

You and I stand on the threshold of that final crisis. For us, earth's darkest hour still lies ahead. All the prophecies of the ages focus on the few years just before us. The issue that confronts you and me, now that we have traced those prophecies to their end, is how the great controversy of those prophecies will be decided in our hearts. On whose side will we be found when it is over? And the answer is very simple: Each of us is even now, by the choices we are making this very day, perhaps this very moment, choosing on whose side we will emerge at the end.

Those who put God ahead of every other interest today are the ones who will keep their relationship with Jesus in earth's darkest hour—the crisis of the end time.

When the morning finally comes, when you and I ascend to meet Jesus in the clouds, and when we finally step into the New Jerusalem, we will declare with one voice, "Hallelujah! Though we obtained it through inexpressible suffering, heaven is cheap enough!" (see *Early Writings*, p. 67).